VICTORIAN CATHEDRAL MUSIC
IN THEORY AND PRACTICE

VICTORIAN CATHEDRAL MUSIC
IN THEORY AND PRACTICE

WILLIAM J. GATENS

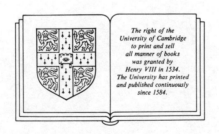

The right of the
University of Cambridge
to print and sell
all manner of books
was granted by
Henry VIII in 1534.
The University has printed
and published continuously
since 1584.

CAMBRIDGE UNIVERSITY PRESS

CAMBRIDGE
LONDON   NEW YORK   NEW ROCHELLE
MELBOURNE   SYDNEY

Published by the Press Syndicate of the University of Cambridge
The Pitt Building, Trumpington Street, Cambridge CB2 1RP
32 East 57th Street, New York, NY 10022, USA
10 Stamford Road, Oakleigh, Melbourne 3166, Australia

First published 1986

Printed in Great Britain at
the University Press, Cambridge

British Library cataloguing in publication data
Gatens, William J.
Victorian cathedral music in theory and practice.
1. Church music – England – History – 19th
century 2. Cathedrals – England – History – 19th
century
I. Title
783′.02′6342   ML2931

Library of Congress cataloguing in publication data
Gatens, William J.
Victorian cathedral music in theory and practice.
Bibliography: p.
Includes index.
1. Church music – England – 19th century.
2. Church music – Church of England.   I. Title.
ML3131.4.G37   1986   783′.02′6342   85-30949

ISBN 0 521 26808 7

Contents

Contents

Preface

A sympathetic understanding of Victorian cathedral music is the intended object of this study. To this end, the investigation has been organised into two broad divisions designated by the terms 'theory' and 'practice'. Some preliminary explanation of the character and scope of material comprehended by these terms may prove to be helpful.

The first division, concerned with theory, seeks to build up a picture of the cultural and intellectual atmosphere in which Victorian church music was composed, by investigating the peculiar attitudes, assumptions, and prejudices pertaining to music in its relationship to religion and worship during the period. In deciding on which issues to examine, preference has been shown for those which seemed most clearly to differentiate the cultural and aesthetic atmosphere of the Victorian church composer from that of the present day, and even from the world of nineteenth-century secular music. Material has been drawn primarily from published sources of the nineteenth century, with emphasis on writings apparently intended to be serious and enduring rather than journalistic ephemera.

The second division examines the careers and works of leading Victorian church composers. These chapters may be regarded as case studies, illustrating in specific instances how the cultural and intellectual theories found their way into compositional practice. The period from 1840 to 1880 is the principal focus of attention. To this has been added the work of Thomas Attwood (1765-1838), who, of the later Georgian church composers, pointed most distinctly towards Victorian characteristics. Also included are works by mid Victorians whose active careers continued well beyond the 1880 landmark, from which point, as most historians seem to agree, new currents of English compositional practice distinct from the mid-Victorian school began to attain prominence. This was the generation of Parry and Stanford, whose careers substantially overlap those of Stainer, Barnby, and Sullivan, but who represent a different artistic tendency. The genres of anthem and service have been chosen as the almost exclusive objects of detailed attention, as these are the most artistically ambitious types of music forming a normal part of Anglican choral worship. Other genres are not completely ignored, but if the Anglican repertory is to be assessed as sacred art, it is on services and anthems that the case must rest, these being in some sense the Victorian counterparts of the masses and motets of the Renaissance or the *concerti sacri* and cantatas of the Baroque.

The selection of composers for detailed examination was determined by two principal criteria. First, professional concern with church music must have constituted a major share of their careers as composers and of their reputations, both in their own time and at present. Second, they must have been among the most eminent figures of their profession. Fortunately, the later Victorian writers, such as W. A. Barrett, Joseph Bennett, Myles Foster, and J. S. Bumpus, are helpful here, as they were in general agreement as to who the leading figures were. Their assessments have significantly influenced the selection made for this study, though of course the list, on their authority, could have been much longer. As it stands, the selection of composers is small enough to permit more than a merely superficial consideration of their work, while facilitating comparison.

In stating that the object of the present study is a 'sympathetic understanding', the author freely admits to finding the repertory in question attractive and congenial, with a claim that this does not preclude a rational treatment of the subject. Neither is it meant to imply that the music in question is 'great' in the usual sense. Sympathetic understanding is not intended to mean myopic partisanship of the sort that induced William Spark and John Broadhouse to maintain in the 1880s that Henry Smart was one of the greatest of composers, though it is historically interesting that they should have thought so. Sympathy rather implies discernment and acceptance of the factors that helped to govern compositional practice, and thus assessment of the music on its own terms.

If sympathy is not a disqualification, outright antipathy can be, in so far as the critic assumes that criteria pertinent to a favoured repertory are universally applicable, and so invokes them in cases where they are not entirely appropriate. Having an antecedent dislike of the Victorian idiom, far too many twentieth-century critics and historians have proceeded to fault the music for lacking some quality admired in, say, the Tudors or Jacobeans. They are somewhat like the seventeenth-century French classicists who deprecated Shakespeare for failing to observe the Aristotelian unities.

Because of the persistence of some fundamental misunderstandings, compounded by the efforts of some latter-day church music propagandists virtually to discredit the Victorian repertory, the fairly broad approach of the present study seemed appropriate. It may be seen as a compromise between a mere survey which risks superficiality by neglecting many of the underlying issues, and a more minute and restricted investigation which risks loss of perspective. With increasing scholarly attention now being given to nineteenth-century music and to Victorian studies of all kinds, one may hope that the present study will prove to be a forerunner of more concentrated investigations of specific facets of Victorian music.

Abbreviations

In the notes and bibliography, frequently cited periodicals and reference works are identified by the following abbreviations:

CC *Church Congress Reports* (N.B. These are identified by venue and year of meeting. In cases where publication was in the following year, this has been indicated in the bibliography but not in the notes.)

MT *The Musical Times*

MW *The Musical World*

NG *The New Grove Dictionary of Music and Musicians*, ed. Stanley Sadie (London, 1980)

PMA *Proceedings of the Musical Association*

Other periodicals are cited in full.

Within a set of chapter notes, the first reference to a work is given in full. Thereafter, the work is identified by the author's surname and the date of publication.

Introduction
Historical background and liturgical framework

The composers of English cathedral music in the Victorian period were inescapably influenced in matters of compositional practice by historical circumstances, assumptions, and attitudes that prevailed during the period. While it may be argued that this applies, to a greater or lesser extent, to virtually any musical repertory, such influences are particularly strong where the repertory in question is conceived and employed within the terms of a prominent institutional framework, and all the more so when music forms only one part of the institution's concerns. Consequently a genuine aesthetic understanding of Victorian cathedral music demands that such influences be taken into account. A major part of the ensuing study will thus focus on those issues which, in the author's opinion, most clearly differentiate the Victorian church composer's creative world from that of other periods and even from the contemporaneous secular-music world, at home and abroad. As a preliminary, it will be helpful to take a somewhat broader view of Anglican church history in the nineteenth century, with glances at direct antecedents, so as to provide a context and background for discussion of the more specific issues.

The shape of this history may perhaps be most readily grasped in terms of the doctrinal parties into which the Church of England was unofficially divided. John Henry Newman (1801–90), in the historical appendix to the 1866 French edition of his *Apologia pro vita sua*, discerned three parties: (1) the Apostolic or Tractarian, with emphasis on the divine origin and guidance of the Church, its traditions, episcopal government, sacraments, and doctrinal authority; (2) the Evangelicals, with emphasis on a subjective and intensely emotional view of faith, almost entirely preoccupied with personal salvation, accepting the Bible as sole and ultimate external authority, and with little concern about the visible Church; and (3) the Latitudinarian or Liberal, with emphasis on the primacy of human reason, even at the expense of revelation, and with an unfailing capacity to adapt the concepts of religion so that they conform with the prevailing secular *Zeitgeist*. Newman identified the animating principles of the parties as, respectively: the Catholic, the Protestant, and the sceptical.[1] These principles, far from being confined to those parties of the first half of the nineteenth century with which Newman was specifically concerned, represent perennial tendencies in church history, and have emerged in distinctive but related forms during different periods.

At the beginning of the nineteenth century, the Evangelicals were the most vital party in the Church. As a distinctive group, their history may be traced to the Oxford Methodists, a group of young university men who, beginning in 1729, met regularly for study and devotion. The real birth of the Evangelical revival, however, dates from the intense spiritual renewal suddenly experienced by John Wesley (1703–91) at a meeting in London of a religious society on 24 May 1738. Wesley afterwards began his celebrated preaching ministry. The necessity for such a decisive personal experience remained a central feature in Evangelical teaching. It was essentially a religion of the heart, often at the expense of the head.

At first, the Methodists and other Evangelicals were objects of public ridicule. The low social status of many of the early adherents, their self-conscious spirituality, and the frenzied manifestations that often accompanied vehement preaching were among the factors that rendered the movement unfashionable. Over the years, however, the movement began to attract more distinguished adherents, the most notable being that group of pious, upper-middle-class Anglican businessmen and professionals led by William Wilberforce (1759–1833) and known as the Clapham Sect.

During the first half of the nineteenth century, the Evangelicals were the dominant party in the Church of England, but earlier their churchmanship had tended to be vague. The overwhelming preoccupation with personal religion caused them to set little store in the corporate aspect of the Church or in the external ordering of worship. The Methodists, of course, eventually separated from the Established Church, as did some other Evangelical groups. Meanwhile, there were many other Evangelicals who were technically within the Establishment, but for whom this fact was of relatively little significance.

The British reaction to the French Revolution and its aftermath was one of the factors that helped to draw Anglican Evangelicals closer in spirit to the Establishment, thus consolidating their status as a party within the Church. There was widespread public revulsion against the Revolution, which was perceived as a threat to religion in general, as the anti-religious sentiments associated with the revolutionary spirit were by no means confined to France. The Established Church was undoubtedly in a state of spiritual torpor during the Georgian period, but it was still popularly perceived as a bastion for defence of the faith, commanding a certain degree of *ex officio* loyalty as an integral part of the British Constitution. Anglican Evangelicals thus made common cause with the Establishment against the forces of irreligion, and eventually gained pre-eminence in the Church.

With its rise in social status and closer identification with the Establishment, Evangelicalism played a major role in shaping the moral and social atmosphere of the Victorian period, even though it was generally in decline as a religious movement through most of the second half of the century. The Evangelical characteristics of piety, seriousness, self-denial, duty, and morality were felt in society at large, since the Evangelicals gained as commanding a place in public affairs as they did within the Church.[2] Thus the Evangelical frame of mind coloured the attitudes even of those who either abandoned or had never been adherents of Evangelical religion.

If the Evangelical movement was the most important development in eighteenth-century English church history, the most influential and far-reaching development in the nineteenth century was the High Church revival, beginning with the Oxford Movement in 1833. The principal published writings of the movement, the *Tracts for the times* (1833–41), lent the convenient name 'Tractarian' to the revival and its adherents. The best-known of the movement's early leaders were John Henry Newman, Edward Bouverie Pusey (1800–82), and John Keble (1792–1866). On 14 July 1833, at the Church of St Mary the Virgin, Oxford, Keble preached an assize sermon entitled 'National apostasy'. Newman regarded this event as the start of the Oxford Movement, and it has generally been regarded as such ever since. Although it was bitterly opposed, especially around the middle of the century, the High Church movement gained ground, on the whole, and may be said to have determined the predominant character displayed by the Church of England in the century's closing years, and for some time after. The influence on church music was particularly significant.

There is a popular impression that the Evangelicals and Tractarians were polar opposites on a High Church–Low Church scale conceived for the most part in terms of ritual, with the 'Broad Church' (i.e. the Liberals) lying somewhere in the middle. In fact, the Evangelicals and Tractarians had more in common than either party had with the Liberals, whom they regarded as the real spiritual enemy. Like the Evangelicals, the Tractarians strongly affirmed the fundamental doctrines of the Christian faith and the divine inspiration of the Bible, and their primary concern was the spiritual welfare and destiny of the individual Christian soul. During his years at Oxford, John Wesley was deeply influenced by the devotional writings of the learned High Churchman William Law (1686–1761), and it is surely significant that many prominent nineteenth-century High Church figures – e.g. Newman, Henry Manning, Henry Wilberforce, Nathaniel Woodard, Thomas Helmore, John Bacchus Dykes, John Mason Neale, Walter Kerr Hamilton – came from a background of Anglican Evangelicalism or even Dissent. In the early years of the Oxford Movement, the Tractarians and Evangelicals were allies against the encroachments of Liberalism within the University. A landmark was their joint opposition in 1836 to the Regius Professor of Divinity, Dr Renn Dickson Hampden (1792–1868), whose Bampton Lectures of 1832 were said to advance theories damaging to the grounds of faith and to deny the authority of the ancient creeds of the Church. The fundamental differences between the Evangelicals and the Tractarians in their views of the nature of the Church, however, were enough to make bitter opposition virtually inevitable between these two parties, given the temper of the times in matters of religious controversy.

3

Whereas the Evangelicals were barely concerned with the visible Church, the Tractarians believed the Church of England to be the unique representative of the 'One Holy Catholic and Apostolic Church' within the realm. This Church, they maintained, was founded by Christ in the persons of the original Apostles, to whom he committed a measure of his divine authority, pre-eminently the authority to minister the absolution of sins and to celebrate Holy Communion. This authority was conveyed sacramentally by the Apostles to the bishops they consecrated, they in turn to their successors, and so on in unbroken sequence to the bishops of the present day. This is the all-important 'Apostolic Succession'.

By virtue of this authority, the Church is more than a human association of believers. By means of its priesthood and sacraments, it is the normal channel of grace for the spiritual nourishment of the individual soul, and by Christ's promise it is under the special guidance of the Holy Spirit to preserve and discern doctrinal truth. Whereas the Evangelicals and Dissenters claimed to reject all external authority other than the word of the Bible, it is fundamental to the Catholic view of the Tractarians that the mind and traditions of the Church, being under divine guidance, are complementary in authority with the letter of Scripture. Indeed, they hold that the Church is divinely empowered to interpret the Scriptures rightly and unfold their meaning to the faithful.

The Tractarians certainly did not invent these doctrines themselves. They are part of the Catholic tradition traceable to the Fathers of the ancient Church and to the teachings of Christ and the Apostles as recorded in the Bible. The Tractarians particularly regarded the High Church divines of the Caroline period as their spiritual and doctrinal ancestors in the preservation and transmission of Catholic truth. This traditional teaching was defended in the eighteenth century by conservative High Church clergy, largely in the context of controversy with Latitudinarians of the day: unitarians, deists, and upholders of 'natural religion'. Apart from the Evangelicals, there was a great mistrust in the eighteenth century of 'enthusiasm' in religion. Consequently, the conservative divines of the period, despite the traditional orthodoxy of their position, were as much creatures of the Age of Reason as were their Latitudinarian opponents. They argued learnedly for the probability of the truth of the traditional doctrines, but with such a lack of spiritual fervour that these conservatives earned for themselves the epithet 'High and Dry'. The Tractarians, in contrast, embraced the traditional Catholic doctrines, but with an urgency and fervour more characteristic of the Evangelicals. The immediate cause for this urgency was the perception of potentially grave spiritual danger consequent upon the wave of secular liberalism that appeared to be sweeping the nation in the early 1830s, landmarks of the tendency being the overwhelming Whig majority in the general election of 1831 and passage of the Reform Bill of 1832.

It is important to note that the great majority of Anglicans in the nineteenth century were not self-conscious adherents of any of the parties described by Newman in 1866. For the average English churchman the national and untheological principle of Establishment counted for more than such party divisions, with the Church perceived, almost primarily, as a national cultural institution, though one with still loftier credentials. Another significant characteristic of the average nineteenth-century Englishman was a somewhat irrationally inflamed abhorrence of Roman Catholicism, which is only to be expected in a nation whose history includes Bloody Mary, the Gunpowder Plot, the Glorious Revolution, and the 'Forty-five' uprising. Since the Tractarian position in all its fullness has never been widely shared or popularly understood, it is hardly surprising that the long-forgotten ideas and practices revived by High Churchmen in the nineteenth century gave every outward appearance of leaning precariously towards Romanism, even to those who should have known better.

According to the Tractarians, the Church of England represents a middle way, a *via media*, between the Church of Rome and the radical Protestants. The Tractarians took pains to distinguish Catholicism itself from what they claimed was the Romish corruption of it, at the same time pointing out that Luther, Calvin, and other extreme reformers repudiated the episcopacy and so cut themselves off from the Apostolic Succession. The Tractarians' pointedly anti-Roman statements, however, were of no avail with those who were convinced that the Oxford Movement was really part of a popish plot to overthrow the Church of England and subvert the British Constitution. Matters were not helped by the numerous Tractarians who, following their position to its apparently logical conclusion and driven by bitter opposition from Low Church Anglicans, became converts to the Roman Church. The most notable and most devastating of them was John Henry Newman himself in 1845. Conspiracy theories seemed, to those who held them, to be confirmed in 1850, when the Roman Catholic hierarchy was restored in England, an action which Lord John Russell characterised as the 'Papal Aggression'.

There was a considerable resurgence of religious Liberalism in the Church of England during the second half of the nineteenth century, when the Evangelicals were declining in power and influence and the Tractarians smarting from a number of serious reversals sustained around mid century. A landmark in this resurgence was the publication in 1860 of *Essays and reviews*, a loosely organised collection of papers by some of the leading academic Broad Churchmen of the day. Their object was to question the orthodox position on numerous subjects in a spirit of free enquiry. Their opponents, with some justification, charged them with making reckless attacks on fundamental tenets of the faith and flatly contradicting the Church's teaching on atonement, judgment, and scriptural inspiration. While increasingly influential as a party, the Liberals had very little effect on the course of Anglican worship and music, since these were so largely extraneous to the principal Broad Church concerns.

Such was certainly not the case with the High Church party, though it is a mistake to assume that the Oxford Movement *per se* was chiefly concerned with the revival of Catholic ritual. It was, in fact, far more concerned with the theological and devotional foundations of Anglo-Catholicism. Indeed, many of the early Tractarians sought to discourage extravagant ritual innovations. While wishing to reform worship to the extent of making it more solemn and reverent, they fully recognised that drastic departures from the customary mode of conducting church services would provoke needless misunderstanding, unsettlement, and hostility on the part of average Anglican churchgoers, who would be sure to equate ritual with popery. Nevertheless, as Francis Warre-Cornish so concisely stated, 'Ritual is the expression of doctrine',[3] and so it was inevitable that the dissemination of the doctrines proclaimed by the Tractarians would find expression, including musical expression, in the efforts of serious Anglo-Catholic priests.

These efforts were closely associated with the ecclesiological revival, beginning essentially with the foundation in 1839 of the Cambridge Camden Society, later renamed the Ecclesiological Society, of which the principal guiding spirit was the Revd John Mason Neale (1818–66). This society was concerned with the manifestation of Catholic conviction in church architecture, furnishings, vestments, and ritual, with a scholarly care for historical integrity. Church music eventually came within its sphere of concern, the first substantial musical article in the *Ecclesiologist*, the journal of the movement, appearing in 1843. Independent efforts towards an Anglo-Catholic choral revival had taken place before then.

It is important to note that the standards of worship at the start of the nineteenth century were commensurate with the spiritual torpor of Establishment conservatism in general. Church buildings, including the cathedrals, were in far too many cases in a state of decay and uncleanliness. Pastoral activity was lax. Services were conducted in a perfunctory and listless fashion. Parish music, if any, was often confined to metrical psalmody dispensed from a west gallery, often inharmoniously, to a generally silent congregation. In the cathedrals, things were typically no better. Although these were institutions with foundations endowed specifically for the observance of the daily choral service, choirs were ill-trained and inefficient; the behaviour of the choristers was often irreverent; most of the canons were non-resident; precentors and minor canons were often incapable of discharging their musical responsibilities; lay singers were lax about attendance; choirs and clergy seldom entered in procession, but casually wandered into their places at service time; and choir books and vestments were often in shabby condition. The Evangelical revival, with its lack of concern for externals, did not have much effect on this state of affairs. Virtually all of the vast improvement in the standards of worship that took place during the course of the nineteenth century, including the revival of the choral service, may be attributed to the direct or indirect influence of the High Church revival.

There were essentially two models for the revival of the Anglican choral service. For convenience, they may be designated respectively the ecclesiological ideal and the cathedral ideal. Of the two, the ecclesiological ideal was the one more closely associated, both in admiration and hostility, with the movement to revive Catholic ritual. It was fundamentally parochial, its prime object being to stimulate the active participation of the whole congregation in the singing of the service. Prayers and versicles were intoned by the clergy, with responses sung by the choir and people. The most celebrated and distinctive feature of this kind of service was the chanting of the daily Prayer Book psalms to Gregorian psalm tones. These were favoured as being more conducive than Anglican chants to congregational singing, and because of their antiquity and solemn character. Fanatics for 'Gregorians' sometimes held them to be the only kind of music suitable for Christian worship. Such music formed a natural complement to the ecclesiologists' efforts in the revival of Gothic church architecture and the care taken to produce chancels of the right shape to accommodate a divided choir on the collegiate pattern. Under this ideal the primary purpose of the choir was to lead congregational singing. Composed settings of the service canticles and choir anthems were not banished, but the favoured repertory consisted almost exclusively of full services and anthems, preferably unaccompanied, in the polyphonic idiom of the sixteenth and seventeenth centuries, including adaptations to English words of Latin motets by English and continental composers. Music in more modern styles was studiously avoided.

One of the earliest efforts to institute this type of daily choral service was in 1839 at the Margaret Chapel in London, later to be rebuilt (1850–9) as the Church of All Saints, Margaret Street. The incumbent was the Revd Frederick Oakeley (1802–80), who published the first Anglican Gregorian psalter, *Laudes diurnae*, in 1843. He was a staunch adherent of Tractarian principles, though in 1845 he was among the many who seceded to the Church of Rome. Oakeley's daily choral services, the first of their kind in London, attracted much attention and a diverse congregation.

An even more influential institution took shape beginning in 1841 with the founding in Chelsea of a Church of England training college for school-teachers, afterwards named St Mark's College. Choral services were held daily in the college chapel under the direction of the Revd Thomas Helmore (1811–90), who was appointed Vice-Principal and Precentor in 1842. Here the ecclesiological ideal was maintained to a high standard by a choir composed of students of the college and pupils of the attached model school, and an active singing congregation comprising the rest of the college and school as well as many of the curious and devout from the general public. There was no organ in the chapel until 1861, an indication of devotion to the *a cappella* ideal.

Singing was a fundamental part of the education at St Mark's, and the students went on from the college equipped to assist with the musical worship of the churches in whose parish schools they were destined to teach. This worship ideal was thus widely disseminated, with much assistance from Helmore's brother Frederick (1820–99), the 'musical missionary', who made a career of travelling to country parishes, founding and training choirs to sing the choral service. In 1849, Thomas Helmore published his own Gregorian psalter, *The Psalter Noted*, which was expanded with supplementary material and published the following year as *A Manual of Plainsong*. Wherever the ecclesiological ideal of the choral service prevailed, Helmore's book was almost certain to be in use.

This type of service met with a mixed reception. While many of High Church predisposition, clerical and lay, enthusiastically took to it as the most sublime, reverent, and spiritually stirring of all modes of worship, to most churchgoers it was an unfamiliar and therefore alien and uncomfortable experience. Associations with Tractarianism aroused suspicions that the choral service was essentially popish. Detractors and defenders waged a lively and often amusing war of words in the public press. Anti-Tractarian hostility rose to a climax in 1850, the year of the 'Papal Aggression', and certain churches noted for their ritualist practices were the scenes of ugly 'No-Popery' riots.

The cathedral ideal of the choral service, entailing elaborate music sung by the choir with little or no congregational singing, is of more direct relevance to the present study. Although not as closely associated with the High Church movement in its extremer forms, the cathedral style of service found some anti-popish opposition, especially when elements of it were introduced in a parochial setting. The re-animation of the tradition during the nineteenth century was due in part to the specific efforts of individual High Churchmen, and more generally to the devotional revitalisation in all branches of the Church that was one of the chief legacies of the Tractarian revival.

It is noteworthy that the lead in choral reform did not come from the cathedrals themselves. Throughout the first half of the century, these institutions were for the most part strongholds of entrenched lassitude. Deaneries and canonries were often lucrative rewards for political favours or personal connections, and were regarded as sinecures, with no duties involved apart from a few weeks residence per year in the cathedral city and a minimal amount of preaching, often done by proxy. As noted before, it is part of the function of a cathedral foundation to maintain daily choral services, but the mixture of incompetence and indifference produced a result that was anything but worthy. Meanwhile, some of the funds that should have been devoted to the musical establishment were all too often diverted to other purposes. The wave of liberal reform in the 1830s saw the formation of an Ecclesiastical Commission which set about rectifying the grosser abuses connected with the cathedral system, reducing the inordinate revenues enjoyed by some foundations and using them to supplement poorer parochial livings and establish much-needed new churches in the growing industrial towns. Cathedral choirs were thus left in an even less efficient state than before. Revival could not be expected to emanate from such quarters.

The initiative in revitalising the cathedral ideal of the choral service came, for the most part, from parochial and collegiate institutions. Possibly the earliest important step was taken in 1841 at the newly built Leeds Parish Church, when a group of parishioners requested that the Vicar, the Revd Walter Farquhar Hook (1798–1875), institute daily choral services. There had been a robed choir of men and boys earlier in the century, but it met with opposition and was not adequately maintained. The services at that time appear not to have been fully choral. Hook himself was thoroughly unmusical – indeed, he was probably tone-deaf – but he had such a keen sense of decorum in worship that he gladly accepted the proposal for daily choral services, on the condition that they be conducted at the highest possible standard, and that no expense be spared for their proper maintenance. Hook chose as a consultant the Revd John Jebb (1805–86), then a Prebendary of Limerick Cathedral, nephew of the late bishop of that diocese, and the undisputed expert on all details of cathedral worship. In 1842, the direction of music was placed in the capable hands of Samuel Sebastian Wesley (1810–76).

The year 1842 also saw the completed restoration in London of the Temple Church. Previously the music had consisted of a mixed quartet in a gallery singing metrical psalms under the direction of the blind organist George Warne. One of the barristers, William Burge, pressed for the reorganisation of the music along cathedral lines. Warne, who was incapable of managing the new arrangements, was retired at full salary in 1843, and Edward John Hopkins (1818–1901) was appointed in his place. Hopkins retained the post until 1898, and under his direction the Temple Church was to become for some years the standard of excellence for the cathedral ideal of worship in London, as St Mark's was for the ecclesiological ideal. It is noteworthy that Westminster Abbey and St Paul's were not at this stage even in the running.

The collegiate foundations at Oxford and Cambridge were, for the most part, in as sorry a state as the cathedrals during the first half of the century, though the appointment of Thomas Attwood Walmisley (1814–56) to the organistships of Trinity and St John's, Cambridge in 1833 marked the beginning of a rise in standards there. In 1848, the chapel of Radley College near Oxford was opened, with music under the direction of Edwin George Monk (1819–1900), who conducted a full cathedral service on Sundays and some weekdays. In 1849, King's College, London appointed twelve choral exhibitioners, and in 1852, choral services were instituted at Lincoln's Inn. In 1850, Gray's Inn began services along ecclesiological lines, with singers from St Mark's. In 1862 the Benchers discontinued this arrangement in favour of forming their own choir under E. J. Hopkins for cathedral-style services. A similar shift took place at the new parish church of St Andrew's, Wells Street (consecrated 1847), which started as a Tractarian stronghold with the ecclesiological ideal. Around 1850, however, the organist John Foster (1827–1915), a former chorister at St George's, Windsor, began to introduce elements of the cathedral style and discontinued use of Helmore's *Psalter Noted*. This tendency continued under Foster's successor, Philip Armes (1836–1908), and if there were any doubts remaining, they must have been dispelled by the appointment of Joseph Barnby (1838–96) in 1863.

Undoubtedly the most remarkable establishment of the period was the Church and College of St Michael at Tenbury, founded by Sir Frederick Ouseley (1825–89) in 1856. As a priest, Ouseley was a serious High Churchman, but he had never been in sympathy with extreme ritualism or the Gregorian psalmody of the ecclesiological choral ideal. His enthusiasm was entirely for the cathedral ideal, and the sorry state of the nation's cathedrals convinced him that a new foundation was needed, dedicated to the perpetuation of the daily choral service according to the cathedral tradition, if that tradition were to survive. St Michael's survived until 1985.

By mid century, the days of lassitude in the nation's cathedrals were near their end. The Cathedral Commission appointed in 1852 urged reforms that would make the cathedrals truly the centres of diocesan life. These included linking definite duties to preferments, involving such things as work connected with the cathedral schools, universities and theological colleges, the parishes of cathedral cities, pastoral training, diocesan charities and societies, the maintenance of decorous cathedral worship, and development of church music. In some cases the cathedral musical establishments were shamed into improvement by the standards achieved by some parish church choirs. In 1865 there took place at Lichfield the first diocesan choral festival, which brought together parish choirs from the district for choral services in the cathedral. These became immensely popular annual events throughout the country in the second half of the century, and may be viewed as a prime example of the cathedral's renewed function as centre of diocesan life. The high standards achieved by the amateurs in these festivals could prove embarrassing to the endowed cathedral choirs.

The year 1872, in which John Stainer (1840–1901) was appointed to St Paul's, may be seen as a landmark. The ground had been prepared by a series of reforms instituted by Robert Gregory, who was appointed canon in 1868. These included cleaning of the fabric, choir processions as the norm rather than the exception, and fines for absence and tardiness of singers. The organist then was John Goss (1800–80), who, though a fine musician and an outstanding composer of anthems, was no choir disciplinarian. At the time of his appointment in 1838, he would have found no support from an unmusical dean and chapter for much-needed reforms, and by 1868 he was too advanced in years to carry out a strenuous reorganisation. Another indication of the change in character at St Paul's was the appointment in 1871 of Richard William Church (1815–90), one of the younger generation of Oxford Tractarians, as Dean. Under his influence, High Church principles, though not extreme ritualism, came to prevail at the cathedral. During Stainer's tenure, the level of music at St Paul's became a model and a challenge to the other cathedrals of the nation.

A most important development in the second half of the century was the increased public approbation of the choral service. Apart from the extreme manifestations of the ecclesiological ideal, choral worship was no longer controversially linked with Tractarianism. Practices that had seemed alien and sinister around mid century gradually came to be accepted as normal, and many of them have been characteristic of Anglican worship ever since.

It might be argued that the one tangible feature uniting the whole Church of England was its Book of Common Prayer, and certainly to understand the role of music in the Anglican liturgy, it is important to know something of the structure and background of the liturgy itself.

Most Anglicans in the eighteenth and nineteenth centuries regarded the Prayer Book as a thoroughly Protestant document, but the Tractarians recognised, and held it to be highly significant, that the Prayer Book services unmistakably display their pre-Reformation sources. While many of the English reformers may individually have been adherents of radical Protestantism, in drafting the Prayer Book they preserved for the Church of England a distinctly Catholic liturgy. So much had this fact been forgotten and neglected that the course of lectures on the origins of the Prayer Book given in the 1820s by the Oxford Regius Professor of Divinity, Charles Lloyd (1784–1829), came as a startling revelation to many.

The principal source for the Prayer Book was the Use of Sarum, the liturgy of the Diocese of Salisbury, codified in 1085 and revised during the reign of Henry VIII. Partly, no doubt, to allay fears about 'Romanising', the Tractarians sometimes emphasised the fact that the English Church has always had a liturgy distinct from that of Rome. The mediaeval English Church was more strongly influenced by the Gallican than the Roman Church, and the Gallican liturgy was claimed to derive from that of the primitive Church in Ephesus. Attempts to enforce the Roman liturgy on the British Isles were never wholly successful, and as the English Reformation took place before the Council of Trent, the Tridentine mass was never the liturgy of the English Church.

In 1542 a Committee of Convocation was appointed under the sanction of Henry VIII for the purpose of reforming the liturgies then in use. Two principal objects of the reform were (1) to furnish a liturgy entirely in the English language and (2) to simplify the liturgy by reducing the number of services and the unmanageable elaboration of rubrics. The fruit of their efforts was the Prayer Book of 1549, the basis for all subsequent revisions. These were made in 1552 (but suppressed by Mary I in 1553 before it came into use), 1559 (under Elizabeth I), and 1604 (a few minor changes under James I). From 1645 until the Restoration, its use or even possession was forbidden by Parliament. A revision was prepared in 1661, after the Restoration of the Monarchy, and adopted in 1662. It is in all essentials the version of the Prayer Book which has continued as the official liturgy of the Church of England to the present day, and which was therefore in use throughout the nineteenth century. The only notable modifications have been a revision of the lectionary in 1871 and the addition and later deletion of special orders of service for some national days, commemorating such events as the Gunpowder Plot, the Glorious Revolution, and the Restoration of the Monarchy.

The daily office hours of the mediaeval Church were the source for the Prayer Book offices of Morning and Evening Prayer. The old offices were better adapted to the communal life of monasteries, where it was feasible to gather frequently throughout the day for prayers and devotions. Under other circumstances, the offices were generally 'accumulated', that is, several of them were said in unbroken succession, resulting in a great deal of repetition of items common to the various offices. The Prayer Book offices do essentially the same thing, but they eliminate the redundancies of the former practice. Morning Prayer (sometimes called Mattins) is thus a synthesis of the old offices of Mattins, Lauds, and Prime. Evening Prayer (or Evensong) is a synthesis of Vespers and Compline. The lesser hours of Terce, Sext, and None were often omitted before the Reformation except in monasteries, and they were not included in the Prayer Book scheme. Here, then, is an outline of the order for Morning and Evening Prayer as found in the 1662 Prayer Book and observed in Victorian churches and cathedrals. Sung items are given in capitals.

> Introductory sentences, bidding, general confession and absolution, Lord's Prayer
> PRECES ('O Lord, open thou our lips...')
> VENITE, EXULTEMUS DOMINO (Ps. 95) [At Morning Prayer only; there is no equivalent of this item in Evening Prayer.]
> PSALMS OF THE DAY
> The first lesson (Old Testament)
> CANTICLE Morning: *Te Deum laudamus* or *Benedicite, omnia opera* (Song of the three holy children)
>   Evening: *Magnificat* (Luke 1:46–55) or *Cantate Domino* (Ps. 98)
> The second lesson (New Testament)
> CANTICLE Morning: *Benedictus* (Luke 1:68–79) or *Jubilate Deo* (Ps. 100)
>   Evening: *Nunc dimittis* (Luke 2:29–32) or *Deus misereatur* (Ps. 67)
> The Apostles' Creed
> VERSICLES AND RESPONSES (Including Short Litany (*Kyrie*) and suffrages)
> COLLECTS (Collect of the day followed by two invariable collects)
> ANTHEM
> Prayers and 'Grace' (II Cor. 13:14)

The lessons were chosen so as to cover the greater part of the Bible during the course of the year. The Book of Psalms was divided into sixty more-or-less equal segments assigned to the morning and evening of each day of the month. Thus if the offices are sung daily, the entire Psalter will be chanted in order each month (except, of course, in February). It is worth noting that the 1662 Prayer Book was the first to make explicit provision for the anthem, though of course anthems were composed and sung in Tudor and Jacobean times.

As Morning and Evening Prayer were derived from the Catholic daily office, so the Prayer Book Communion Service was derived from the Catholic mass, but as the following outline of the 1662 order shows, it was considerably simplified and the items arranged differently.

> Lord's Prayer (without doxology) and Collect for Purity (said by the priest only)
> THE TEN COMMANDMENTS
> Collect of the day
> The Epistle
> The Gospel
> The Nicene Creed
> Sermon
> Offertory, preceded by one or more offertory sentences
> Prayer for the Church Militant (a general intercession)
> Bidding, general confession and absolution, followed by 'Comfortable Words'
> Eucharistic Canon: *Sursum corda*, preface, *Sanctus*, prayer of institution (consecration), communion of priest and people, Lord's Prayer with doxology, prayer of oblation and thanksgiving
> *Gloria in excelsis*
> Benediction

The *Kyrie* of the Anglican service consists of the responses to the Ten Commandments rather than the short litany of the mass. The response to each of the first nine is: 'Lord, have mercy upon us, and incline our hearts to keep this law.' The response to the tenth is: 'Lord, have mercy upon us, and write all these thy laws in our hearts, we beseech thee.' Notice that the *Gloria in excelsis* is placed near the end of the service, when in the Roman mass it occurs immediately after the *Kyrie*. The *Benedictus qui venit* and *Agnus Dei*, normally sung portions of the mass, are omitted altogether from the Prayer Book service.

The outline above represents typical practice in cathedrals during the first half of the nineteenth century. In contrast with the continental practice of devoting the greatest attention to choral settings of the Mass Ordinary, the paucity of sung items in the English service and the practice of speaking items that one would expect to be sung are immediately striking. This may be taken as reflecting the prevailingly Protestant spirit of most Anglican worship at the time, tending to place minimal emphasis on the sacraments and on Eucharistic worship in particular. This tendency was notable from the later seventeenth century onwards. By the early nineteenth century, the normal Sunday morning service consisted of an accumulation of Morning Prayer, Litany, and Holy Communion. In many places, there might be an actual communion as seldom as four times a year, in which case, the weekly Communion Service (or more properly, the ante-Communion) would end after the Prayer for the Church Militant. Even where there was a weekly communion, the choir generally dispersed at this point, and the remainder of the service would be conducted without music. Thus the choral items of a typical cathedral Communion Service of the time would consist of a *Sanctus* (transplanted from the Eucharistic Canon to become a kind of introit marking the transition from the Litany to the Communion Service), and the *Kyries* (responses to the Ten Commandments). The Creed might or might not be sung.

English cathedral music has generally placed the greatest emphasis on the canticles and anthems for Morning and Evening Prayer, these being the most artistically ambitious genres in regular use, and consequently the objects of principal concern in the ensuing study. Indeed, from the time of the Restoration, the weight of emphasis was concentrated on anthems at the expense of canticles, which were increasingly treated in the perfunctory 'short service' idiom that became normal in the late seventeenth century and throughout the eighteenth. A 'complete' Anglican Service, as a musical genre, consists of settings of the canticles for Morning and Evening Prayer plus the sung portions of the Communion Service. Many services are not complete in this sense, in that they comprise only settings of the morning and/or evening canticles. Anthems, of course, offer considerable freedom in choice of text and manner of treatment, and this may explain their greater popularity.

One of the effects of the Tractarian revival was to place greater emphasis on Eucharistic worship, with a resulting desire for musical elaboration. As there was a lack of suitable settings of the Communion Service by English cathedral composers of the past, as compared with the wealth of morning and evening services, many High Church establishments turned to mass settings by continental composers, adapted to the Prayer Book texts. A landmark in this development was the liturgical performance in 1866 of Gounod's *Messe solennelle de Ste Cécile*, including a harp, at St Andrew's, Wells Street, under the direction of Joseph Barnby. Before long, as choral worship gained wider acceptance, churches other than those of Tractarian leanings began to make use of such adaptations, sometimes with mixed reaction. Again Barnby was in the vanguard with the elaborate choral services presented at St Anne's, Soho, where he was appointed in 1871.

Finally, it is worth noting in general that English cathedral music is not essentially music rendered by large forces in the presence of huge congregations, which is sometimes the case with elaborate church music in other countries, Catholic and Protestant. The English daily choral service is typically an intimate affair, associated not with the cavernous naves of the great cathedrals but with their enclosed or semi-enclosed choirs, or college chapels, with a small choir and clergy seated in fairly close proximity in facing stalls. A congregation is welcome but not strictly essential, because the statutory duty of the collegiate body, the choir and chapter, is to render daily choral praise for the glory of God, not primarily for the edification of human listeners.

Introduction

It is a remarkable development of the Victorian period that cathedral music came to be regarded as the normal music of the Anglican Church as a whole, not just the preserve of the choral foundations. The ecclesiological ideal, while essentially parochial, was destined not to gain wide acceptance. It was too closely tied to a much misunderstood and widely unpopular strain of churchmanship, and too firmly bound to a musical repertory of the remote past. While it was impractical, even undesirable, for all parish churches to adopt the cathedral ideal wholesale, it was this ideal that had the potential for public enthusiasm, as adopted in the diocesan choral festivals, and as the cathedrals themselves raised their musical and devotional standards. Elements of the cathedral ideal found their way into the typical parish churches of the land to produce that varying mixture of congregational and choral worship that had become the norm by the end of the Victorian era, and that may only now be showing serious signs of disintegration.

PART I

Victorian cathedral music in theory: issues that shaped the composer's creative world

1

The malaise of neo-puritanism

The state of English musical culture in the nineteenth century

Are the English a musical people? This is a question that has been raised, sometimes with polemical intent, by many observers, native and foreign. It is a question of some relevance to the theory and practice of Victorian cathedral music, since one may reasonably expect that the status of music in the life of the Church of England will stand in close relation to the status of music in general culture. Indeed, it is with respect to this general status that the question has any meaning at all, since it is clearly not a question about the quantity of musical talent in a population, but rather about the importance that society attaches to musical activities and interests.

In the nineteenth century, it is notable that many musical Englishmen, either directly or implicitly, answered this question in the negative. This was so even quite late in the century, when the amount of serious musical activity in England was much greater and more widely diffused than during its earlier years. For example, Hugh Reginald Haweis (1838–1901), a Broad-Church clergyman in the West End of London and an enthusiastic musical amateur, wrote in 1871:

Although we are inclined to admit that the English are on the whole a Religious People, we arrive at the sad conviction that, however improving and improvable, the English are not, as a nation, an artistic people, and the English are not a Musical People.[1]

Similarly, Frederick J. Crowest (1850–1927), a professional singer and organist, literary editor, and writer on musical subjects, declared in 1881 that 'we are not essentially a musical people, as are, for instance, the Italians: musicians do not spring up on English soil near so rapidly as do capitalists, clergymen, shopkeepers, and mechanics'.[2] Other observers deplored the fact that much ostensibly musical activity in England was not motivated by a devotion to the art, but pursued for ulterior motives: mercenary in the case of professionals, and as a superficial 'accomplishment' in the case of many non-professionals. William Spark (1823–97), once an articled pupil of S. S. Wesley at Exeter and Leeds and later organist of Leeds Town Hall, writing in an essay of 1870, inveighed against the legions of incompetent music teachers on precisely these grounds for furnishing faulty and insubstantial instruction using only cheap and trivial music.[3] In 1883, Sir George Grove (1820–1900), frustrated by the difficulties of raising endowment funds for the new Royal College of Music, declared that 'the national intellectual bias is opposed to what it is pleased to consider non-essentials', and that 'to the ordinary educated Englishman, music is an abstraction until united with some essential, such as sectarian opinion, or utilised for some charitable purpose, or made incarnate in a brass band ministering to the works of the flesh and of fashion'.[4] In the *Pall Mall Gazette* of 14 October 1884, he observed that 'a musical nation in the sense in which Germany and Italy are musical nations, that we most certainly are not'.[5]

England has been called the 'land without music'. As there has always been music in English life, perhaps it would be more accurate to say that, through much of the eighteenth and nineteenth centuries, England appeared to be without a national sense of music. The illusion of a country without a music of its own was reinforced prior to the later nineteenth century by a peculiar preference for foreign composers and performers. This placed native musicians at a disadvantage, while foreigners knew only too well that some of the richest fees in Europe were to be had in London.

While many Englishmen sincerely believed that fine music, like fine wine, is a luxury the native soil will not produce, many English musicians were convinced that this pro-foreign prejudice was mainly the result of ignorance clinging to fashion. In an essay on early Victorian music, E. J. Dent remarked that the English public tend to base their devotion to performers and composers more on affection than genuine critical discernment.[6] They could be remarkably obtuse about recognising native talent. It is notorious, for instance, that William Sterndale Bennett (1816–75) found a more receptive audience for his music in Leipzig than in London.[7]

There was always, of course, a significant English minority, both professional and amateur, which was seriously interested in fine music, a minority which grew considerably during the second half of the nineteenth century. Many were convinced of the need to produce a more musically intelligent public capable of appreciating music on its merits rather than mindlessly following the commercial arbiters of fashion. This was a goal to be achieved through the wider dissemination of musical instruction and increased cultivation of amateur musical activity. Such developments were urged by proponents of amateur music like Augusta Mary Wakefield (1853–1910), one of the pioneers of the competition festival movement,[8] and Frederick Crowest.[9] It was a position consistent with the more overtly moralistic arguments in favour of the sight-singing movement of the 1840s, and the campaign for more and better musical education in the nation's schools.[10] Many of the reformers looked to Germany in these respects as a model of healthy musical culture. It is important to distinguish those who urged emulation of the German example from those who were content merely to import the German product.

The background of nineteenth-century
neo-puritanism

However depressed the state of English musical culture may have been in the nineteenth century, this had not always been so. In Tudor and Jacobean times, musical skill and discernment were normal accomplishments of a lady or gentleman. Whereas legend has it that the Puritans stamped out music making in mid-seventeenth-century England, Percy Scholes has proved the opposite. The Puritans did abolish all church music but unaccompanied metrical psalmody sung in unison, but they did not object to music as such. On the contrary, they supported a flourishing secular-music culture, and Scholes has documented the fact that most of the Puritan leaders were lovers of music and even of social dancing, many of them being keen amateur musicians.[11] English music publishing flourished during the period, and it is worth noting as an example that John Playford's *The English dancing master* first appeared in 1651, at the height of the Interregnum.

In the eighteenth century, however, the picture had changed. The practice of music, far from being an edifying recreation for the cultivated gentleman, was seen as simply beneath his dignity. Lord Chesterfield's notorious remarks to his son were typical and authoritative.[12] Music was at best a pleasant noise to be provided by hirelings, preferably foreign. A musical nobleman like the Earl of Mornington (1735–81) was regarded as something of an oddity. When Charles Burney (1726–1814) proposed in 1774 that the Foundling Hospital be developed as a school for the training of young musicians on the pattern of schools he had seen in Naples and Vienna, his ideas met with jeers and ridicule, including the publication of a vulgar satire.[13] To some extent, such attitudes survived throughout the nineteenth century, though they may have been slightly less virulent, and the growing devoted minority was a mitigating factor.

It is difficult, even precarious, to assign external causes for the depressed state of English musical culture in the eighteenth and nineteenth centuries. There is no guarantee that classic social, political, economic, and religious factors will be adequate to account for cultural phenomena which, while certainly influenced by such forces, may to some extent be said to have a life of their own. Nevertheless, one can identify some persistent attitudes inherited from the past that had become obstacles to Victorian musical culture.

The truisms and slogans that elicit widespread assent in one age can sometimes be recognised as the popularised and generally distorted forms of sophisticated philosophical positions of the past. A metamorphosis of this kind seems to have played a part in producing the state of musical culture inherited by nineteenth-century England. Thus while music flourished in English culture of the seventeenth century, its respectability among the educated was probably being undermined even then by the growth of what, for convenience, may be termed rationalist thought. The term as used here will denote a propensity to confine the notion of ideas, and hence the province of the intellect, to what is expressible in verbal form, this being regarded as the pre-eminent vehicle of human reason. It will also imply that the very highest value is accorded such kinds of mental activity in comparison with all others.

Proceeding from ostensibly Aristotelian principles, many rationalist thinkers assessed the merits of the arts according to their capacity to imitate nature. Music, being severely limited in its representational powers, compared with poetry and painting, was perceived by such a frame of mind as nothing more than a play of meaningless sounds, pleasing in a sensual way, but incapable of seriously engaging the mind, and thus beyond the pale of reason. At most it might serve to raise the passions, but such emotional activity in the absence of rational ideas was something to be regarded with cautious circumspection. Thus in the opinion of John Locke and many other thinkers, music was the least worthy of accomplishments, and eighteenth-century writers on aesthetics often ranked instrumental music lowest in the scale of the arts.

Although seventeenth-century Puritans cannot be blamed directly for the general decay of musical culture in subsequent centuries, the state of affairs inherited by the Victorians probably does owe a great deal to currents of religious thought and events unique to England. This, coupled with a rationalist intellectual temper, helped to distinguish the characteristics of English musical culture from those elsewhere in Europe, and it is highly likely that Puritanism was not unrelated to what transpired.

The stereotype of the Victorian spirit – 'earnest, moral, not overly refined, but still forward-looking'[14] – is commonly characterised as puritan and middle-class, though closer examination reveals that it is not coextensive with any social class defined according to hereditary, residential, economic, political, or occupational criteria.[15] Still, like all stereotypes, it has a basis in fact. Numerous historians agree that the Victorian spirit may be linked to the moral reformation that was an important social consequence of the Evangelical movement, both inside and outside the Church of England. It gradually worked a transformation in society at large from the promiscuous ethos of the Regency period to the strict propriety of the Victorian.[16]

Eighteenth-century Evangelicalism, however, was significantly different from the classic Calvinist Puritanism of the seventeenth century. Erik Routley has made the following intriguing observation:

The Wesleys publicly repudiated classic Puritanism, but nobody was a more consistent temperamental Puritan than John Wesley, except his brother Charles. Puritanism was a theology and a way of life up to the end of the seventeenth century. In the eighteenth century it was transformed – one might well say corrupted into a temperament...The irrational and emotional philistinism which later associated itself with the word 'Puritan' was an eighteenth-century manifestation, which continued into the nineteenth century.[17]

If the puritanical temperament described by Routley was an integral part of eighteenth-century Evangelicalism, this goes some way towards explaining the earnestness of much eighteenth- and nineteenth-century philistinism, and in particular the deterioration of musical culture. The blurring of rigorous Puritan divinity into a serious but essentially intuitive and emotive temperament seems consistent with a tendency to blur the classic Puritan strictures against music in public worship and expand them into a general attitude towards music itself, while the tone of religious seriousness might be claimed to have blurred and expanded the rationalist intellectual verdict on music into an emotive moral conviction. For convenience, this temperament and its associated attitudes and prejudices will hereafter be referred to as 'neo-puritanism', and will especially denote the conviction that music as such is morally questionable, effete and enervating, a squandering of energy that could be better expended in worthier directions, at best an innocuous and trivial pastime not to be taken seriously, and hence fundamentally at odds with religious devotion if not kept within severe bounds. The arguments most often chosen by those Victorians who sought to promote music were that it is conducive to morality, edifying, uplifting, serious, and hence worthy of earnest attention and cultivation, thus answering neo-puritanism on its own terms and appealing to its own values.

The musical consequences of neo-puritanism were not confined to the Evangelical movement, which appears to have been rather a result than a cause of the temperament. As if in the wake of the Glorious Revolution, the anti-aesthetic temper came to predominate even in the highest reaches of the Establishment. The momentum of Restoration church music may be perceptible in the works of composers like Blow and Croft, but in the eighteenth century, it is generally agreed, English cathedral music entered its worst decline, mitigated only by works of a few composers like Greene and Boyce and the professionalism of several less inspired musicians like Nares, Dupuis, and Arnold. The state of affairs inherited by Victorian church musicians was hardly encouraging, the anti-aesthetic temper being manifested not only in church music but in musical life generally. Neo-puritanism was more than a religious disposition; it was a broad set of cultural habits.

Neo-puritanism and the case against it in the Victorian Church

The malaise of neo-puritanism as it affected English church music in the nineteenth century is most conspicuously manifested in two principal categories of opposition: (1) objection to music in general as a part of worship, and (2) objection to the choral principle in worship. The misunderstandings underlying these objections were deepened by the fact that in the eighteenth century and well into the nineteenth, most English parishioners and many clergy were simply unaccustomed to elaborate music or the continual chant of the choral service as a part of worship.[18] Strong associations of choral worship with Tractarians and ritualists, bringing many suspicious fears of creeping popery, helped to sustain the anti-aesthetic temper. It was largely owing to the passage of time that these prejudices lost some of their force as the choral element became a more normal part of Anglican worship, as did many of the ceremonies, vestments, furnishings, etc., once thought 'advanced' and controversial. In 1881, the architect G. F. Bodley remarked, 'We live at a time when Puritan prejudices, as far as externals go, are passing away.'[19] There were throughout the century, however, those who continued to object along these lines. Indeed, increasing popular acceptance of things they considered objectionable roused neo-puritan hard-liners to a renewal of urgent attacks during the 1880s and 90s.

The two categories of opposition proceeded from essentially the same neo-puritan premises, and might be regarded as different in degree rather than kind. The difference in practical emphasis, however, justifies the distinction. The first category entails rationalist preconceptions, that music by its nature is fundamentally alien to worship and illegitimate because of its meaningless sensuality, while true worship consists of prayer and preaching, essentially verbal activities. Many of those arguing along the lines of the second category outwardly professed a high regard for the role of music in worship as a means of inspiring religious devotion, but they tended to assume that such spiritual benefit as music is able to impart is confined to those actually doing the singing, and so insisted that all worship music be congregational, at least in parish churches. Practicality requires that such music be technically simple enough to permit the participation of the musically untutored, but many of the arguments advanced by advocates of exclusively congregational music reveal the presence of the same anti-musical preconceptions as in the first category. They go beyond practical necessity to allege that all sense of aesthetic artifice in music constitutes interference with devotional quality by diverting attention away from the sacred words, thus implying in addition that music lacks an expressive power of its own which may be turned to devotional purposes, and that art cannot but be antagonistic to religion unless confined within the severest limits.

A prime exhibit of the first category of opposition, together with a forceful and erudite refutation, appears in the tract *An apology for church music and musical festivals in answer to the animadversions of the Standard and the Record* (1834) by Edward Hodges (1796–1867), who was an organist, composer, and contributor to musical journals. He spent a substantial part of his career (1838–63) in North America, where he became the first organist of Trinity Church, New York, in 1846. On 31 March and 2 April 1834, the editor of the *Standard*, an organ of old High-Church Toryism, published scathing attacks on music in general and church music in particular, responding to a forthcoming festival at Westminster Abbey and to a defence of church music from a correspondent. The editor deplored the efforts of some clergymen to increase the amount of music in worship by chanting the canticles in Morning and Evening Prayer, 'and other portions of the church service, so eloquent, so full of masculine dignity in their composition, that music, or any other added ornament, cannot fail to deform them'.[20] He further claimed that music is an obstruction to devotion because it is purely sensual and does not 'convey any definite idea to the understanding', while such powers as music actually does exert are thus 'objections to its admission as part of an intellectual service'.[21]

Hodges refutes these charges by assembling an impressive array of literary witnesses, arguing for the stature of music as a worthy occupation of the mind and source of nourishment for the spirit. These include the anonymous *Praise of musicke* (1586) and writings by Sir John Hawkins, Lord Bacon, Richard Hooker, Shakespeare, James Harris, and numerous learned eighteenth-century clerics. Perhaps even more significant is Hodges' counterattack on the rationalist presuppositions of the *Standard*'s editor, particularly the odious and dangerous notion that Christian worship is essentially or exclusively an intellectual activity. He invokes the shade of the French Revolutionists' deification of reason and its dire consequences, a comparison which must have stung the Tory editor. Hodges agrees that the Christian faith should engage the mind of the believer in the rationalist sense, but insists that it demands more: the affections rather than the understanding, resting in the heart rather than the head, driven by love rather than cogitation.[22] Music is not repugnant to the intellect, but its influence over the affections is completely in accord with that warmth of feeling indispensable to true Christian worship, yet beyond the reach of cold reason. Hence music has a rightful place in the services of the Church.

A book worthy of notice in this regard is *The music of the Church* (1831), a comprehensive and often morally impassioned treatise by John Antes Latrobe (1799–1878). Having received the Oxford M.A. and ordination in 1829, Latrobe in 1831 was at the start of a clerical career during which he served in several curacies before his appointment to the living of St Thomas's, Kendal, in 1840, where he remained until 1865, becoming an honorary canon of Carlisle in 1858. His book is of considerable historical importance as a detailed discussion of the state of English church music in the years immediately preceding the Oxford Movement. Although the book is not specifically a defence of church music against direct neo-puritan attacks, Latrobe does seek to uphold the cause of church music at a time of indifference and neglect. While the mode of presentation is more homiletic than philosophical, Latrobe's discussions of principles are of more than ephemeral value, since they raise most of the perennial issues which engaged contemporary and later defenders of church music.

One of the fundamental issues for Latrobe is that music in worship is not just a permissible option, but a solemn duty owed by the worshipper to God, who implanted the gift of music to be used to his glory.[23] He invokes histori-

cal precedent for church music, noting that from earliest antiquity, music has
been associated with worship, with documentary evidence of musical worship in the early Church from the New Testament, Pliny, Justin Martyr, etc.[24]
More importantly, Latrobe maintains that music is a means of spiritual
edification. It may not impart religious knowledge, but it does arouse religious affections.[25]

How are the spiritual gifts of God bestowed upon man? By an imperceptible influence,
or by working upon the affections? Can the two great commandments of the law, love
to God, and love to the neighbour, be fulfilled without feeling? If then feelings are
under divine influence, is not that mode which most deeply impresses upon those feelings, the truth and majesty of the divine word, the best under God's blessing for the
transmission of His Spirit?[26]

Latrobe does not confine the capacity for spiritual edification to congregational music; the remarks above were made with specific reference to the
chanted psalmody of the cathedral tradition. He insists on the value of
anthems as a means of spiritual communication, on the grounds that the
expressive power of music can deepen the impression of the sacred text on the
hearer.[27] Furthermore, Latrobe claims that one does not require a knowledge
of musical technicalities to derive spiritual benefit from hearing an anthem.
He cautions against attributing to the fault of the compositions themselves
problems arising from abuses in performance and from erroneous notions as
to the function of anthems, a problem for which the negligence and ignorance of the clergy may in large part be blamed.[28]

One of the most articulate early Victorian defenders of church music was
Dr Robert Druitt (1814–83), a physician by profession, but a keen musical
amateur and conscientious High Churchman. He was a co-founder in 1846
of the Society for Promoting Church Music, and editor of its journal, *The
Parish Choir*, which appeared from 1846 to 1851. His systematic refutation of
the prejudices and misconceptions of popular neo-puritanism is found in
Conversations on the choral service, a series of articles in dialogue format in
The Parish Choir, republished in book form in 1853. He had raised many of
the same issues in *A popular tract on church music with remarks on its moral
and political importance and a practical scheme for its reformation* (1845).

Like Latrobe, Druitt maintained that the use of music in worship is a duty,
a conclusion he reinforced by contrasting prayer and praise. He declared that
prayer, as intercession, is concerned with the earthly life, sins, and needs of
mortals, while praise is concerned with God's goodness and mercy. From this
point of view, praise is the higher form of worship, and of the two, it is the one
which will endure in eternity, when all need for intercessory prayer will have
vanished. Thus that form of public worship is best in which praise, expressed
communally, is the distinguishing feature. The most solemn and dignified of
all forms of public praise is the choral service of the Church.[29] A contemporary illustration of the opposite sentiment is supplied by the reply from
Canon Sydney Smith of St Paul's to a request by William Hawes in 1844 to

increase the number of cathedral choristers. Hawes cited the size of other choirs in support of his proposal. Smith answered in a letter of 21 August: 'It is a matter of perfect indifference to me, whether Westminster bawls louder than St. Paul's. We are there to pray, and the singing is a very subordinate consideration.'[30] Smith thus implies that worship is virtually synonymous with prayer.

Druitt was not advocating the installation of cathedral-type choirs in every parish church. He was emphatic in his insistence on the congregational basis of the choral service and the demolition of the popular fallacy that there is a fundamental difference between cathedral and parochial worship. He points out that there is one Book of Common Prayer, therefore one liturgy for both and one ideal for its execution. Any difference should be in degree, not in kind, with all observances of the liturgy as solemn and elevated as means permit. He heartily endorses the elaborate music of the cathedral tradition, saying of anthems that '*good* Church Music is essentially necessary; it is an offering due from us; a debt; a thing we owe to the service of the Church, if we enjoy it anywhere else'.[31] He joins Latrobe, Hodges, and many others in affirming that the feelings deserve to be addressed in religion as well as the mind, that the love of hearing church music should not be condemned by the connoisseurs of pulpit oratory, that 'anthems are themselves sermons, only more eloquent'.[32] Cathedrals and other institutions with endowed choral foundations are, of course, obliged to maintain worship to a high standard of musical professionalism. Parishes, however, are not exempt from maintaining such music in the service as they can. Druitt defends his position by appeals to history, propriety, and practicality, and he is careful to pre-empt accusations of 'Romanising' Anglican worship, a very sensitive issue around the middle of the century. He does not reject the use of a trained choir in the parish church for the singing of more elaborate music than is feasible for the congregation, but his ideal is for the congregation to assume all the functions of a choir.[33]

Attacks on church music did not cease later in the century. Consider, for instance, an address to the Newcastle Church Congress of 1881 by Edward Henry Bickersteth (1825–1906), a prominent Evangelical clergyman and editor of the widely-used *Hymnal Companion to the Book of Common Prayer*. He presents his sentiments as a defence of church music, but he soon reveals his neo-puritan colours.

I grant you, there may be too much of music and song in our parish churches. I think there is too much when it 'cribs, cabins, and confines' the sermon, the preaching of the everlasting Gospel, God's chosen instrument for the salvation of souls, and for the building up of His people in their most holy faith...Up to a certain limit, music is the greatest help to devotion; beyond that limit music depresses and dissipates religious fervour.[34]

The chief ingredients are stated or implied: the notion that music is inherently dangerous and debilitating, implicit denial of its capacity for spiritual edification beyond a severely limited degree, a tendency to regard it as an optional frill, and its unequivocal subordination to a purely verbal medium, not of prayer or praise, but of instruction.

At the Portsmouth Church Congress of 1885, there was a session on the theme 'Religion and art – their influence on each other'. The discussion following the main papers turned into a veritable chorus of neo-puritan attacks on art, in which music received its share of the abuse. Many of the arguments were ostensibly against the choral principle in worship, and some of the speakers professed to defend the role of music, but the nature of their remarks reveals a more general anti-aesthetic attitude. Their axiom seems to be that beauty, as revealed in the highest achievements of the fine arts, is fundamentally alien if not positively antagonistic to worship, on grounds that a devotion to art will supplant religious devotion. The remarks of Canon Edward Hoare of Tunbridge Wells are typical. He refers to the experience of attending a service in which a choral Te Deum was sung.

As an artistic performance it was capital. But what was the effect? Fifteen hundred people stood there in silence, and not one of them could sing. Well, I say the very per-fection of the art destroyed the worship...Art may hinder worship in producing an impression upon the mind which is substituted for the reality of communion with God...Let the thrill produced by [the power of music] become to a man a substitute for the real intercourse of his soul with the living God, and his religion is damaged by the success of the art employed. You have given him that which is spurious in the place of that which is true.[35]

He is obviously unwilling to allow that the finest art may be a medium of genuine, not spurious spiritual edification. The notion of a duty to render praise with the finest means available is at odds with neo-puritan prejudices as to what constitutes worship. Hoare praises the aid to devotion provided by fine hymns, but on the whole his unmistakable message is that art is admis-sible to worship only if it is not too much and not too good. J. Johnston Bourne, also of Tunbridge Wells, flatly denied that any spiritual edification can come from art. The Revd Arthur J. Robinson, Rector of St Mary's, Whitechapel, insinuated that preaching and preaching alone is the means of such edification. The Dean of Wells, chairman of the session, capped the proceedings with the dubious assertion that 'the triumphs of art have never coincided with the intensity of faith'.[36]

The second category of opposition specifically concerns objections to trained choirs singing artistically ambitious music as part of public worship. The misunderstanding arises from a failure to comprehend the spiritual edification and genuine worship attainable in the reverent contemplation of a performance of music too complex for congregational participation, but thereby richer in expression and loftier in concept than might otherwise be possible. As Canon Hoare's remarks illustrate, the overlap with the first category of opposition is considerable, in so far as the arguments run against the propriety of aesthetic artifice as such, but the distinctive feature of the second category is to represent choral music as a deprivation of the congregation's inherent rights of participation.

Around the middle of the century, when feelings were running particularly high, choral worship was often condemned as a Roman corruption. This was the position, for example, of Steuart Adolphus Pears, an assistant master at Harrow, in a tract of 1852 entitled *Remarks on the Protestant theory of church music*. He deplores choral music as worship by proxy and a usurpation of congregational rights. He urges disbandment of parish choirs, and displays his anti-aesthetic streak by saying, 'Better to hear the praise of God heartily sung by the people to a vulgar tune, than an anthem of the highest order performed in the purest style by a dozen select singers.'[37] Pears, like many others, inconsistently exempts cathedrals from his ban on choral music. Surely what he holds to be so intrinsically vicious cannot be less so in another setting. It seems likely that Pears's arguments arise as much from cultural habit inflamed by party spirit as from pure principle.

Similar lines of thought were developed at greater length by the Revd Edward Young of Trinity College, Cambridge, in a book entitled *The harp of God: twelve letters on liturgical music, its import, history, present state and reformation* (1861). Young's misunderstanding of the choral principle is matched only by his misunderstanding of music history in general. He claims to defend church music, citing biblical evidence for its status as a gift from God. He maintains that Ambrosian chant, like the music of the ancient Jewish temple, was highly rhythmical, and that this accounts for its extraordinary capacity to move listeners and singers. It was Pope Gregory who robbed music of its rhythm, and later generations of composers, culminating in Palestrina, who reduced the vital music of ancient times to an obscure art of mere harmony, devoid of rhythmic and melodic character. The implication is that this devitalisation of the divine gift into an abstruse occupation for trained choirs is the result of a popish plot. Young seems to regard as legitimate liturgical music only that which is utterly determined by the structure of the text. Once the music shows any degree of independence, he condemns it as pedantic and artificial, and he refuses to acknowledge it as liturgical at all. Hence he praises Jackson's Te Deum in F but condemns the masses of Mozart.[38] He declares that anthems are by nature a dramatic exhibition, and therefore false in expression and a feigning of worship.[39] He does not explicitly seek to do away with choirs, but attacks the choral principle just as effectively by seeking to disqualify the greater part of their repertory.

Although the opponents of the choral principle were mostly Evangelicals, there were High Churchmen whose allegiance to the ecclesiological ideal of the choral service, entailing Gregorian psalmody, plainsong hymns, and an atmosphere of severe solemnity in worship, was a loyalty so intense and exclusive as to be, in some cases, equally hostile to more elaborate forms of worship music. The more moderate proponents of this ideal tended also to be the more musically inclined: men like Robert Druitt and Thomas Helmore.

They did not object to trained choirs and their repertory, but neither were they champions of elaborate modern church music. Plainsong and sixteenth-century polyphony were more in keeping with the flavour of worship they were intent on cultivating. Other High Churchmen, often the least musical ones, were just as hostile towards elaborate choral music as the most vehement neo-puritan Evangelical. Such a one, for instance, was the Revd Nathaniel Woodard (1811–91), founder of a network of public schools for the middle classes, who amazingly once referred to Sir Frederick Ouseley as the 'sworn opponent of Church Music'.[40] In so far as the enthusiasts for plainsong insisted on the exclusive or nearly exclusive employment in public worship of a severely restricted form of music, not for its intrinsic aesthetic merit but for its consonance with the devotional atmosphere of antiquarian asceticism, one can justly refer to their attitude as a paradoxical variant of neo-puritanism.

Statements critical of elaborate church music sometimes come from unexpected sources. J. B. Dykes (1823–76) was unquestionably in favour of the cathedral tradition of the choral service, and in a paper of 1871 he warmly endorsed the use of anthems in parish churches, but on the subject of the Communion Service he had other ideas. On the one hand, he disliked the 'uncouth crudities' of plainsong, but he was equally opposed to elaborate settings of the mass, especially the adaptations of Mozart and Haydn masses for English use, on the grounds that this service is far too solemn to risk having it 'degenerate into a mere occasion for sensuous and aesthetic gratification'. In the end, he preferred to have the organ alone. 'The fewer that are off their knees then, the better.'[41]

Frederick Crowest, advocate of amateur music, insisted that choral music in parish churches is inappropriate. Services should be entirely congregational because 'the Church of England Services are for the laity, and not alone for the clergy and their choirs'.[42] Similar sentiments were voiced by church musician William Henry Gladstone (1840–91) in a Church Congress paper of 1884, noting that choirs often discourage congregations from singing.[43] He expressed disapproval of adaptations of foreign masses as well as long and elaborate canticle settings, even in cathedral services.[44] At the same session, Walter Parratt (1841–1924) opined that choral services have too much music, so that those portions which naturally lend themselves to musical treatment thereby lose most of their special effect.[45] Such sentiments, from expected and unexpected sources, might be collected *ad nauseam* from Victorian documents.

By the same token, defenders of choral music were not wanting. In the 1830s, J. A. Latrobe seems to have had some misgivings about extremes of technical complexity in anthems, especially when the text is obscured and distorted, but on the whole he favoured the genre for parochial as well as cathedral worship.[46] In a very curious tract of 1837 entitled *Music and the Anglo-Saxons: being some account of the Anglo-Saxon orchestra, with remarks on the church music of the nineteenth century*, Francis Diedrich Wackerbarth deplores the neglect by the contemporary church of the rich heritage of English church music and the decay into which choral institutions had then fallen, a condition attributed to 'a want of zeal among Protestants for the service of God'. He is careful to dissociate himself from Roman inclinations, but he commends as worthy of emulation the care the Romans show over the details of musical worship and the spirit of self-sacrifice such care betokens. He favours the use of music from other religious traditions, especially Haydn, Mozart, and Bach, to enrich the repertory of the English Church.[47]

The most extensive Victorian treatise on choral worship is *The choral service of the United Church of England and Ireland: being an enquiry into the liturgical system of the cathedral and collegiate foundations of the Anglican Communion* (1843) by the Revd John Jebb (1805–86), an Irish High Churchman and future canon of Hereford Cathedral. This book was preceded by *Three lectures on the cathedral service* given at Leeds in 1841 and published that year in the *Christian's Miscellany*. This was evidently in connection with the opening of the new Leeds Parish Church, for which Jebb was a consultant on matters of choral worship. The lectures reappeared in book form in 1845, and present in more popularly accessible form essentially the same principles which underlie the monumental treatise.

Jebb makes it plain that he regards the choral service in absolute terms as 'the highest, most perfect, and most ancient' mode of worship, and that anything other than the fully choral service, while permissible on grounds of practicality, should be understood as falling short of the ideal.[48] Like Druitt, Jebb considers any attempt to separate the ideals of parochial and cathedral worship to be specious and unhistorical, maintaining that before the Reformation, the choral service was the norm in most parish churches.[49] Unlike Druitt, however, Jebb emphasises the special role of the choir as distinct from the congregation. He dissents vehemently from the popular notion that the congregation must always be taking an audible part in the music in order to be worshipping.

Those who cannot sing well, must remember that it is no part of their duty to make the attempt. All may join in heart and sentiment; all may join, though inaudibly, with their lips. But if music be really an adornment of divine service, it ought not to be hindered of its due effect, by the inharmonious or unmelodious discords of the unskilful.[50]

The choir, however, are not giving a performance for their own amusement or for the congregation's entertainment. They are performing a sacrificial act of worship on their own behalf and that of the congregation. The technical limitations which must be imposed on congregational music would, if the service were to be completely congregational, disallow the finest and most distinguished specimens of the ecclesiastical repertory, and the service would thereby be robbed of a great part of its beauty and dignity, qualities which Jebb maintained are an integral part of worship.

Even Thomas Helmore, an advocate of plainsong and the congregational ideal of the choral service, was just as warm in his defence of the choral principle.

I fear...many pious persons have not fully realized the fact that it is as possible, and as right (abstractly considered,) to stand before the altar in worship silently, while a choir is raising some solemn or joyous strain to the praise and glory of Almighty GOD, as it is to stand silent...while the Scripture Lessons or the Epistle are read.[51]

He reiterates that choral worship is not just for cathedrals, but an obligation of parish churches 'as the means, ability, and zeal of the ministers and people, together with a choir, if there be one (voluntary or official), will allow'.[52]

Later in the century, just as there was no scarcity of those attacking music in worship and the choral principle, so there were those who defended it along much the same lines as these. In *Music and morals*, H. R. Haweis fervently defended anthems against the attacks of the exclusive congregational position.[53] At he Rhyl Church Congress of 1891, C. H. Hylton Stewart, Precentor of Chester, argued for the coexistence of congregational and choral music in parish churches, claiming that the 'contemplative' choral repertory 'is too good not to have in our worship, because it has a power of edification different from that of congregational music but no less valuable'.[54] At the Exeter Church Congress of 1894, a most eloquent defence of church music in general and choral music in particular was delivered by Sir John Stainer.[55]

John Spencer Curwen (1847–1916) was a Congregationalist, and therefore a direct heir of English Puritanism. He was certainly not hostile to music, not even to sacred choral music as such, but he had serious misgivings as to the extent to which a congregation listening to a choir could actually be said to worship, claiming that it is 'very hard to sustain that elevated mood which draws spiritual good from listening to others singing', and that 'we are always tempted to shrink from worshippers into critics'.[56] In a Glasgow address of 1883 he attempted to account for differences in attitudes to music in worship on lines of religious orientation according to two theories of worship: the Ritual and the Puritan.

The Ritual appeals to the senses, the Puritan to the soul. In the one you have the *sight* of a gorgeous building, and an altar blazing with light; the *sound* of bewitching music; the *smell* of incense; the *touch* of holy water; the *taste* of the wafer. In the other, in its purest form, you have the senses completely ignored, the forms of worship, such as they are, appealing straight to the intellect and the soul. The Ritualist treats man as if he were an animal; the Puritan treats him as if he were an angel. Unfortunately for the theories of each, man is neither: he is a mixture of both.[57]

To be fair, Curwen recognised that some accommodation must be reached that takes account of both elements in human nature, but the serious flaw in his analysis is to treat the externals of worship necessarily as forms of self-indulgence. This point of view underlies many of the attacks on church music cited above. An answer to the objections implicit in Curwen's analysis was supplied some forty years before in a letter of 7 October 1841 from the Revd Walter Farquhar Hook (1798–1875), Vicar of Leeds.

Now it is of the essence of Protestantism, to refer everything to self; it is of the essence of Catholicism to refer everything to God. A Protestant goes to church to get good to his soul, a Catholic to glorify God; a Protestant to have his own mind impressed, a Catholic to do God service; a Protestant desires to have the service addressed, as it were, to himself, a Catholic to offer a sacrifice to God; a Protestant desires to have his ecstatic feelings excited, since he judges of the state of his religion by the state of his blood; a Catholic desires to have everything so done that he may be solemnly reminded, at every point of the service, that he is engaged with saints and angels in an unearthly work. He confesses his sins, but it is with the Church; he praises God but with the Church, he prays, but with the Church, in the Church's own peculiar language and peculiar tone. According, then, as your feelings are more Catholic or more Protestant, you will like or dislike cathedral service. A Protestant must hate Choral Service, though, if he likes music, he may commit the sin of going to church unworthily to hear the anthem; a Catholic, though he knows nothing of music, will go far to attend regularly the choral service, because it accords with his feeling of performing a service. During the last century the mind of England became thoroughly Protestantised, therefore choral service fell into disuse; it is now becoming again Catholicised, and choral service is coming in.[58]

As the evidence indicates, the Protestant frame of mind described by Hook and exhibited by Curwen did not disappear from the Church of England in the nineteenth century, and this often made the work of church musicians difficult and frustrating.

2

Morality, singing, and church music

The ethical implications of music, while largely neglected in modern times as irrelevant to aesthetic understanding and appreciation, were a serious concern to the Victorians. Moral considerations often entered into philosophical interpretations of the musical phenomenon and helped determine modes of musical practice. Some Victorians believed in distinct moral benefits to be derived from the study of music, and in particular from participation in choral music. Their belief was strong enough to stimulate a flourishing sight-singing movement beginning in the early 1840s under the leadership of men who acted on this conviction with missionary zeal. The movement provided training for many members of the virtually innumerable amateur choral societies and volunteer church choirs of the period. The proportion of amateur to professional singers in the great festival choral societies increased steadily during the course of the century, fed by this more modest but more widely-flung choral activity.[1] Such activity helped to create a large demand for printed music, encouraging the firm of Novello to develop the means of producing choral scores cheaply in octavo format, a development which affected British choral activity at every level. Moreover, the increase in amateur choral activity did much to stimulate the national musical sense and counteract neo-puritan prejudices. This abetted an improvement in the standard of cathedral music and worship, providing a notable stimulus to new church composition, especially in the second half of the century. The perception of a moral dimension in music thus had far-reaching ramifications.

Victorian theories on music and morals

The overwhelming majority of Victorian musicians seem to have held what may be broadly termed a hermeneutic rather than a formalist view of music. That is to say, they believed that music has a significance – for example, emotional expression – which is dependent on the deployment of musical materials but which transcends mere formal design. Many believed that this significance has a capacity to influence the listener's character directly for good or ill. In other words, it has a moral effect; and if it be one's object to employ music in a morally beneficial way, great care must be taken over how the materials are deployed.

33

The most celebrated nineteenth-century statement of the opposing formalist view is Eduard Hanslick's *Vom Musikalisch-Schönen* (1st edn, 1854). Hanslick sought to confine the legitimate province of music to a narrow aesthetic band concerned with a beauty derived entirely from the operation of musical design on the cognitive faculty. He claimed that musical design exists for its own sake, not as a mediator of something else; an end, not a means. While Hanslick allows that emotional expression may take place in music, this is outside its legitimate aesthetic province and thus extraneous to any respectable intellectual formulation about its essential nature and unsatisfactory as a foundation for musical aesthetics. If, as Hanslick claims, musical design cannot mean or signify anything other than itself, it is hard to see how there can be any direct link between it and morality, which is well outside the scope of pure musical design. The strictly formalist position thus excludes the possibility of a moral dimension in music, although Hanslick does not say so explicitly.

Hanslick was in England in 1862, but it is noteworthy that he seems to have been better known than his book, which did not appear in English translation until 1891. Furthermore, the most eminent musical Victorians appear not to have been greatly exercised by a need either to defend or rebut his or any other formalist thesis. On the contrary, some trans-formal property seems to have been taken for granted, even if not always emphasised. The English Victorians did have a strong sense of formal order in the classical sense and in connection with prescriptive musical grammar. They also delighted in scientific investigation of the physical properties of music and their relation to aesthetics,[2] as well as in psychological and anthropological speculations about musical experience.[3] In none of these, however, does one encounter the negative aspects of Hanslick's formalism.

The most celebrated Victorian exponent of the direct moral influence of music was the Revd Hugh Reginald Haweis (1839–1901) in the first section of his book *Music and morals*, probably the most widely read of his published works. It first appeared in 1871, went through some sixteen editions during the author's lifetime, and was still being reprinted well into the twentieth century, at least as recently as the 1930s. While hardly academic philosophy, Haweis's theory is fundamentally sensible and coherent, written in lucid and animated prose easily comprehended by the average reader. One may surmise that for these reasons, his ideas were possibly more in keeping with widely prevalent attitudes than subtle and intricate philosophical speculations would be.

For Haweis, the pre-eminent significance of music is emotional, so that his position on musical morality depends on his theories about the nature and behaviour of the emotions. These may be summarised in four main propositions:

1 That emotion is coextensive with consciousness; that in all our waking moments, we are in some emotional state. It is a mistake to regard emotion

only as intermittent occurrences of intense feeling, as if other moments, characterised by milder feelings, were emotionless.

2 That emotions can exist in the abstract, as in cases of elation or depression for which we are unable to assign an adequate cause.

3 That emotional experiences leave an enduring impression on one's character.

4 That emotional states can be deliberately cultivated; that in so far as emotional behaviour is volitional, it has a moral aspect.

Haweis invokes what he confidently believes to be the shared values of his readers when he insists that the moral exercise of the emotions requires discipline, balance, and restraint, asking the reader 'to condemn as immoral the deliberate cultivation of unbalanced emotions for the sake of producing pleasure'.[4] Extremes of emotion should not be cultivated to excess, nor should they be left without the counterbalance of their complementary opposite. At the heart of the matter is what Haweis calls the battle between 'realism' and 'sentimentalism'. The essence of realism is precisely this healthy balance of emotional impulses, with a sense of due proportion between feeling and action. Sentimentalism, on the other hand, consists of an enervated wallowing in exaggerated and unbalanced emotions. Habitual indulgence in sentimentalism will have a deleterious effect on one's moral character.

Haweis claims that music, of all the arts, is best suited to arouse the emotions because it shares their properties more closely than any other. While music can express the emotional states to which definite thoughts and images give rise, 'absolute music' is unique among the arts in its capacity to arouse abstract emotion in the listener. Music thus involves the manipulation of emotional atmospheres, and to the extent that emotional behaviour has a moral aspect, so does music.

On this basis, then, Haweis is prepared to give a moral characterisation of the principal schools of European music. In a lengthy discussion, he concludes that the Italian school offends by being exaggerated and voluptuous in expression, while the French school is frivolous and sentimental. He makes it clear that these are general characterisations, not wholesale condemnations, and he is glad to acknowledge the merits of outstanding composers like Rossini, Verdi, Auber, and Gounod. As a national school, however, he maintains the superiority of the Germans for the balance and realism of emotional expression in their music, with the moral power of Beethoven standing unsurpassed.

Haweis's remarks on sacred music are brief and somewhat disappointing, since he deals only broadly with genres and makes no stylistic discriminations. He defends oratorio as 'a form of art capable of expressing the noblest progressions of the religious sentiment in the highest planes of emotion'.[5] and insists on its dignity in being dramatic without being theatrical. He speaks of the mysterious emotional bond that unites a congregation during the singing of a hymn. He expresses enthusiastic approval of the cathedral-style choral service, noting the spiritual edification that can come from attentive and reverent listening. What would be most instructive, and what he does not offer, is comment on the contemporary style of church composition, as epitomised in the works of Stainer and Barnby. Later criticism has tended to deplore this idiom as weak and sentimental, and since sentimentality is a characteristic anathema to Haweis, it seems reasonable to expect that he would have been eager to urge its banishment from worship music. He is often highly critical of the taste of the contemporary public, and would not have been likely to miss an opportunity to commend the correction of an abuse in a sphere of musical activity which was so close to him professionally and in which moral and spiritual integrity are of the utmost importance. Tentatively, the lack of condemnation may be construed as fundamental approbation, possibly indicating that what later generations perceived as weak and sentimental was not always so perceived by contemporaries.

Haweis claimed that the ideas elaborated in *Music and morals* were the fruits of his solitary meditations, without recourse to prior or contemporary written authority,[6] but he was certainly not the first to maintain such ideas. The notion that music can arouse, or at least signify, emotional states has a long history which includes the baroque *Affektenlehre*, associating the various states of the human passions with quite specific musical figurations, as well as the tendency of many eighteenth-century Enlightenment thinkers to regard music pre-eminently as the language of human feeling. As early as 1752, Charles Avison, in his *Essay on musical expression*, attributed intrinsic moral benefits to music, claiming that it has the capacity to raise the 'sociable and happy passions and to subdue the contrary ones', but is incapable of stimulating morally impeachable passions such as selfishness, jealousy, or cruelty.[7] In the Victorian era, such sentiments were eagerly put forth by the proponents of choral singing, as witness numerous short items in the early years of the *Musical Times*, which began publishing in 1844.[8]

There were many thinkers – Haweis among them – who believed that the moral effect of music is not always and automatically good. On the contrary, music itself is morally neutral, but its powerful moral influence depends on the intent of the composer or performer and the way he makes use of the art, 'in the same sense in which a drug given one day as a poison and another day as a medicine is in itself perfectly un-moral'.[9] If music has an enormous power to influence moral character, but a power which may be misused either by design or negligence, then matters of taste have serious moral consequences. Hence, discussion of these matters, especially matters of musical education of the young, could and did assume a note of great moral urgency.

There is no better illustration of this than the example of Adolf Bernhard Marx (?1795–1866) in his book *Allgemeine Musiklehre* (1839), or *General music instruction* as translated by George Macirone and published in London by Novello in 1854. While primarily a textbook on the rudiments of music, it contains a group of philosophical chapters of great moral fervour, rising at times to a passion and earnestness of religious devotion. These chapters were serialised in the *Musical Times* from 1859 to 1861.

According to Marx, music is an emanation from the profoundest reaches of the human spirit, full of transcendental significance. Human corruption often debases this spiritual communication by confining music to the level of corporeal sensation and shallow virtuosity. Marx considers this tantamount to blasphemy that dulls the artistic sense, flatters the ego, and so is morally deleterious. The wrong kind of musical training can have a catastrophic effect on the young.

Parents should weigh well, in the choice of a teacher, what power is given him through his art over the mind of their child; that he may elevate the youthful mind to the most noble sentiments, or defile and lower it to the most grovelling: how prejudicial it is merely to leave the mind vacant, while music is acting irresistibly upon the senses and the mind. Listlessness, thoughtlessness, sensuality, vanity, unbridled passion, may be implanted and fostered by the teacher of music; but we may also be indebted to him for awakening and cherishing the noblest powers and sentiments of the soul.[10]

Thus the cultivation of musical taste is not to be taken lightly. As William Holman-Hunt observed, 'What the people are led to admire, that they will infallibly become.'[11]

Marx's characteristically Germanic mystical earnestness may seem foreign to the British temperament, but it is important to remember that the Victorians had the highest regard for German authority in musical matters, of which the publication and diffusion of Marx's book is but one of many examples. From 1857 to the early 1860s, for instance, the *Musical Times* published a series of essays entitled *Truth about music and musicians*, the work of an unnamed German correspondent, translated by Sabilla Novello. Their tendency is along much the same lines as Marx. This sense of music as a mystical religion and reverence for German authority suffuses every chapter of Elizabeth Sara Sheppard's 1853 novel *Charles Auchester*, which is based very loosely on the life and character of Mendelssohn. Haweis's German predilections have already been noted – he was an ardent admirer of Wagner – but his book manages to present these kinds of ideas in a more genially British flavour of seriousness, soft-pedalling the mystical earnestness in favour of a somewhat more mundane and accessible, but no less vehement notion of morality.

It is worth noting that John Ruskin (1819–1900), in some of his later writings,[12] developed theories of music and morals derived not from German sources but from classical: Plato, especially the *Laws*, and the interpretation of Greek mythology. Being true to Plato, Ruskin insisted that music derives its dignity entirely from the words of a text, that wordless music amounts to undisciplined passion: irrational, sensually seductive, and morally enervating. He claimed that musically elaborate text setting is a corruption in which reckless passion takes the lead over sense, and he specifically condemned the genres of sacred oratorio and elaborate church music as sirenic blasphemy, dangerous to the soul. He even wrote a handful of original songs which presumably put his theories into practice.[13] Like Plato, Ruskin stressed the importance of music in general education for building moral character, and he sincerely regarded himself as a music lover upholding the only true principles of the art, but because of his outright hostility to the prevailing norms of nineteenth-century musical practice, Ruskin had virtually no real influence.

At least one Victorian writer denied that the emotional or expressive content of a piece of pure music has any direct bearing on the moral character of the listener. This was Edmund Gurney (1847–88), who developed a highly sophisticated psychology and philosophy of musical experience in his book *The power of sound* (1880). He was unusual among the Victorians in advancing an outwardly formalist view of music, but unlike Hanslick with his closed system of abstract sound patterns, Gurney sought to link the significance of musical form with the most profoundly emotional human experience imaginable, namely sexual desire. He took issue specifically with the theories presented by Haweis in *Music and morals*. Significantly, Gurney did not insist that music and morals are unrelated, but that their relationship is different from that alleged by Haweis.

On this question of morality it is important to avoid confusion between the effects of Music when produced and the causes that bear on its production. Morality tells in the *production* of all work; and of course a naturally-gifted musician is failing in duty if through a failure of earnestness he shirks his responsibilities and writes down to his public, as though a schoolmaster should bring up his pupils on fairy-tales: but the fact that his public are satisfied is the result of their being children, not the cause of their being naughty children. So again a deep moral fervour, as in the case of Beethoven, may accompany and inspire the composer in his work...But Mr. Haweis contends that the symphony of Beethoven stands in direct relation to the *morality* of the *listener*; while I maintain that it is in the greater *beauty* of the work, and the consequently deeper and more enduring *pleasure* of the listener that Beethoven's strenuous labour, patient self-criticism, and general moral superiority...take effect.[14]

If, as Gurney maintains, expressive content in music does not have a direct effect on the morals of the listener, music may still have a powerful but indirect moral influence to the extent that beauty of the highest order will produce pleasure of the noblest order.

I am...anxious not to seem to ignore the indirect moral and social power of Music, already enormous and capable of enormous increase. I believe as firmly as any one that if in life we may promote happiness through morality, in Art we may promote morality through happiness.[15]

Whatever the merits of Gurney's argument, it is important to recognise that direct and indirect moral influences are not mutually exclusive. Haweis, in addition to the emotional and moral theories already described, was deeply concerned with the moral, cultural, intellectual, and spiritual betterment of the lower classes. He felt that mere exposure to good music would be sufficient to work a transforming effect, so he urged the establishment of institutions to make concerts and other edifying recreations widely accessible. Haweis thus affirmed both the direct and indirect moral effects of music, and would surely have seconded Gurney's call to promote morality through happiness by means of music. Indeed, it is likely that Haweis and many other writers did not recognise the sharp distinction that Gurney attempted to make between direct and indirect effects. Whatever their differences in theory, there was a fundamental agreement as to the moral value of music in practice.

Morality in sight-singing and church music

The Victorian conviction concerning the moral benefits of musical activity found its most conspicuous embodiment in the sight-singing movement beginning in the early 1840s. Percy Scholes described it as a 'most extraordinary mania', and insisted that 'mania is *not* too strong a word'.[16] The principal leaders of the movement were Joseph Mainzer (1801–51), a German emigré who was active in Paris before coming to England in 1841; and John Pike Hullah (1812–84), a native English musician and educator, who became interested in the Paris singing classes, and who also in 1841 began his own classes in London. To these may be added the Revd John Curwen (1816–80), who, in seeking a method to teach hymn tunes to children, adapted a system devised by Sarah Ann Glover (1785–1867) of Norwich, and so invented Tonic Sol-fa, which eventually drove all other systems from the field and became something of a national institution which even now is not entirely dead.

Briefly, the sight-singing movement consisted of singing classes which succeeded in training a vast number of people in the rudiments of music, and so stimulated a great many amateur choral societies and church choirs. In a speech to the House of Lords in 1842, Lord Wharncliffe noted that some 50,000 persons were then attending the classes of John Hullah and those of his graduates,[17] and this does not count the pupils of other singing methods. It is noteworthy that the early chapters of *Charles Auchester* involve the protagonist as a participant in a singing class under the direction of a man alleged to be modelled after Hullah. Indeed, Hullah's name became so much a household word that Charles Kingsley could mention it with no further explanation in Chapter 14 of *Alton Locke*, in complete confidence that his readers would fully understand the reference. The movement even gave birth to the *Musical Times*, the Novello publication which originated as a means of making choral scores available at the cheapest possible price to members of singing classes, and whose literary content began more or less as a newsletter of the movement.

The moral dimension of the movement was present from the beginning. As Scholes observed, sight-singing should be seen as part of a larger movement for the general betterment of the working classes. It was naturally associated with the mechanics' institutes and even with the temperance movement.

Mainzer, for instance, was a temperance activist, sometimes appearing at movement rallies. His message, one that was echoed by many proponents of choral singing, was that music is an inherently wholesome and edifying activity, whose cultivation would not only bring direct moral benefits, but would also supplant morally harmful leisure-time diversions. In his treatise *Music and education* (1848), in which he put forth his philosophical arguments concerning the nature of music and the moral value of music as part of general education, Mainzer wrote:

If the people of Great Britain had learned music as an amusement only, they would not want to seek amusement in public houses; and there is the source of their ruin, ruin in health and in character...Shut up public houses, teach the people sober habits for those of intemperance, and soon you will have to close the greater number of the [lunatic] asylums and jails...Teach them in your schools those innocent pleasures which music gives, and you will make their home more attractive. Where is the husband debased enough, who would seek pleasure abroad, when the mother sits by the fireside, surrounded by her children, and sings sacred hymns or songs, appropriate in music and poetry, to time and circumstances![18]

In general, Mainzer's philosophical outlook on music was very similar to that of A. B. Marx, both in content and temperamental character.

Mainzer's career brings together the practical aspects of the sight-singing movement in the British Isles, its link with self-help and social reform movements, a German philosophical flavour, and a crusading temperament tinged with political and social radicalism. In 1826 Mainzer was ordained a priest and became singing master to the seminary at Trier. In 1833 he renounced the priesthood and was forced to flee Germany as a consequence of his political activism. He lived first in Brussels, then in Paris, where, in 1834, he began workmen's singing classes. He reached England in 1841 and began classes in London. From 1842 to 1847 he was active in Edinburgh, and in 1842 began to publish *Mainzer's Musical Times*, the direct ancestor of the Novello periodical. He stood unsuccessfully for the Reid Chair of Music in 1844. From Edinburgh, he moved to Manchester and died in Salford on 10 November 1851.

Hullah's career and outlook were in many ways similar to Mainzer's, but the differences were highly significant. Hullah studied singing at the Royal Academy of Music, and in the later 1830s he composed several operas, including *The village coquettes* (1836) to a libretto by Charles Dickens. In 1839 he travelled to Paris to observe the singing classes conducted according to the system of Guillaume Louis Bocquillon Wilhem (1781–1842). Upon his return to England, he made the acquaintance of Dr James Kay (later Sir James Kay-Shuttleworth, 1804–77), the eminent physician and educationist. In February 1840 he began teaching music to the students of the Battersea Training College, of which Kay was co-founder.

In contrast with Mainzer's radicalism, Hullah was a social and political conservative. As a boy, however, he had been subjected to the inculcation by his Brixton schoolmaster of the radical egalitarian philosophy of Claude-

Adrien Helvétius (1715–71), who held that all native human ability is essentially equal, that apparent differences are the result of environment and upbringing, so that 'placed under the same or like circumstances from infancy, the powers of a Milton and a Tupper might be found equal'.[19] Hullah did not long retain such a radical view, but he was convinced that 'anybody could do anything he put his mind to',[20] that disadvantages of social or economic status are not insuperable obstacles to achievement, and that they are irrelevant to the existence of inherent talent. These convictions became the indispensable foundation for his efforts in the sight-singing movement. While he did not stress the transcendent spirituality of music in the same way as Mainzer and Marx, Hullah did place just as great emphasis on the moral benefits of musical experience.

The impulses and convictions that might easily have led Hullah into fully-fledged radicalism were, in effect, offset by his deep love of civilised culture, especially its music. He greatly prized the gentleness and refinement which for him gave life its humanity, and which he believed it was music's special capacity to bestow. In contrast, his experience of popular radical movements and their aftermath filled him with revulsion, owing to his perception of their tendency to promote and even exalt coarseness and boorishness. He was as much opposed to this inverse snobbery as to the exclusiveness of higher society, both being in his view inimical to humane culture. On balance, he saw that the institutions of society tended better to preserve those things he valued so highly than did their overthrow; hence his conservatism.

Another aspect of Hullah's career, without an exact parallel in Mainzer's, is of special interest in the present study. In addition to his own singing classes, Hullah was engaged to teach sight-singing to the students of St Mark's College in Chelsea, which has already been noted as an important early centre of the ecclesiological ideal of choral worship under the direction of the Revd Thomas Helmore (1811–90), the college's Precentor and Vice-Principal. Hullah's career thus provides a tangible link between the secular singing-class movement and the contemporaneous High Church movement to revive choral worship in Anglican parish churches. Also previously noted was the career of Thomas Helmore's brother Frederick (1820–99), the 'Musical Missionary', whose activities in forming and training choirs in rural parishes were very much an ecclesiastical variant of the sight-singing movement, especially as so many of the choirs trained by him were composed of farm and other labourers and their sons, many of whom had no prior active musical experience.

Hullah's connection with St Mark's College, however, should not lead one to conclude that he was a proponent of the ecclesiological ideal of the choral service. He had his own ideas about church music and of the musical responsibilities of worshippers. These he set forth formally in a lecture of 1846, under the auspices of the Leeds Church Institution, which was published the same year as *The duty and advantage of learning to sing*. The Leeds Parish

Church has already been mentioned as an important centre for choral worship according to the cathedral ideal, boasting Samuel Sebastian Wesley (1810–76) as organist from 1842 to 1849. The Revd John Jebb (1805–86), previously noted as an eminent authority on cathedral worship, had served as consultant in the initiation of choral worship at Leeds and in 1841 had there given his *Three lectures on the cathedral service*. Hullah refers to these lectures approvingly at the start of his own address.

Neither Hullah nor Jebb objected to Gregorian music as such, but they did oppose those extremists who were attempting to promote plainsong as the only form of music appropriate to Christian worship. Hullah surmised that one important reason for the zealots' insistence on the exclusive use of plainsong was their own limited musical capabilities. He notes an inconsistency in the ecclesiologists' attitude towards music as compared with other kinds of church art.

For, be it observed, they are not called upon to build churches, carve finials, or paint frescoes; theirs is the easier task of talking about them. But the delegation of Church singing to others is another matter. There has happily grown up a feeling of late, that they should do this duty for themselves; and seeing no ready mode of raising their powers to the standard of what the Church requires, it is not very surprising that they should have striven here and there to lower the standard to their powers; and so, because every body is not qualified to take part in them, the 'service high and anthem clear' are to be banished from the sanctuary, and we are to take to the Gregorian Chant in unison.[21]

For Hullah, the answer lay not in the complete relegation of church music to trained choirs, though he certainly did not disapprove of them, but in a genuine raising of standards.

It is the duty of a Christian to *qualify himself* for every part of a Christian's duty. If public worship be one part of that duty, and if music be an integral part of public worship, unless we study to take part in that music, how can we be said to worship 'with all our heart, and all our soul, and all our strength?'[22]

This attitude is entirely consistent with the convictions on which he grounded his efforts on behalf of sight-singing, and knowledge of the achievements of his singing classes must have lent additional force to his exhortation.

Hullah used the occasion of his Leeds lecture to express his more general ideas about the moral effects of music and the benefits of learning to sing. Against the charge that music is just a trivial pastime that detracts from more important pursuits and tends towards weakness of character, Hullah cites a list of famous men – Charlemagne, Alfred the Great, Richard Coeur de Lion, Charles V of Spain, Dante, Sir Philip Sidney, Sir Thomas Gresham, John Milton, Sir Thomas More, Bishop Ken, Dean Aldrich, and Martin Luther – who were known practitioners of the art, and submits as further evidence the most glorious period of English history, the age of Elizabeth, as one in which music was most widely and assiduously cultivated.[23]

In an address to the Bristol Church Congress of 1864, Hullah reiterated several of these points. He expressed his disapproval of the antiquarian position of the ecclesiologists. He urged reforms in congregational singing, implying training to enable congregations to sing in harmony, and he even advocated church seating by vocal parts! He favoured the inclusion of women in church choirs, and stressed the moral and social benefits of participation in keeping members from falling into less wholesome pastimes.[24] It is clear from these addresses to church groups that the issues of church music, the countering of neo-puritanism, and the moral benefits of music were closely related in Hullah's mind.

As the examples of Hullah and the Helmores indicate, the moral case for choral singing applies as much to church choirs as to secular singing classes and choral societies. In addition, the philosophical issues pertaining to music and morals have their ecclesiastical counterparts. John Jebb, for instance, affirmed music's transcendent capacity, blending the language of the theologian with that of the philosopher.

Is it not most certain, that ideas allowing of no verbal expression are communicated to the mind by music, so as to be auxiliary either to good or evil; conveyed indeed by the sense, but not themselves sensual, because they are abstract conceptions of the mind, though ministering to the senses, in those unhappy cases when the soul is in subjection to the body...The senses are each an independent channel of some peculiar instruction to the human soul; of which, perhaps, even in her original glorified state she may be incapable except through them; for even in heaven she will be clothed with a body.[25]

Likewise, Robert Druitt (1814–83), in the context of a defence of choral worship, ascribes the origin of music to spontaneous emotional expression, and affirms that music is both the expression of an emotional state and the medium of its communication to the listener, there being a direct relationship between the characteristics of the music and the type of emotional expression communicated.[26] This being the case, music may enlist the feelings in the worship of God, not at the expense of reason, but as its essential complement, in the manner of poetry.

Poetry, especially that of the Bible, is not mere dry pedestrian narrative; it clothes fact with the graces of imagery, similitude, and metaphor; instead of coldly addressing the reason, it rouses the passions; appeals to our love, fear, hope; works not on our knowledge but on our emotions. The mode of using poetry must naturally be that which gives it life and animation; by the beauty and grandeur of musical sound. Music is the very language of elevated feeling, to use a much abused quotation – ''Tis nature's voice, and understood alike by all mankind.'[27]

This line of thought blends into many of the arguments against neo-puritanism, especially those of Edward Hodges discussed previously. In the end, it is only a difference in choice of words whether one says with Haweis that music can be morally beneficial because of the wholesome stirring of the feelings, or with Druitt that it can be spiritually edifying for the same reason.

The parallel may be followed a step further. Haweis maintained that some kinds of music are morally healthy while others are not, depending on the balance and realism of emotional expression as mediated by musical style. Likewise, not all music is equally edifying spiritually or equally appropriate for use in worship. Stylistic and critical discriminations thus come into play in securing the finest and most appropriate music possible for use in worship. Sir John Stainer (1840–1901) put the case with eloquent urgency in an address to the Leeds Church Congress of 1872.

It will, I suppose, be generally admitted that English churchmen have a right to ask that the influence exercised by our cathedrals, whether on art or religion, shall be of the highest and purest character. Knowing as we do the extraordinary effects music is capable of producing on the emotions, on the mind, on the very soul itself, it is of the utmost importance that these effects, this power, should be guided and handled to the best possible purpose. The world of pleasure is fully alive to the allurements of sweet sounds, and very often uses their attractions to no good purpose, and, in so doing, is able to secure the services of the best composers, singers, and instrumental performers. If the Church is content to stand still in matters of music, she is allowing a valuable weapon to be wrested from her hands and used by her adversaries. Our duty, as churchmen, is plain; we must strive to keep the standard of our music as high or higher than that of secular music, and so extend the influence of the Church, as against that of the world. I know there may be many here who will object to this view, as offering aesthetical temptations to worshippers: but should we not compete with the aesthetics of the world? I think we must do so. We should draw into the service of the Church, not only the most promising composers, but also painters, sculptors, and poets, should make art subservient to morality, and make all that is beautiful exemplify and inculcate all that is good.[28]

On this front, then, the issues of music and morals merge with those of stylistic propriety of church music, the subject of a subsequent chapter. It is important, especially in the present day, to remember that these moral considerations were a persistent part of the atmosphere in which the urgent debates on the style of church music were conducted. The flavour of the moral arguments may usually be detected even if they are not always affirmed explicitly. To that extent, at least, they had a significant bearing on compositional practice.

3

Orthodoxy and the composer

The romantic stereotype of the creative artist in the nineteenth century implies a spirit of genius soaring above the constraints of convention, obeying the promptings of the inner muse, independent of imposed authority, under no obligation to gratify the myopic whims of patron or public, subject to no laws but those of genius and art. He is priest, prophet, and creator, not a craftsman producing a serviceable object. This image may have been little more than a gratifying self-delusion for composers of symphonies, chamber music, or opera, who were probably less free of external constraints than they might have been willing to admit. For the composer of church music, however, even the pretence to such freedom is foreign, since his product must fit into and enhance a liturgical action, so that artistic autonomy is more obviously bounded by function. According to the romantic stereotype, this is a burdensome constraint on the artist's supreme creativity, keeping in fetters a spirit that yearns to soar free.

Consider, however, the possibility of composers whose temperamental inclinations and creative aspirations correspond closely with the conditions set by the functions and sentiments of the liturgy, composers whose personal conviction and education conduce naturally to modes of creativity consonant with the ecclesiastical ethos. For such composers, conformity with the requirements of a liturgy would not be a stifling constraint, but a fulfilment, even if a perfect congruence between artistic aspiration and liturgical requirement cannot always be expected in practice.

While somewhat idealised, this description fairly characterises the chief Victorian church composers, most of whom were not only steeped from childhood in the ways of Anglican church music, but were also believers in the essential doctrines of the Christian faith according to the conservative orthodoxy of the Anglican tradition. Some were conspicuously and actively pious, while others seem to have given more routine assent, taking orthodoxy more or less for granted. What is not conspicuous among Victorian church composers is a sceptical religious liberalism or overt manifestation of unbelief. It is worth adding that when the actual state of church music falls so far below the ideal that reform is imperative, it can be carried out better by musicians with a sympathetic insight into the ecclesiastical ethos, having an aspiration to realise it more perfectly, than by those seeking to demolish constraints, pursuing a substantially different ideal. John Stainer did for St

Paul's Cathedral what Franz Liszt would have been temperamentally incapable of doing.

Church music as an act of faith

Many nineteenth-century English writers insisted that participation in church music must be a genuine act of worship. John Antes Latrobe deplored the irreverence of hired singers in fashionable London churches.[1] John Jebb suggested that lay singers in cathedrals ought to be regarded as in a kind of minor orders, 'clergy of the second form', rather than merely hired singers.[2] Thomas Helmore and others urged that all members of church choirs, especially volunteer parish choirs, ought to be communicants, or in the case of younger children, catechumens.[3] Many Victorian sermons and addresses stressed the duty and privilege of rendering choral worship. In a sermon of 1874, for instance, Sir Frederick Ouseley likened the chorister's surplice to the Jewish ephod, a white linen garment set apart for holy use and worn by all who serve in the Lord's temple, both being types of the white robes worn by the angels and saints in the apocalyptic visions of the Old and New Testaments.[4]

Essential as sincerity, integrity, and the avoidance of secularism may be to choristers, choirmasters, and organists, many Victorians maintained the even greater importance of these virtues for composers. William Henry Gladstone eloquently epitomised the ideal in an address of 1884.

It will be evident then, I think, that the spirit of one who writes for the Church, must not be that of a mere musician. He must be this, but he must be something more. His office has some analogy to that of the preacher. He, too, has to select, expound, and illustrate his text, to dive into its inner meanings, and clothe it in a vesture of song...[His work] must be founded on canons of taste and right feeling that will endure amid fluctuations of fashion. This, I think, our best musicians feel. Such was the spirit in which one, whose name has been endeared to thousands by his hymns – Dr. Dykes – approached his task. Dr. Wesley confesses the same. 'It is an act of worship,' says he, 'when the musician in his private chamber, devotes his whole mind to his vocation.' Hear also the great Palestrina: 'Nothing, most Blessed Father,' he says in his Dedication of the Vesper Hymns, 'is so congenial to me, as to be able to give myself to that study of music...when I can abide by my purpose of embracing topics which most fully show forth God's praise, and which, pondered in all their weightiness and dignity of word and idea, and embellished with some amount of musical art, may well move the heart of man to devotion.'[5]

The echo of the 'Comfortable Words' in the Prayer Book Communion Service cannot have been accidental.

There is written evidence to establish the personal conviction of the principal Victorian church composers. Among the most noteworthy for piety were two clergymen of High Church persuasion: John Bacchus Dykes (1823–76) and Sir Frederick Arthur Gore Ouseley (1825–89). Dykes seems to have been shy and self-effacing but a gifted and devoted pastor, judging from the Revd J. T. Fowler's biography, with its ample quotation of letters and diaries.[6] Dykes's life of piety and service determined the attitude he brought to the composition of hymn tunes. He perceived theological and mystical significance in musical theory and practice, and appears to have taken pleasure in speculating on these correspondences in sermons and lectures.[7]

Ouseley, while not as absorbed by pastoral work as Dykes, did feel a strong pastoral responsibility for the students and choristers at St Michael's, Tenbury, the school and church he founded in 1856 to be a model for choral worship in the English cathedral tradition. In an essay published in 1872, he maintained that the education of choristers should not be just academic and musical, though these aspects of it must be of the highest standard, but should incorporate moral and devotional training by precept and example as well as comprehensive instruction in religious knowledge.[8]

Although not an extreme ritualist, Ouseley was a conscientious High Churchman, deeply concerned with the difficult issues that faced Anglo-Catholics around the middle of the century. In 1850, while a curate at St Barnabas, Pimlico, a church where Tractarian and ritualist principles governed teaching and worship, Ouseley was particularly exercised by the issue of Erastianism and the Royal Supremacy. This was brought to a head by the notorious Gorham Judgment in March of that year. In this case, a secular court overturned the decision of a diocesan bishop (Henry Phillpotts of Exeter, 1778–1869) and an ecclesiastical court when a priest, George Cornelius Gorham (1787–1857), was refused institution to a parochial living on the grounds that he held heretical views on the sacrament of baptism. It thus appeared that the Crown had assumed the authority of making final pronouncement in a matter of religious doctrine, a step intolerable to the Tractarians. The depth of Ouseley's concern is documented in extant correspondence with his friend and confidant, the Revd James Wayland Joyce, Rector of Burford, where Ouseley had done the greater part of his preparation for Holy Orders.[9] Had it not been for Joyce's personal influence and learned arguments, Ouseley might have been impelled by conscience, at this critical point in his career, to leave the Anglican Communion for Rome.

At the end of 1850, Ouseley was in a state of near-nervous exhaustion owing to the tumultuous events during his London curacy, culminating in the 'No Popery' riots in November of that year. He resigned shortly thereafter, and in 1851, in part to recover from the strain of the previous months, undertook a year's travel on the Continent, having first established the choristers of the disbanded St Barnabas choir temporarily at Lovehill House, Langley, Buckinghamshire, under the tutelage of his friend and colleague, the Revd Henry Fyffe. This was the first step towards the founding of St Michael's. Meanwhile, during this year of travel, Ouseley settled his thoughts and made decisions that may, without exaggeration, be said to have determined the remainder of his career. His disenchantment with the Roman Church, on first-hand experience of it, confirmed him in the Anglican position,[10] and it was during this time that he felt most strongly the duty to devote his talents to the improvement of choral worship. Writing from Munich on 26 September 1851, he declared:

I have no talent for teaching, no powers of preaching, and no health for hard parochial work. But God has given me one talent; and that I am determined to devote to His service, and offer it up to adorn His Church. I should never forgive myself, if I did otherwise; my conscience exacts it of me.[11]

The direct perception of musical activity as a religious vocation is perhaps more significant for the present study in Ouseley's case than Dykes's, since for Ouseley it was the centre of his career, most of his compositions being in the ambitious genres of cathedral services and anthems.

Such piety was not confined to priestly musicians. For example, T. A. Walmisley said of his godfather, Thomas Attwood (1765–1838):

[He] was a man of sincere piety, and, when engaged in the composition of music for the Church, always felt that he was employing the genius given to him by God for the noblest purpose to which it could be devoted – His service; and his great aim and hope were that he might be enabled to praise Him worthily.[12]

Edward Copleston (1776–1849), Dean of St Paul's from 1828 to 1849, characterised Attwood as 'a sincerely religious and conscientious man'.[13]

John Goss (1800–80), Attwood's successor as organist of St Paul's, was also noted for his piety and mildness of character. Sir John Stainer affirmed the connection between Goss's convictions and his work as a composer: 'That Goss was a man of religious life was patent to all who came in contact with him, but an appeal to the general effect of his sacred compositions offers public proof of the fact.'[14]

Mary Elvey, widow (the fourth wife!) and biographer of Sir George Job Elvey (1816–93), organist of St George's, Windsor from 1835 to 1882, said of her husband and his first wife, Harriet Skeats (d.1851): 'This union was a truly blessed one, for the young pair were not only congenial in their musical tastes, but their hearts were united on the all-important point of love to their Saviour.'[15] Lady Elvey attributed a like sincerity of faith to Sir George's brother, Stephen Elvey (1805–60), Choragus at Oxford and organist of New College and the Church of St Mary the Virgin, saying that he was a man 'not only of splendid musical attainments, but a devout and earnest Christian, and he devoted all his splendid powers to his work'.[16] The final reference is to the preparation of a pointed psalter, a task performed with painstaking care, occupying Elvey for some seven years.

In his obituary of Sir John Stainer (1840–1901), F. G. Edwards cites several letters testifying to the composer's gentleness, generosity, kindness, and piety. Religious devotion and sacred music seem to have been so closely bound in Stainer's mind as to be inseparable. An old Magdalen College chorister wrote to Lady Stainer after the composer's death: 'Over and above his unapproachable playing, he was one of the very few touched with the radiance of the inner life of sacred music.' Another correspondent, Mr Edward Chapman, MP, who had known Stainer at Magdalen, described the musician's rapture during the extemporisation of anthem introductions and the sensitivity of his psalm chant accompaniments, underscoring remarks about Stainer's piety and its expression in music.[17]

Other Victorian church musicians, not as noted for conspicuous piety, seem at least to have been believers in the routine sense. Many had been cathedral choristers, so during their most impressionable years, the habits of worship were ingrained and continued throughout their careers, making them feel at home in the ecclesiastical setting. Despite the tempestuous and self-pitying aspect of his personality, this is essentially true of S. S. Wesley (1810–76), and the careers of T. A. Walmisley (1814–56), E. J. Hopkins (1818–1901), Joseph Barnby (1838–96), G. M. Garrett (1834–97), and many others, seem to follow a like pattern, even if specific evidence of their religious conviction is not abundant.

Victorian biographers and eulogists undeniably made careful selection of material to give a favourable impression of their subjects. Nevertheless, it is unlikely that reports of specific instances of piety and devotion are untrue, whether or not there is a neglected darker side to the subject's character. Indeed, such accounts inform us that these are among the characteristics highly valued by the writers themselves, and presumably by their contemporary readers. The general impression left by such literature suggests that the cases presented here are typical. On the whole, Victorian church musicians apparently believed in the doctrinal implications of their professional musical activities.

Artistic consequences of orthodoxy: classic or romantic?

Granting that most Victorian church composers were Christian believers, one may question whether or to what extent this might affect the intrinsic character of their work, not just their predisposition to conform with the requirements of the liturgy. In an essay of 1939, C. S. Lewis considered this question with respect to literature, and concluded that while the Christian faith imposes no canons of artistic or literary value, there are aesthtic attitudes which tend to be discordant with the Christian outlook.[18] The conflict emerges clearly in considering the element of originality. One of the most enduring legacies of romanticism is the exaltation of originality to an absolute virtue in art. Indeed, Sir Maurice Bowra has argued persuasively that the exaltation of the subjective imagination and its products to the highest order of metaphysical dignity is the definitive characteristic of romanticism, that for the romantic the imagination is the supreme discerner of transcendent truth and the creator of a world more real than the external objects of sense perception.[19] While Bowra confined his attention to poetry, it is notable that a host of romantic musicians made similar claims for music. This exaltation of the artist's imagination is conducive to a radical egoism that goes severely against the grain of Christian orthodoxy. Lewis observed that the Christian must believe the ultimate source of truth, beauty, and goodness to be external to himself. Thus the Christian artist tends not to conceive of himself as creating beauty *ex nihilo*, but rather reflecting in his work an existing beauty of a higher order, whose ultimate source is divine. A Christian artist may well be as original as a non-Christian artist with respect to independence from existing conventions and models, but probably for different reasons. The Christian will be original if originality is most conducive to his end, but he will not make it an end in itself, or art a religion in its own right, as so many of the romantics did. The chief value of his work will lie in its theme or substance, not its novelty of expression or technique, so he will be the more inclined to emulate procedures already established in the language of his art, so as to facilitate communication.[20] Christian art may thus be expected to have an inherently conservative bias, and Victorian church music generally fulfils this expectation.

Assertions of this sort may seem to say more than is intended: namely that Christian art obeys totally different aesthetic laws from non-Christian art. Since Christianity does not specify an aesthetic canon, the Christian artist must adopt and possibly adapt for his own use the artistic principles and procedures furnished by his culture in so far as these are not in fundamental conflict with his convictions. Composers of Victorian church music, therefore, did not have grave moral reservations about originality as such. On the contrary, since originality was highly valued in art of the nineteenth century, the Victorian church composers prized it in their own work,[21] but as Lewis's theory implies, there was that ingredient in their conviction which acted as a safeguard against the deification of originality.

Romanticism was clearly the predominant musical aesthetic in the nineteenth century, and one cannot deny the inescapable influence of romanticism in Victorian church music. Still, if one is constrained to give a simple answer to the question 'Is Victorian church music romantic?' the answer must be 'No'. If there is a fundamental conflict between romanticism at its most characteristic and the Christian understanding of self and external reality, the philosophical case need not be formally stated or apprehended by the composer for its implications to influence the temperamental atmosphere in which he works, thus affecting the character of his work almost subliminally. Moreover, it is likely that much misunderstanding of the Victorian repertory comes from inappropriate application of romantic critical criteria.

Romanticism may have been the predominant musical aesthetic in the nineteenth century because it was primarily a German phenomenon, and German music was widely acknowledged to lead the field. There were, of course, many instances of romantic influence in English music: the brooding and melancholy in some of the songs and piano works of the tragically short-lived George Frederick Pinto (1785–1806), the delicate, nostalgic wistfulness of the piano nocturnes of John Field (1787–1837), the emotional intensity and supernatural literary subjects in some of the songs and operas of John Barnett (1802–90), the gentle flavour of Mendelssohnian romanticism in much of the music of William Sterndale Bennett (1816–75), and among church composers, the highly individual expressive diction of S. S. Wesley (1810–76). When one thinks of English romanticism, however, the work of poets, not composers, probably springs first to mind. Far from being the central tendency as in Germany, romanticism was at best a periphery of English music.

Bowra discerns a significant difference between the English and German varieties of romanticism. The Germans, in their preoccupation with the infinite, sometimes cultivated unsatisfied longing for its own sake, a delight in hallucination, or nihilistic detachment from life. The English, on the other hand, felt compelled to state their visions and prosecute their transcendent quests in terms at least commensurate with objective reality, to convince the reader that the vision is 'not absurd or merely fanciful'.[22] One might thus conclude that the verbal medium of poetry is the ideal vehicle for the English variety of romanticism, for which music is ill-suited, while music is admirably suited to evoke the intense emotion, sense of the infinite, and unfulfilled longing of the German variety. The Germans were far readier than the English to recognise in music a revelation of infinite truths beyond the reach of words, an immediate manifestation of the movements of the will (Schopenhauer), the essence of poetry without the interposition of limiting verbal contingencies (Liszt), an order of meaning not too vague but too precise for words (Mendelssohn).

The prevailing conservatism of English musical culture, moreover, can hardly be said to have favoured the adventurousness of romanticism. The persistence of old styles and genres, an affection for the orderly and familiar, and corresponding apprehensiveness of innovations, are characteristic traits among English critics and audiences of the nineteenth century. A related ingredient is academicism, the increasing institutional organisation of musical education and practice, with the almost inevitable tendency to canonise correctness and sometimes to confuse this with inspiration. Nineteenth-century England saw the foundation of musical schools, examining bodies, an important learned society (the Musical Association), and substantial reforms in the requirements for musical degrees at the universities. Given the neo-puritan tendency of educated English society, it is understandable that an effective way to promote music's intellectual and cultural respectability was to ensure its academic rigour: to suffuse the study of music with something of the atmosphere of classical philology – to make the academic fugue, motet, and canon the counterpart of the Latin prize poem.

The Victorian church composers dealt in genres more thoroughly English and more inclined to conservatism than virtually any other, with the possible exception of the glee. Furthermore, the historical association between ecclesiastical and academic musical activity was extremely close. Long before the reforms in the second half of the century, the Oxford and Cambridge professorships, as well as subsidiary university musical posts, were often held by practising church musicians, often the organists and composers in charge of one or more of the college choral foundations. S. S. Wesley went so far as to recommend that the professors ought to be elected by the nation's cathedral organists.[23]

One modern critic has claimed that the Victorian cathedral repertory is romantic because its musical expression is coercive, that it prescribes the listener's emotional response.[24] This is essentially the criterion advanced by Friedrich Blume – though he is certainly not its originator – to distinguish classical from romantic modes of musical expression. Classical utterance is idealised and sublimated, engaging the creative participation of the listener. Once the means of expression become exaggerated, personal, and mannered, as is generally the case in romantic art, this relationship between artist and listener is disturbed. A 'superabundance of means threatens to upset the balance of statement', and the listener is no longer engaged in a creative participation in the work of art, but overwhelmed into passive receptivity.[25]

The classical principle as described by Blume corresponds with the theory of choral worship that many English writers advanced in the nineteenth century in opposition to neo-puritanism: namely, that the members of the congregation, while listening in silence, are supposed to be participating in the act of worship performed on their behalf by the choir, just as they are supposed to share in the collects and other prayers read by the presiding clergyman. John Jebb, in an 1841 lecture on choral worship, anticipated Blume's argument when he likened the expression of modern non-classical music to the 'importunate guides in a show place' who 'put the imagination in leading strings, prescribe its sphere of observation, and endeavour to define those matters upon which perhaps no two persons...can be perfectly agreed'. In contrast, 'the ancients lead the imagination to the point from which the prospect is obtained, and leave it there in solitude to select for itself the most congenial objects of its contemplation'.[26]

The Victorians' compositional practice is, on the whole, consistent with their theory, as subsequent discussion will attempt to demonstrate in greater detail. While the anthem may sometimes address the congregation in the manner of a sermon, not merely offering up their praises vicariously, it cannot be automatically assumed that Jebb's remarks about 'importunate guides in a show place' are applicable. Just as the safeguard of orthodoxy restrains the preacher from eccentric doctrinal speculations, so it checks the composer's egoism and induces a voluntary adherence to traditional proprieties. Given their stylistic norms, the Victorians generally employed a conservative economy of means, and even the much-maligned later Victorian idiom was employed more as a classical than a romantic musical diction. This becomes apparent when most Victorian cathedral music is compared with the genuinely romantic sacred music of Berlioz, Liszt, Verdi, or Elgar.

This Victorian character displays a striking similarity in spirit to that cultural phenomenon in Germany and Austria during the first half of the nineteenth century generally called Biedermeier. Both were fundamentally conservative in temper, associated with the rise of the middle classes, characterised by a desire for order, tranquillity, and a certain homeliness. Writers such as Horst Heussner and Carl Dahlhaus have argued that the Biedermeier is a distinct cultural and aesthetic orientation that cannot be understood according to romantic critical norms.[27] Nevertheless, the characteristics shared by Biedermeier and romanticism can be misleading. Some composers (e.g. Schubert, Mendelssohn, Spohr) seem to have one foot in each camp, so it is hardly surprising that Biedermeier music, like Victorian, has often been dismissed as an inferior, watered-down version of romanticism. In contrast, however, with the intense subjective compulsion of romanticism, the Biedermeier composer seeks an essentially classical order and poise, employing a variety of formalised gestures to suit different expressive circumstances, much as the classicist idealises and sublimates spontaneous personal expression.[28] Romantic-biased criticism calls this insincere, and the Victorians have often endured the same accusation.[29] At their worst, Biedermeier and Victorian music could be sentimental 'kitsch', but at their best, each was a continuation of the classical ideal into the nineteenth century, employing a distinctly nineteenth-century musical language, and achieving expressiveness without the crudity, excess, or technical chaos their practitioners perceived in unrestrained romanticism. Biedermeier composers tended to trace their musical ancestry to Mozart, while romantics preferred to claim descent from Beethoven,[30] so it is noteworthy that the influence of Mozart on English music of the nineteenth century, and especially on early to mid-Victorian church music, was exceptionally strong, as Nicholas Temperley has demonstrated.[31]

The importance attached to emotional experience in life and art is the characteristic whereby the Victorian church composer's temperament probably comes closest to romanticism. It is a characteristic shared with the High Church revival as a whole, derived in turn from the Evangelicals, a point stressed by Owen Chadwick in the introduction to his anthology *The mind of the Oxford Movement*. Emotional fervour was the chief distinction between the Tractarians and the 'High and Dry' conservatives of the eighteenth century. Reacting against the rationalistic smugness of the early-nineteenth-century Liberals, the Tractarians urged the necessity for mystery and poetry in the devotional life. The externals of worship thus took on a new significance, 'in the desire to turn the churches into houses of prayer and devotion, where men would let their hearts go outward and upward in worship, instead of preaching houses where their minds would be argued into an assent to creeds or moral duties'.[32] This clearly corresponds with some of the Victorian arguments in favour of choral worship: that the feelings and not just the mind should be engaged, and that music as a mediator of feeling has a vital role in worship as a complement to the purely verbal and rational.

In this sphere also, orthodoxy acts as a check to excesses. Just as it was a safeguard against the metaphysical deification of the romantic imagination, likewise it was a safeguard against the deification of the emotions, yet Victorian church composers could prize aesthetic originality and individuality as well as imparting an unabashed warmth of feeling to their music. Even a critic who is not flattering to the Victorians acknowledges that they hardly ever fall into the perfunctory dullness of so much run-of-the-mill cathedral music in the eighteenth century.[33]

The predominant flavour of most Victorian writing about music, both sacred and secular, is unromantic, as many of the passages quoted in this study might suggest. Nevertheless, it is equally evident that classical order and restraint do not account for the whole Victorian temper. While unchecked romanticism can run to egoistic extremes, seeking a reality as far removed as possible from material reality, the extreme extension of classicism involves the neo-pagan assumption that the human spirit can be fully satisfied with a completeness or perfection of beauty attainable through an idealised material reality. This, of course, goes equally against the grain of Christian orthodoxy. On the whole, Victorian church music avoids both extremes, though one could argue that it leans more to the classic than to the romantic side. To the partisans of either side, it may seem an unsatisfactory compromise. Indeed, it is the direct warmth of romantic aspiration indissolubly joined with classical order and restraint that can make Victorian church music aesthetically uncomfortable to many listeners, but it is exactly this mixture which makes it as authentic and appropriate a vehicle for Christian worship as any which has ever existed.

The context of orthodoxy

Thus far, consideration of orthodoxy as an influence on musical composition has concentrated on the composer's personal conviction. The manner in which religious convictions are expressed or reflected in music, however, is influenced not only by the composer's conscience but also by its relation to the general state of religious conviction in society: whether orthodox belief is a prevalent and popular characteristic of the times or an embattled minority position.

In an essay of 1921, Ernest Walker (1870–1949) analysed the aesthetic implications of the relationship between personal belief and the state of religious faith in society of his time. He speaks of 'profoundly important changes in religious thought' as having undeniably taken place during the course of the last generation, assuming the form of 'radical refusals of the old

Temperley, the English ecclesiastical adoption of Mozart's instrumental style assumed a degenerate or weak form. In particular, what he calls 'the weaker church style of the early Victorian period' comes directly from Mozart, as illustrated by a list of pieces in teacher-to-pupil succession:

> Mozart: 'Ave verum Corpus' or, even more aptly, the A♭ theme from the variations in the organ fantasia (K.608)
> Attwood: 'Come, Holy Ghost'
> Walmisley: 'He remembering his mercy' from the Magnificat in D minor
> Dykes: 'Gerontius' (tune for 'Praise to the Holiest in the height').

Temperley further observes that, once one recognises the Mozartian element in Victorian church music, 'it is difficult to hear a Victorian anthem without thinking of it as a watered-down Mozart string-quartet'.[5]

This observation is valid to an extent, but it is incomplete and perhaps even misleading as an account of the stylistic character of the Victorian repertory. An anthem is not, after all, a string quartet. Its function as a text-setting intended to take place within an existing liturgical context of distinct character dictates that Mozart's instrumental idiom, even as perceived at the time, will not be adopted wholesale, but adapted to the different purpose. Furthermore, Mozart was not the only influence on the Victorian church style, or even on Attwood. As J. S. Bumpus observed,

Attwood received his early musical education in the choir of the Chapel Royal under English musicians. That this education was extended and completed under foreign masters is visible in the numerous compositions which he wrote from time to time for the Church. The union of these styles produced a third, which may fairly be given to him as his own. It made an agreeable variety, without departing much from the manner and gravity of that harmony which one could always wish to remain as the foundation of all our devotional music.[6]

Thus 'Come, Holy Ghost' may be linked stylistically to Mozart, though one would not be likely to mistake it for genuine Mozart. At the same time, it shows at least as much melodic affinity to some eighteenth-century triple-metre psalm tunes (e.g. 'Richmond'). The influence of Mozart on nineteenth-century English church music is undeniable, but it is only one of several, and the final product is a category in its own right. It is not really helpful to characterise it as a watered-down version of something else.

The conception of Mozart attributed here to Attwood's contemporaries appears to have persisted, at least among some English critics, throughout the nineteenth century. To an early Victorian like William Mullinger Higgins, author of a curious volume entitled *The philosophy of sound* (1838), Mozart was notable for his romantic emotional intensity, exercising a 'despotic influence over the passions of the auditor'.[7] It is noteworthy that Mozart claims more space in Higgins's survey than any other composer, while Beethoven is not even mentioned! A subsequent remark on Mozart as a child helps to clarify the nature of Higgins's predilection.

This singular child was not less distinguished for the mildness of his disposition than for his extraordinary musical genius. To the warmth of his affections we may in a great measure attribute the touching sweetness of many of his compositions and the power which he afterwards exercised over the feelings of others.[8]

The emotional intensity is manifested in outward gentleness and refinement. This characteristic seems to have captured the nineteenth-century English imagination, and may help to explain the popularity enjoyed by Mendelssohn, Spohr, and Gounod among the Victorians, and the ambivalence, sometimes the hostility, with which many of them approached Berlioz, Liszt, Schumann, Wagner, and even Brahms, at least initially.

Sentiments consistent with this predilection were voiced by Joseph Bennett who, writing in 1897, discussed the influence of Mozart as being

not so much directly exerted...as indirectly, through English composers trained in his school, and mingling with it English elements of expression. No safer influence could have been brought to bear than that of Mozart. The purest and most serene of the classics, he was, at the same time, a harbinger of romanticism in right of poetic spirit, of a fascination which bespoke the intense humanity of his music.[9]

Such refined yet intense expressiveness constituted, in Bennett's view, the chief Mozartian characteristic reflected in Attwood's music. To the modern ear, this passage (ex. 1) from the Deus Misereatur of Attwood's Service in D (1831) may seem to have Mozartian overtones. J. S. Bumpus, however, in a publication of 1891, cited the quartet verse (ex. 2), which comes only a few pages later in the same work, as 'perhaps the most tender and Mozart-like of them all'.[10]

These Mozartian characteristics are not conspicuous in Attwood's earliest major church compositions, notably the Service in F (1796), which is very much in the traditional Georgian style. As it was Attwood's first official offering as newly-appointed composer to the Chapel Royal, it is understandable that he should have stayed well within the bounds of custom.

Attwood was particularly noted for his care in matching the expressive character of his musical settings to the changing sentiments of the words. Stainer pointed out, however, that this often resulted in a restless, disjointed, and seemingly fragmentary setting.[11] The Service in F is susceptible of this criticism, especially the Te Deum. Attwood moves from verse to verse, setting each almost in isolation. There are attractive musical ideas, but hardly any development beyond mere statement and sometimes antiphonal repetition, leaving an impression of short-windedness. The tonal organisation of the Te Deum shows careful planning, and involves key relationships typical of those found throughout Attwood's church music. He begins solidly in F, and apart from a few secondary dominants and touchings on the relative minor, stays firmly in the tonic until reaching 'the Holy Church throughout all the world', where he moves to B♭ by introducing the flat seventh in the bass. This occurs in the fifth short section of the canticle, initiating an excursion on the flat side of the tonic. He modulates to C minor at 'Thou art the

Ex. 1 Attwood: Service in D, Deus Misereatur

Ex. 2   Attwood: Service in D, Deus Misereatur

King of glory', and launches 'When thou tookest' immediately in A♭. Attwood always sets this part of the Te Deum in triple metre, and here it is the setting's first departure from duple metre. At 'When thou hadst overcome', he prepares an arrival in C minor, but in keeping with the spirit of the words, he sets 'Thou didst open the kingdom of heaven to all believers' in C major, and so initiates the turn sharpwards. 'We believe that thou shalt come to be our judge' is set in A minor, which becomes A major at 'Make them to be numbered with thy saints'. This turns to F♯ minor at 'O Lord, save thy people'. 'Day by day' is in D. Attwood does not hesitate to juxtapose keys a third apart, but in this case, the arrival has been anticipated by a turn to B minor in the preceding section, including a sequence which had passed through D major. At 'O Lord, let thy mercy', Attwood approaches a dominant pedal through an augmented sixth on B♭, suggesting D minor. In continuing, however, he uses the favourite tonal device of following an unmistakable minor key preparation with its relative major, so the final section returns quietly to the home key of F. Attwood shows great sensitivity for the character of the words in choosing his changes of key and mode, and the total scheme smoothly traverses considerable tonal ground, but this does not adequately mitigate the discontinuity resulting from his sectional treatment.

Another early composition which adheres to the traditional Georgian style is the verse anthem 'Teach me, O Lord' (1797). Its opening choral movement, one of Attwood's best-known compositions, might be considered a specimen of Mozartian lyricism. Its neat, carefully balanced, and compact structure could derive from the example of a work like 'Ave verum Corpus'. Such lyricism, however, is no less typical of Handel when writing in the Beautiful Style (according to Crotch's categories), and the balanced compactness is found equally in pieces like 'He shall feed his flock' or 'How beautiful are the feet' from *Messiah*. It would be rash to deny Mozart's influence in the opening of 'Teach me, O Lord', but one can hardly detect it in the subsequent bass verse (ex. 3), whose Georgian formality is more characteristic of the anthem as a whole.

Ex. 3　Attwood: anthem, 'Teach me, O Lord', bass verse

The change in musical diction between these end-of-the-eighteenth-century compositions and Attwood's later church music is well illustrated by the harmony of a passage (ex. 4) in the Te Deum of the Service in A (1825). The affective diminished harmony over the pedal F♯, the rising chromatic bass with its series of chromatically altered seventh chords to punctuate the supplication 'help thy servants', reaching the dominant of A major in $\frac{4}{2}$ position with the root approached from a chromatic alteration of itself – these features help to produce a stylistic flavour foreshadowing the Victorians.

Attwood's contrapuntal writing leaves a mixed impression. In three anthems of 1814, setting Prayer Book collects, he demonstrates a confident

Ex. 4   Attwood: Service in A, Te Deum

contrapuntal fluency, and it is worth noting that he was well-trained in the grammar of strict counterpoint. His exercises for Mozart are extant and in print.[12] Nevertheless, much of the fugal writing in his church compositions sounds uneasy and halting. At times he seems almost unable to think in linear terms, the fugal texture lurching chordally from downbeat to downbeat. The 'Amen' to the Gloria Patri of the Jubilate (repeated for the Nunc Dimittis) from the Service in C (1832) furnishes an example. The character of the subject itself (ex. 5) seems conducive to such a treatment. By the time of the

Ex. 5   Attwood: Service in C, Gloria Patri of Jubilate (or Nunc Dimittis)

third (treble) entry, the other parts are reduced to block harmony. The bass is silent during the second (alto) entry, its accompanimental role passing to the tenor, who never has the subject in the exposition. Thus a three-part fugal exposition is distributed over four voices, a procedure Attwood also follows in his 'Cathedral Fugue' in E♭ for organ and in the concluding fughetta from the anthem 'They that go down to the sea' (1832), whose third (treble) entry is curtailed, the third bar of the subject becoming the basis for a short-breathed descending sequence over a dominant pedal, which seems out of place so close to the beginning of the fughetta (ex. 6). Moreover, there are two places, roughly half-way and three-quarters of the way through this section, where all the voices halt on semibreves, having the effect of dividing the fughetta into small segments.

Ex. 6   Attwood: anthem, 'They that go down to the sea'

In addition to his theatrical and ecclesiastical activities, Attwood was a noted composer of glees, and it seems possible that some of the features noted in his church compositions may owe something to the habits of a glee composer. Glees of the so-called 'Golden Age', epitomised in the works of the elder Samuel Webbe (1740–1816), usually possessed a good deal of lively motion in the inner parts as well as the outer ones, including some imitation, but the fundamental organising principle was usually harmonic progression. In later generations of glee composers, the homophonic principle gained ground, and the history of the glee merged into that of the part-song. According to William Alexander Barrett (1834–91), who appears to have been the leading Victorian authority on the history and stylistic character of the glee, a true glee was almost invariably a piece of more than one movement, the various parts of the text being set according to their affective character, with distinct breaks between the short movements. In contrast, the madrigal, as purveyed by Georgian composers like William Beale (1784–1854), to name one of the most adept, was set as a single movement, with the successive lines of the text frequently treated to overlapping points of imitation.[13] It might be said that, whereas the Georgian madrigal consisted of harmonically saturated counterpoint, the glee was composed of contrapuntally enlivened harmony. Attwood's propensity for setting the canticles as a string of short, detached sections, closely following the character of the text, as well as the short-windedness and leaning towards homophony in some of his fugal writing, would seem natural for a glee composer.

Certain of these characteristics are turned to good account in the aforementioned anthems of 1814 on Prayer Book collects: 'O God, who by the leading of a star' (Feast of the Epiphany), 'Grant, we beseech thee' (Twenty-first Sunday after Trinity), and 'O Lord, we beseech thee' (First Sunday after the Epiphany). Most collects consist of three distinct parts: (1) an address which calls upon the Almighty, naming one of his attributes or citing one of his acts, (2) the central petition, and (3) a closing formula. In each of these anthems, Attwood treats the parts of the collects sectionally, but presents them as subdivisions of a single movement rather than a joining up of separate short movements. He introduces no changes of metre, and sometimes he links the sections thematically.

Of the three, 'O God, who by the leading of a star' is the most compact. The printed extract (ex. 7) gives the first two sections complete, correspond-

Ex. 7   Attwood: anthem, 'O God, who by the leading of a star'

94

Ex. 7 (*cont.*)

by the lead-ing of a star ___ *f* didst ma - ni -fest thy

who by the lead-ing of a star a star, didst ma - ni-fest thy

by the lead-ing of a star, of ___ a star, didst ma-ni-fest thy

who by the leading of a star, *f* didst ma nifest thy

on - ly be-got-ten son to the gen -tiles; *p*

on - ly be-got-ten son to the gen -tiles; mer - ci-ful-ly

on - ly be got - ten son to the gen -tiles;

on - ly be-got-ten son to the gen -tiles; *p*

cresc.
may af - ter this

grant that we, which know thee now by faith may af - ter this ___

may af - ter this

cresc.

life *f* have the fru - i - tion of thy glo - - rious

life have the fru - i - tion of thy glo - - rious

life have the fru i tion of thy glo - - rious

f may af - ter this life have the fru - i -tion of the glo - rious

god - head,

god - head, thy glo - rious god - head.

god - head,

god - head

95

ing to the first two parts of the collect. Attwood separates them with a semi-
breve rest in all parts, then changes the texture from free counterpoint to
homophonic block chords to mark the beginning of the petition, but he has
calculated the phrasing and harmony sufficiently well that there is no sense of
discontinuity. The rest at the half cadence seems to punctuate the musical
thought without dissipating the energy involved, in much the same way that
the semicolon marks the end of the verbal clause, yet leaves no doubt that
there is more to follow. The principal musical interest of what follows is
harmonic: an indirect route from E major to E minor by way of A minor,
which serves a pivotal function as ii of G major before settling in the relative
minor of that key. The unisons at the end of the section are an example of a
device so frequently used by Attwood for formal articulation or text emphasis as to be almost a fingerprint of his style. The remainder of the anthem,
setting the concluding formula of the collect, 'Through Jesus Christ, our
Lord', is more expansive, resuming the contrapuntal texture of the opening
with similar but not identical material. The 'Amen' is a sixteen-bar contrapuntal coda in which Attwood touches on the principal keys and harmonies
from earlier in the work, most notably those of the petition. On the whole,
it is a finely crafted work whose style and character seem to foreshadow similar works by John Goss, like the brief, unaccompanied 'These are they
which follow the Lamb' (1859). Indeed, in the closing bars of the petition in
Attwood's anthem, one might almost detect a pre-echo of Goss's 'O Saviour
of the world' (1869).

The other collect-anthems are considerably lengthier. In the collect for the
Twenty-first Sunday after Trinity, the address and petition are not grammati-
cally separate, so a brief, introductory opening section like that of 'O God,
who by the leading of a star' would not be appropriate. Attwood sets the
words 'Grant, we beseech thee, merciful Lord' as a fugue of considerable
dimension – nearly fifty bars in moderate $\frac{4}{2}$ metre – on a concise subject (ex. 8),

Ex. 8   Attwood: anthem, 'Grant, we beseech thee'

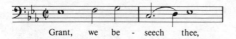

Grant,   we   be - seech   thee,

which coincidentally reappeared some fourteen years later in a Schubert
symphony. In contrast with the Attwood fugues mentioned earlier, this one is
remarkably fluent, owing at least in part to the subject itself: concise, dignified, and pliable, as compared with the busy but unyielding material often
found elsewhere, such as the subject from the Service in C. No new text is
introduced until the bass has a dominant pedal D with the words 'to thy faithful people', leading to the quiet homophonic continuation of the petition
with the words 'pardon and peace'. After this, the subject returns for the
closing of the collect, 'Through Jesus Christ, our Lord'. There is no new fugal

exposition, but free counterpoint based on statements of the subject as well as inversions and diminutions plus melodic ideas which clearly grow out of it. An effective interrupted cadence on Cb, following V of Eb, is continued by a unison statement of the subject in Cb major (*pp*) by alto, tenor, and bass. A German sixth produced by an A♮ in the treble restores Bb as a lengthy dominant pedal, leading to the quiet conclusion in Eb.

The same general charactcristics, especially fluent part-writing, are found in the third collect-anthem, 'O Lord, we beseech thee'. Here some of Attwood's stylistic fingerprints might be faulted as mannerisms: the use of sequence, repetition of short musical ideas, and a tendency to repeat a short passage of text over and over, set syllabically or nearly so, with little or no rhythmic variety.

Attwood has tended to be best known to later generations through some of his slighter achievements: melodious miniatures that have an immediately attractive appeal if sometimes a minimum of musical substance. Such works were generally the earliest of his church music to be published – the principal exceptions were the coronation anthems of 1821 and 1831 – while his more substantial works had to wait until 1851 for the publication of T. A. Walmisley's edition of Attwood's *Cathedral music*. Among these slighter works, the best-known is 'Come, Holy Ghost', written for an ordination at St Paul's on Trinity Sunday 1831. It was originally a treble solo for one of the cathedral choristers, J. G. Boardman. The choral arrangement of the familiar published version was produced subsequently. Although a felicitous melodic inspiration, the work is little more than a strophic hymn tune, which would appear to have cost the composer little labour or concentration, since it was composed, at least in part, on the morning of its première, while Attwood was driving into town from his home in Norwood. He collected Boardman on the way, and that was the first sight the soloist had of the new score.[14] 'Turn thee again, O Lord, at the last' was composed for the funeral of Princess Charlotte of Wales on 19 November 1817. It is also in gently lilting $\frac{3}{2}$ metre (larghetto), in straightforward AABA form. 'Turn thy face from my sins' (1834) was composed for *Sacred Minstrelsy*. It is in simple AABB form, with the first of each pair for solo voice and the repetition harmonised in four parts. 'Enter not into judgment' was published in *Sacred Minstrelsy* in 1835. It is also in AABB form. The first A is in unison while the second is in parts. The Bs are in parts and repeated literally.

In the absence of documentary evidence, it is difficult, even precarious, to say anything about Attwood's attitude towards pieces such as these, which have tended to be the most popular of his works. His sacred music does seem to divide fairly neatly between artistically ambitious works like those published in Walmisley's collection, and these more lightweight compositions, which are conventional in form and, while solemnly dignified, are more smooth and pretty than deeply expressive. It should be emphasised that the difference is not necessarily one of length. The verse anthems and cathedral services are, of course, larger-scale works than the slighter anthems, but 'O God, who by the leading of a star', one of Attwood's finest works and included in Walmisley's collection, is at fifty-four bars, no lengthier than most of them. The difference is one of musical substance. The compositions in Walmisley's collection, whatever their flaws, are proof of what Attwood was capable of achieving. The same cannot be said of 'Come, Holy Ghost', 'Turn thee again', and 'Turn thy face', though these anthems did elicit praise even from late Victorian commentators, while some historians give the false impression that they represent the limit of Attwood's creative ability.

The two coronation anthems with orchestra hold a conspicuous place in Attwood's output. 'I was glad', the earlier of them, begins with an introduction based on 'God save the King'.[15] The main body of the work is not notable for subtlety of effect, but it is solidly crafted along symphonic lines, in the sense that virtually the whole of the musical material is built up from a few germinal motives. The opening choral phrase is broad and triadic (ex. 9a). It is soon complemented with a faster-moving phrase in contrary motion (ex. 9b). The accompaniment is full of fanfares in dotted rhythms. The quiet middle section is based on a new theme (ex. 9c). There is a Gloria Patri, and

Ex. 9   Attwood: coronation anthem, 'I was glad'

it is for this section that Attwood reserves his sense of harmonic drama. The sudden flatward plunge comes as something of a surprise after the harmonic straightforwardness of most of the work (ex. 10). The strings contribute semiquaver tremolandi starting at 'As it was in the beginning', and the anthem concludes with a busy symphonic/operatic coda.

The Attwood anthem which comes perhaps closest to the Mozartian Viennese flavour is a late one: 'Let the words of my mouth' (1835). The compositional procedure is more like that of 'I was glad' than of the collects, verse anthems, or cathedral services. Attwood is not concerned here with the sectional exposition of the character of successive clauses of a text. Instead, he builds up a symphonic structure from germinal motives, in this case, closely associated with the rhythm of the specific phrases of the text. The

Ex. 10   Attwood: coronation anthem, 'I was glad'

printed extract (ex. 11) gives an idea of the flavour of the work, its brightness and lyricism, while illustrating something of how it is put together. This passage presents in combination ideas that had earlier been presented separately. The melody in the first bass part opened the work as a treble solo. Notice its inversion in the second treble part. The figure in the alto and tenor to the words 'O Lord' had formed the basis for an earlier contrasting section. The music certainly has a life of its own, and thematic procedure as a determinant of the anthem's structure is a notable feature in many of the anthems of Goss and other Victorians.

Ex. 11   Attwood: anthem, 'Let the words of my mouth'

In assessing Attwood's place in history, it is worth remembering that the state of English cathedral music during his lifetime was as bad as it has ever been since the Commonwealth. The principal late Victorian writers agree in giving Attwood a large share of credit for initiating the improvement of cathedral music in the nineteenth century. W. A. Barrett noted that he 'set a good example by approaching the duties he felt called upon to perform, with an earnestness of purpose and piety of intention that could not fail to be effective in course of time, if not at once'.[16] Bumpus listed Attwood among the composers who upheld a worthy standard of church music in a generally undistinguished period. Among others to whom he gave favourable notice were T. S. Dupuis, Benjamin Cooke, Samuel Arnold, Edmund Ayrton, John Alcock, Jonathan Battishill, J. C. Beckwith, J. Clarke-Whitfeld, Samuel Wesley, J. Stafford Smith, Joseph Pring, and William Crotch.[17] If the greater number of these maintained a reasonable standard of achievement along lines inherited from Greene and Boyce, Attwood breathed new life into the old system by means of the fresh impulses assimilated during the course of his continental study. Myles Foster gave Attwood the major share of credit for the improvement of compositional standards.

From about the year 1770 to 1817, or, in other words, during the best part of the reign of King George III., there followed a period of forty years' dearth in Anthem writing: a famine longer than that of the Egyptians, and in which no Joseph arose to help; no one, with the exception of Jonathan Battishill and Dr. Crotch, appeared on the 'trackless desert' to render any support or supply any strength to what must be considered as the very weakest part of the History of the Anthem, until at length Attwood returned to England from the Continent and began to write and redeem the situation.[18]

The influence of Crotch was not an unmixed blessing. John Jebb had speculated on the unrealised potential of Jonathan Battishill (1738–1801) to invigorate the ailing condition of cathedral music.[19] Battishill's finest works (e.g. 'O Lord, look down from heaven') have an impressive dramatic vividness, but he devoted relatively little of his efforts to cathedral music, not enough to establish a foundation for future development. While Attwood's ecclesiastical output was not massive, it was substantial, and his professional commitment to the cathedral and the Chapel Royal made his the stronger influence. This influence was stressed by Frederick George Edwards.

In many respects he may be regarded as the father of modern church music. As Sir John Stainer says: 'Attwood deserves an important place in any sketch of the history of Services for the bold attempt to attach to the words music which should vary as to their character. This had, of course, been done to some extent before his time, but nearly always with a polite leaning to the conventionalities of the past. Attwood struck out a fresh path.' The same remarks may be applied to his melodious anthems.[20]

Bumpus, while acknowledging Attwood as a pivotal figure, suggested that his influence on the Victorians was belated, since most of his major cathedral compositions were virtually unknown prior to the publication of Walmisley's edition in 1851.[21] Against this it might be argued that Attwood's most significant influence was exerted directly on pupils like Goss and Walmisley, who were themselves eminent and influential. Likewise, Attwood's services and anthems must have been well known to the choristers of St Paul's and the Chapel Royal in the first half of the century, among whom were many individuals, like S. S. Wesley and E. J. Hopkins, who later rose to prominence in the world of Victorian cathedral music.

Even his contemporaries recognised something different about Attwood's church music in comparison with others of his generation. The writer of his obituary in the *Musical World* remarked:

His Italian education and want of intimacy with the great Protestant school of eccle- siastical music, as exhibited in the works of Sebastian Bach, led him to reject the energetic dissonances derived from the organ; hence his Church vocal music, although marked by a serene and elegant outline, is without that unction and raciness of spirit which distinguished the kindred effusions of his contemporaries, Charles and Samuel Wesley. The intricacies of counterpoint he had perfectly overcome, but he had not a mind of the character which leads its possessor to mould out of old conceptions the shapings of new and great thoughts. His strength lay in the elegance of his cantilena and the pure orchestral structure of his harmonies. The anthems 'Be Thou my Judge, O Lord', 'Grant, we beseech Thee', 'Bow down Thine ear', 'Teach me, O Lord', and the Cantate Domino, are severally learned and elaborate compositions, well worthy the study of the amateur, while for correctness and chastity they are models, which stand unequalled in modern times.[22]

The writer may have wished for sterner stuff, but he recognised that Att- wood's music is distinctive and different, possessing an excellence of its own kind.

In determining Attwood's historical stature, it is important not to exagger- ate the intrinsic merits of his work as a composer, and yet to give credit where it is due. The eulogist of 1838 sets a tone found in the writings of later Vic- torians, who wish to make clear their respect and esteem for Attwood and the importance of his achievement, and yet make it equally clear that he was not, after all, one of the very greatest of composers. Joseph Bennett traced to Attwood a softening of the formal Georgian style, making 'a decided step towards the freedom, pliancy, grace, and, as regards structure, simplicity which the sacred compositions of various masters displayed later on'. Bennett notes the pre-eminence of Attwood's influence in the music of John Goss, and even says that it was as master to Goss that Attwood made perhaps his greatest contribution to the history of English cathedral music.[23] Neverthe- less, Attwood's music is worthy of attention for its own considerable merits.

6

Thomas Attwood Walmisley (1814–56) and John Goss (1800–80), the first Victorian generation

Of Attwood's pupils, the two who achieved the greatest eminence as composers of church music were Thomas Attwood Walmisley and John Goss. Each was decisively influenced by Attwood and by a generous childhood exposure to the heritage of traditional English cathedral music as practised, for better or worse, in the late Georgian period. While both pursued careers as continuers and developers of this tradition, the differences in their professional circumstances and creative personalities may help to account for the significant differences in the character of their works and in the influence exerted by each on successive generations of church musicians.

Goss spent the whole of his career in London. He was born in Fareham, Hampshire, and in 1811 was admitted to the Chapel Royal as a chorister. After leaving the choir, he had lessons in composition from Attwood. Following a number of London parish organistships, Goss was appointed to St Paul's shortly after Attwood's death, and was later appointed an organist and composer to the Chapel Royal. He had been a professor of harmony at the Royal Academy of Music from an earlier date, and was thus a notable figure in London musical life, even if by choice and temperament he restricted himself largely to the ecclesiastical sphere. As a composer, he carried the style of the mature Attwood onwards toward the High Victorian idiom. He was, almost literally, the link between Attwood and Stainer.

Walmisley, on the other hand, although born and educated in London, spent the greater part of his career in Cambridge. He was the son of Thomas Forbes Walmisley (1783–1866), the distinguished glee composer and organist of St Martin-in-the-Fields. After an unsuccessful attempt in 1832 to launch a career in London theatre music, and after two years as organist of the Croydon Parish Church, Walmisley was elected in 1833 organist of Trinity and St John's Colleges, and shortly thereafter proceeded to the degree of Mus.B. In 1836, on the death of John Clarke-Whitfeld (b.1770), he was elected Professor of Music in the university. He received the B.A. in the same year, having previously matriculated as a student in arts, and he proceeded to the M.A. in 1841. He became Mus.D. in 1848. As Professor, Walmisley strove to improve the low esteem in which music was then held in the university. One of his innovations was illustrated lectures in music. As a graduate in the arts, he commanded a respect which a musician, however eminent or scholarly, would not otherwise have been accorded. Still, Cambridge was not London, and a musician must inevitably have felt cut off there. In the isolation of Esterháza, Haydn claimed that he was forced to become original. Walmisley, however, was not Haydn, and in the isolation of Cambridge, where music tended to be taken less seriously than at Esterháza, Walmisley's compositions never quite escape a certain provincial flavour. This is often due to an apparent self-consciousness in matters of tonal and harmonic technique.

The quantity of Walmisley's extant church compositions is not very great. There are nine services, two of them with the full complement of morning and evening canticles plus Communion Service items, and twenty-two anthems, of which fifteen were published in the nineteenth century.[1] It may at first seem fussy to divide so small an output into stylistic periods, but considered chronologically, the anthems and services fall into three successive groups. The works of the early to mid 1830s are in the traditional Georgian vein, with the influence of Attwood strong in places. The later 1830s and early 40s are dominated by anthems with an oratorio-like sense of drama and the unmistakable stylistic influence of Mendelssohn. Beginning with the Service in D major of 1843, Walmisley turns away from Mendelssohnian flavour, not in the direction of richer chromatic harmony, but rather to a fluent diatonicism, sometimes with a faint shade of ancient polyphony. It is an idiom of some individuality. Unlike Goss, therefore, Walmisley did not form a direct link to the music of the immediately succeeding generation, although his works were highly regarded throughout the second half of the century, from the publication in 1857 of the folio edition of his *Cathedral music*, collected and edited by his father, to the appearance later in the century of new Novello octavo editions of the most important works. If Walmisley had an influence, it was belated. His later style seems almost to foreshadow the post-Victorian idiom of certain works by Stanford and Wood, both men associated with Cambridge, where, if anywhere, Walmisley's reputation would have been high. Meanwhile, it is noteworthy that T. Tertius Noble (1867–1953) modelled his own Service in B minor, at the urging of his teacher Walter Parratt (1841–1924), on the diatonic idiom of Walmisley's famous Evening Service in D minor.

Walmisley's early services adhere more closely to the idiom of the Georgian short service than do those of Attwood. Whereas Attwood took pains to characterise each of the varying sentiments of the text by means of sectional divisions involving changes in harmony, texture, key, mode, and metre, Walmisley's settings seem perfunctory, even mechanical in comparison. The Te Deum from the Morning and Evening Service in C (1831), for instance, is in $\frac{4}{2}$ metre throughout, and indeed, the only departure from duple metre in the entire service is an ATB verse ('To be a light') in the Nunc Dimittis. Walmisley confines deliberate expressive characterisation to isolated passages. In his Te Deums, for instance, at the words 'When thou hadst overcome the sharpness of death: thou didst open the kingdom of heaven to all believers', he generally employs some affective harmony at the word 'sharpness', then brightens the harmony and texture for the second half of the verse. The afore-mentioned Service in C and the Morning Service in B♭ (1834) furnish examples. Apart from such moments, however, the music of these early services might almost be described as expressively neutral, and the greater part of them could pass for work of the mid eighteenth century.

At times Walmisley seems more interested in abstract technical devices than with expressive considerations. In the Magnificat from the Service in C, for instance, beginning at 'He hath put down', he uses the chord of B♭ prominently within a short space to exploit several of its possible functions: VI of D minor, the tonic of B♭, and III of G minor. A similar device occurs in the anthem 'O give thanks unto the Lord' (1833). The concluding movement for double chorus, 'Blessed be the Lord God of Israel', has a quiet introductory section centred on the single note D. Unison Ds in Choir II are answered by full chords in Choir I, incorporating the D in different ways: first as the root of D minor in root position, then the third of B♭, next the root of D minor in $^6_4$ position, and finally the fifth of G minor.

This work is one of two verse anthems dating from 1833 that are cast in the traditional Georgian style. The other one is 'Behold, O God, our defender', composed for the annual observance of the Royal Accession.[2] The anthem consists of a group of very short movements, of which two ensemble verses – 'Grant the Queen' (ATTB) and 'In her time let the righteous flourish' (SAATB) – show the influence of Attwood in their triple-metre lyricism and carefully balanced structure.

Two single-movement anthems of the 1830s are distinguished from the foregoing by giving full sway to gentle lyricism without the formal grandeur – or sometimes the mechanical stiffness – of these other works. 'O God, the King of glory' (1834) is a setting of the collect for Ascension Day. It is notable for smoothly flowing phrases and harmonic fluidity. The Attwood work it most nearly resembles is 'Let the words of my mouth', which dates from the *following* year (1835). There are significant differences, however. The structure of Walmisley's anthem is derived from that of the collect, and his harmony is more enriched than Attwood's. The opening section begins in F and includes a deceptive cadence on D♭ which proves to be IV of A♭. The section ends in E♭. A brief quotation (ex. 12), beginning with the passage for solo

Ex. 12 T. A. Walmisley: anthem, 'O God, the King of glory'

Ex. 12 *(cont.)*

seech thee leave us not com - fort - less;

voices that serves to link the opening section with the main choral setting of the collect petition, gives some idea of the flavour of the anthem as a whole.

There seems to be fairly general consent that Walmisley was one of the few English composers of the second quarter of the nineteenth century not to have been markedly influenced by Spohr. The cited passage and others, however, may furnish reason enough to revise this assessment. Mozart is a common denominator between Spohr and Attwood, since Spohr regarded Mozart as his musical exemplar in preference to Beethoven. This might well have predisposed Walmisley to Spohr's music. His oratorio *The Last Judgment* (1826) had a profound impact on the English public and critics after its first English performance in Norwich in 1830, making him familiar to a far wider public than the relatively small number of serious musical enthusiasts who had known the few English performances of some of his instrumental works in previous years.[3] If Walmisley was not present at the Norwich performance in 1830, it is highly likely that he heard *The Last Judgment* at the Philharmonic Society the following year, which was prior to his removal to Cambridge. By 1843, he was using the work as a sight-reading exercise for his Cambridge choristers.[4]

Further on in 'O God, the King of glory', Walmisley returns to the home key from Db by treating the V_7 of Db enharmonically (Gb = F#) as the German sixth of C major, itself the dominant of the home key. Still further on, a chain of secondary dominants leads back to F after another excursion on the flat side of the tonic. Such devices alone cannot prove an indebtedness to Spohr, but they are typical of his style. Attwood's brand of post-Mozartian style is not noted for the conspicuous use of such harmonic devices. Attwood's influence on Walmisley is beyond question, and the chromatic enrichment of a style derived from Attwood produces something very like Spohr.

The other lyrical single-movement Walmisley anthem mentioned above, 'Father of heaven' (1836), is based on a rhyming metrical text from the *Church of England Christian Remembrancer*. It is pleasant, free of lofty pretensions, and possibly open to the same criticisms as certain of Attwood's smaller anthems: that it attempts to obtain more mileage from a brief text and slight musical material than is entirely warranted.

Another anthem of 1836, 'Hear, O thou shepherd of Israel', marks a significant development in Walmisley's style. He calls it a verse anthem, and in outward format, it proceeds as a succession of short sections: recitative, brief lyrical ariosi, a passage of choral declamation, and a short concluding chorus. In feeling, however, it seems to derive a sense of drama from the oratorio. It unfolds in the manner of a composite scene on the theme of penitence, with a profound psychological and devotional progress from sadness and desolation to comfort and resolve to amendment. Traditionally, the verse anthem tends to be a relatively static multi-movement setting of a text, supplying its varying shades of sentiment with music of appropriate character. If a parallel be sought, the traditional verse anthem seems closer to the succession of contrasting movements in a Corellian concerto or sonata than to the purposeful dramatic progress of baroque opera or oratorio. While some eighteenth-century verse anthems, such as Greene's 'How long wilt thou forget me', involve something like the psychological progress attributed to Walmisley's anthem, this cannot be considered a customary feature of the genre. A very similar effect, however, is produced by the series of short solo numbers from Part II of *Messiah*:

> Recit.: 'Thy rebuke hath broken his heart'
> Air: 'Behold and see if there be any sorrow'
> Recit.: 'He was cut off out of the land of the living'
> Air: 'But thou didst not leave his soul in hell'

The last-named air, in a spirit of conservative understatement, quietly marks the turning point of that part of the oratorio. It is no less dramatic for being understated, and is thus representative of a species of non-theatrical drama that could be appropriated for use in the church anthem. History furnishes a parallel in Erdmann Neumeister's ideal of the Lutheran church cantata as resembling a segment of an opera, with recitatives and arias to dramatise the sacred message. It would be rash to call Walmisley an English pioneer in this, especially as excerpts from oratorios had for some time done service as cathedral anthems. Still, the general tendency in the nineteenth century was for anthems to assume a greater degree of emotional warmth and for the oratorio to shed most of the theatrical associations of its early history in England, and to be regarded more and more as a devotional exercise. In effect, the two genres drew closer together in spirit, and 'Hear, O thou shepherd' is a noteworthy specimen of this tendency.

The anthem begins in C minor with a tenor recitative giving the opening of Psalm 80, from which the text of the whole anthem is selected. Ending on the dominant via a German sixth, the recitative is followed by a short (24-bar) andante aria in ¾ time, 'Thou that leadest', flowing directly into the E♭ major chorus 'Turn us again' (andante larghetto), still in ¾ time, in the familiar vein of Attwood lyricism. The mood is of calm but penitential supplication. The succeeding alto recitative (ex. 13) is one of Walmisley's most remarkable passages. It is rare to find him striving so deliberately to match the sentiment of the text with harmonic colour, employing affective irregular progressions

Ex. 13 T. A. Walmisley: anthem, 'Hear, O thou shepherd of Israel'

that invite comparison with S. S. Wesley. There follows a short, impassioned choral declamation of the same words. Next comes an alto aria, 'Thou feedest them with the bread of tears', once again returning to a placid lyricism reminiscent of Attwood.

Watkins Shaw alleges an incongruity in this aria between the sentiment of the text and the style of its musical setting.[5] Such a criticism might be convincing, were it not for the fact that Walmisley has just given an example of his ability to project a sense of anguish by musical means. The most reasonable assumption is that the change of mood was deliberate, and that the expressive rationale is not so straightforward as expected. Could it be that Walmisley interprets the phrase 'bread of tears' as a form of comfort in the midst of adversity, in contrast with the desolation evoked in the recitative, the consequence of divine anger? There is a tenderness in the imagery of the text, and the psychological progress rings true. Genuine penitence requires genuine sorrow. The general confessions in the Prayer Book have at their centre words of desolation: 'And there is no health in us' from Morning and Evening Prayer; 'The remembrance of them is grievous unto us; the burden of them is intolerable' from the Communion Service. If true penitence is a fruit of divine grace, then there must be a special comfort in being fed with the 'bread of tears', the necessary preamble to absolution. Seen in this light, Walmisley's setting makes a great deal of sense, and the remainder of the anthem tends to sustain this interpretation. The alto aria is followed by a bass recitative in A♭, 'Let thy hand be upon the man of thy right hand', which seems to exude a sense of renewed confidence. The concluding chorus in E♭ is one of quiet resolve, beginning with four bars of block minims (largo), 'So will we not go back from thee', followed by the main section (andante), 'O let us live, and we shall call upon thy Name', in the idiom of a homophonic part-song.

An anthem similar to 'Hear, O thou shepherd' in its apparent use of the oratorio as a model and also in the nature of its spiritual drama is 'Remember, O Lord', which won the prize offered by the committee of the Dublin Ancient Concerts in 1838. Following an introductory chorus for men's voices in four parts, there is a bass recitative ('Our fathers have sinned') that could almost have come directly from a Mendelssohn oratorio. It is possible that Walmisley was influenced here by Mendelssohn's *St Paul*, which had its first English performance under the direction of Sir George Smart at Liverpool in October 1836. It was published by Novello the following year.

The influence of Mendelssohn is even more apparent in two slightly later anthems. The undated anthem 'If the Lord himself had not been on our side' is the subject of the following remarks by William Glover in his *Memoirs of a Cambridge chorister* (1885).

I addressed our Professor in the following terms: 'Surely in our good cathedral music we must in future add something of a modest orchestral effect to the organ part. Whether we are more restless than our fathers or not, certain it is that we are apt to become impatient when we hear long, drooping notes, like those in Kent's "Blessed be Thou". How different is the effect from that produced in the chorus, "Help, Lord", in "Elijah", where a few bright notes on the violins sustain the voices for a length of time.'...The Professor seemed for a time inclined to defend an imitation of the ancient, unassisted church music. But...in a few months he produced an anthem based on these conditions. It contains a short, effective solo, 'If the Lord Himself had not been on our side'...I am bound to say that the Professor, having once left the beaten track, proceeded to overwork his steed in a course of incessant labour. He went far beyond my intention. I did not mean to imply that a kind of perpetual movement should be introduced, without many grateful reliefs and pleasant resting-places. This restless motion is almost as wearying as the tedious calm of our older writers.[6]

To judge from his mentioning a chorus in *Elijah*, one might assume that Glover's suggestion could not have been made before August 1846, when that oratorio had its first performance at the Birmingham Festival. What makes this unlikely is another Walmisley anthem, 'The Lord shall comfort Zion', dating from 1840, which is written along the same stylistic lines as 'If the Lord himself'. There would have been no reason for Glover to make his suggestion and Walmisley his mild protest in 1846 or later if 'The Lord shall comfort Zion' had been composed six or more years previously. The likeliest explanation is that Glover (b.1822) was simply inaccurate in his recollection of the details of an event that took place about half a century before, a supposition reinforced by the eccentric, rambling, and haphazard arrangement of his two volumes of memoirs, notable for the absence of exact dates.

In addition to the orchestral effects in the accompaniment, 'If the Lord himself' is not lacking in drama and harmonic colour, though Glover is justified in his criticism of the *moto perpetuo*, which sometimes is more busy than expressive. It is highly effective, however, in the emotional climax of the opening chorus, at the words 'They had swallowed us up quick', employing diminished seventh harmony in rising sequence. An arresting specimen of harmonic dramatisation occurs in the concluding chorus, 'Our help standeth in the Name of the Lord'. Following a cadence in Eb major, the voices enter quietly in Eb minor with the words, 'The dead praise not thee, O Lord: neither all they that go down into silence.' This turns to the relative major (Gb) before making a new start in Eb major. This is respelt D♯, so that the flat VI, previously Cb, becomes B major, to function as IV of F♯. The F♯ major chord then acquires a seventh (V_7 of B), but this resolves as a German sixth – though not spelt as such – in the concluding key of Bb major. Here again, one suspects the influence of Spohr's harmonic diction. In general, Walmisley seems to have favoured the German sixth modulation as a climactic device.

'The Lord shall comfort Zion' (1840) is the largest in scale of Walmisley's anthems, and the one which most closely resembles Mendelssohnian oratorio in its style and expressive progress. Indeed, one can identify specific movements of *St Paul* that might have furnished models:

Chorus: 'The Lord shall comfort' – cf. 'How lovely are the messengers' (ii/26)
Bass solo: 'Lift up your eyes' – cf. 'Consume them all' (i/12)
Soprano solo: 'Hearken, ye that know' – cf. 'I will sing of thy great mercies' (ii/27)
Chorus: 'Awake, awake' – cf. 'Rise! Up! Arise!' (i/15)
'The redeemed of the Lord' – cf. 'Bless thou the Lord, O my soul' from 'Not only unto him' (ii/45)
'And everlasting joy' – cf. 'Behold, now, total darkness' from 'Rise! Up! Arise!' (i/15)

As for orchestral effects in the accompaniment, the organ part looks throughout like a keyboard reduction of an orchestral score, including, for instance, tremolandi in the bass solo. Bumpus implies that it is not a reduction when he says that it 'would lend itself well to orchestration',[7] and when one considers that a major portion of the organist's repertory in 1840 would have consisted of arrangements of orchestral pieces, Walmisley's accompaniment as intentional organ writing becomes even more credible. Most of Walmisley's other organ accompaniments, both of earlier and of later works, are more in keeping with what is customarily regarded as idiomatic for the instrument, but as Walmisley was himself a celebrated organist, he would not have perpetrated infelicities out of ignorance.

In general, Walmisley does not bring a dramatic Mendelssohnian flavour to his service settings. The Morning, Communion, and Evening Service in F (1839) is conservative alongside the larger anthems Walmisley was writing around the same time. Like John Jebb and many others, he may have thought that the service texts require a more formal and communal treatment than anthems, which can offer greater scope for subjective expression.

The Morning, Communion, and Evening Service in D major (1843) seems to mark another stylistic turn, this time toward that fluent, mostly diatonic idiom prevailing in much of Walmisley's later work. The Te Deum, however, is a reworking of an unpublished setting of 1830, and is in the perfunctory short service idiom. There are passages of Spohrish chromaticism in the Communion Service, but in the evening canticles, the composer most clearly shows his new face. There is an effective enharmonic German sixth modulation toward the end of the Magnificat, but more characteristic of the later style is an entirely diatonic sequence (ex. 14) occurring earlier in the setting. Its fluency contrasts decidedly with the stiffness of much of Walmisley's earlier neo-Georgian diatonic writing. In this new idiom, even when chro-

Ex. 14   T. A. Walmisley: Service in D major, Magnificat

111

matic and modulatory, as in the next cited passage (ex. 15) from the Nunc Dimittis, the stylistic flavour is not at all Spohrish or Mendelssohnian. Rather, it seems almost a foretaste of Stanford.

Ex. 15   T. A. Walmisley: Service in D major, Nunc Dimittis

Two unaccompanied anthems date from 1844. 'Not unto us, O Lord' is in two short sections, both in triple metre recalling Attwood. A more remarkable work is 'Hail, gladdening light' for five-part choir (SSATB), more thoroughly in Walmisley's later diatonic idiom. It appeared in John Hullah's *Vocal scores* (1846–7) where it is dated 1 January 1844. The text is John Keble's translation from the third-century Greek. A sense of flow is achieved largely by diatonic dissonance arising from fluid part-writing. Some aspects of the texture, the alternation of block harmony with contrapuntal motion, and the striking and often unexpected juxtaposition of harmonies, bear comparison with Charles Wood's well-known setting of the same text for unaccompanied double choir. Did Wood know and admire Walmisley's setting?

The work which may claim to be Walmisley's supreme achievement in this later idiom is the Evening Service in B♭ for double choir with organ. Evidently Walmisley himself thought highly of it, since he published it in 1845, partly to gauge the potential reception of a whole volume of his cathedral music. Presumably the results were disappointing, since the projected volume did not appear during his lifetime. The service is broad and dignified in concept, making effective use of the various textural possibilities of homophonic and contrapuntal eight-part writing as well as double choir antiphony. The harmonic language is restrained, though Walmisley does not hesitate to introduce a dash of diminished seventh colour at 'hath exalted' following dramatic unisons. He achieves real tenderness in the diatonic antiphony of the ensuing 'He hath filled the hungry' (ex. 16). The Gloria Patri, which serves for both canticles, opens boldly with canonic passages for two voices punctuated by massive eight-part block-chordal addresses to the first two Persons of the Trinity. The effect is not unlike that of the Gloria Patri from Bach's Magnificat in D. As Walmisley was a Bach enthusiast, he probably knew the work.

Ex. 16   T. A. Walmisley: Evening Service in B♭, Magnificat

Ex. 16 *(cont.)*

fill - ed the hun - gry, He hath fill - ed with good things.

He hath fill - ed the hun - gry with good things.

Two compositions for treble voices date from 1849 and 1850. The anthem, 'Ponder my words', which includes four-part treble writing, reverts to the idiom of the Georgian verse anthem. The absence of Mendelssohnian influence in writing for trebles is itself noteworthy, with such models available as 'Lift thine eyes' from *Elijah* and 'Hear my prayer'. The second piece is a Morning Service in E for trebles in two parts. The independent organ accompaniment might be seen as a precursor to that of the Evening Service in D minor. Another similarity is the frequent juxtaposition of keys a third apart.

'Blessed is he that considereth the poor' (1854) is noteworthy as a full anthem in Walmisley's later idiom. It was composed for a festival service of the Choir Benevolent Fund held at King's College. The SATBB scoring ensures a richness of sonority.

Walmisley's last important completed composition, the Evening Service in D minor (1855), is, of course, the one chiefly responsible for keeping his name in modern cathedral music lists. It has been accorded sometimes extravagant praise by critics and historians generally unfavourable towards Victorian church music. Watkins Shaw, for example, writes:

It calls for some effort of historical imagination to realise the considerable originality, both of style and technique, which lies behind this great composition. It is, of course, well known that Walmisley here breaks new ground by writing an independent organ part to form an indispensable and integral element in the work.[8]

This is a strange remark, considering that S. S. Wesley in E, to name but one outstanding specimen, was published ten years earlier in 1845. Moreover, Shaw is fully aware of the elaborate accompaniments of Walmisley's own Mendelssohnian anthems, which he adversely criticises in the same article from which the foregoing quotation comes. Might it be that the D minor service finds favour, not because it is innovative, forward-looking, and highly original, but for the very opposite reason: that it attempts, with a degree of success, to conjure up an ethos of ages past, the one piece of Victorian cathedral music which sounds so utterly unlike Victorian cathedral music? Whatever may be said of the organ part, it does not point forwards to Stanford in Bb,[9] but backwards to the idiom of early verse services like Byrd's Second, though Walmisley amplifies the reserved, chamber-organ idiom of the Tudor and Jacobean accompaniments with pedal and some massive chordal effects. The SSA semi-chorus passages are reminiscent of ensemble verses found in some seventeenth-century 'full with verse' services, like Purcell's in G Minor and Bb. The fluent diatonicism noted in other of Walmisley's later works here loses its tenderness. What many critics praise as sturdy grandeur can just as easily be perceived as hard and forbidding. The principal exception is the quartet verse, 'He remembering his mercy', repeated by full choir, pianissimo, in the Magnificat: one last nod in the direction of Attwood, and arguably incongruous in its surroundings. There is some evidence of deliberate professorial antiquarianism. Footnotes inform us that the Glorias of both canticles contain basses borrowed from Henri Dumont, hardly a household word in Victorian England. The work concludes with a Phrygian-mode cadence that is highly satisfying, though as Bumpus implies, it was not satisfying to all later Victorian ears. He reports the custom at King's of reversing the Glorias of the two canticles so as to secure a conclusion in the tonic.[10] The piece is clearly a unique production and somewhat eccentric. Whether it is indicative of a stylistic direction that Walmisley would have pursued even further, had he not succumbed to the consequences of dipsomania in 1856, it is impossible to say.

The works of John Goss present a different picture from those of Walmisley. Both men absorbed the rich heritage of the English cathedral repertory as well as the influence of Mozart, especially as mediated through Attwood. Walmisley's music, however, is the more derivative – his late diatonic idiom notwithstanding – while in Goss's the external influences are discernible, but they seem to be more thoroughly assimilated within a style more distinctly his own. While this may be partially explained by the fact that most of Goss's church music was written when the composer was an older man than Walmisley – indeed, after the Cambridge professor's death – a more adequate explanation seems to lie in Goss's more settled temperament. One simply does not encounter the drastic changes of style in Goss's church music that have been observed in Walmisley's, but rather a gradual development over the years: the slow growth and maturing of tendencies often present from the beginning.

On the whole, Goss's harmonic language is restrained and prevailingly diatonic, though of course, he does not completely eschew chromatic harmony. Nevertheless, his music usually sounds unmistakably Victorian even when completely diatonic, largely as a result of his handling of diatonic dissonances, especially over pedal basses. This is well illustrated by a brief excerpt from the organ part of 'The glory of the Lord' (1869), which doubles the voice parts and adds a few notes of its own (ex. 17). The effect can be similar, though perhaps less pronounced, when the bass line is not completely static. Whereas Walmisley, in his earlier works, grafts some modern harmonic touches on to a stock derived from the eighteenth century, Goss's idiom is modern at its foundation. His works demonstrate that the essential early Victorian flavour does not depend on technical extremes.

Ex. 17   John Goss: anthem, 'The glory of the Lord' (organ part)

Attwood and Walmisley divided their work as composers almost evenly between cathedral services and anthems. Goss, in contrast, was pre-eminently an anthem composer. Most of his service settings were intended not for cathedral choirs but for amateurs: unison settings for the annual Charity Children's service at St Paul's or simple four-part settings, often partly in chant, for the use of parish choirs. The principal exceptions are the Evening Service in E (1854) which, unusually for Goss, is very much in the Georgian short service idiom, and the Te Deum composed in 1872 for the Queen's service of thanksgiving for the recovery of the Prince of Wales. Goss afterwards added a Benedictus to make a standard morning service. Even in anthems, the picture is different. Large-scale verse anthems hold a commanding place in the works of Attwood and Walmisley. Goss, in contrast, excelled as a miniaturist and as an exponent of somewhat more extended single-movement forms.

Goss certainly did not neglect the multi-movement genre. Among his anthems of this type are:

Forsake me not (c.1823–4): solo, duet, chorus
Have mercy upon me (1833): chorus, quartet with full choir, recitative and choral declamation, chorus
Blessed is the man (1842): chorus, trio, choral declamation, chorus
Praise the Lord, O my soul (1854): chorus, semi-chorus, choral recitative, chorus
The wilderness (1861): recitative, trio, recitative, choir with quartet, choral recitative, chorus
Lift up thine eyes (1863): double chorus, recitative, chorus
Come, and let us return unto the Lord (1866): chorus, recitative, chorus, recitative, quartet with full choir leading directly to recapitulation of first chorus

The glory of the Lord (1869): chorus, semi-chorus with full choir, choral declamation, chorus

Fine as many of these works are, either as wholes or in their individual movements, it is noteworthy that none are conceived on as grand a scale as the
larger anthems of Walmisley or S. S. Wesley. Goss appears to have brought no
exceptional insights to the verse anthem genre, nor was his inspiration unfail-
ingly fresh and spontaneous in these works. Of the anthems composed after
1842, only 'The wilderness' has a considerable proportion of solo writing.
The rest mostly present a sequence of choral movements, sometimes with the
connection of recitative, and even this is often choral.

The through-composed miniature, deriving its formal structure from that
of the words being set, was a genre in which Goss produced many fine specimens, including 'God so loved the world' and 'Let the wicked forsake his way'
(1850, as contributions to Henry John Haycraft's *Sacred harmony*, 1851),
'Almighty and merciful God' (1858), and 'These are they which follow the
Lamb' (1859). Goss's finest achievements, however, arguably lay in single-
movement anthems constructed according to tonal and thematic plans essentially musical in origin rather than derived from the text, and yet handled so
as not to neglect or obscure the sense of the text. Some of these are miniature
in scale, like 'O Saviour of the world' (1869) and 'I heard a voice from heaven'
(c.1877), while others are more extended. Anthems of this sort begin to
predominate in Goss's output from 1852 onwards, and he often organises
individual movements of multi-movement anthems according to such plans.
Among anthems having a ternary structure involving either literal or varied
recapitulation after a distinct middle section are 'O praise the Lord, laud ye'
(1856), 'Stand up and bless the Lord' (1863), 'I will magnify thee' (1864), and
'O give thanks unto the Lord' (1866). 'Fear not, O land' (1863) is a rondo, with
two reappearances of the opening section. 'O taste and see' (1863) follows the
binary plan AABB with some slight variation, a scheme more often adopted
by Attwood than Goss.

Of greater structural interest are those anthems with a binary plan involving recapitulation, or ABAB, allowing for variation in the restatement of
material. In many cases, Goss uses the scheme to produce anthems in sonata
form. As one might expect, a sonata-form anthem differs considerably from
an instrumental movement in sonata form, and it is important to clarify those
aspects of sonata procedure which Goss incorporates in anthems.

Sonata form is both a thematic and a tonal process. Thematic material is
presented in the exposition so as to execute a modulation. Distinct first and
second themes are not necessary, as witness so many of Haydn's first movements. Thematic development is frequently the heart of an instrumental
sonata movement, where motivic argumentation is of primary interest. This
is not, however, a procedure well adapted to anthems, where it can easily
interfere with the clear projection of the text, and it is something Goss does
not attempt. It is not crucial to the tonal structure of a sonata movement, and

indeed, sonata form without development is a fairly common plan in Mozart slow movements. A short modulatory passage may perform the tonal function of the development in a sonata anthem. The recapitulation confirms the structure. If any one principle may be held as definitive in sonata procedure, it is the recapitulation in the home key of thematic material that was originally stated in another key, however adapted and varied it may be on its return.

Not all of Goss's recapitulating binary-form anthems fulfil the conditions for sonata form. Among those which cannot convincingly be called sonata anthems, even though some may incline in that direction, are 'Christ, our Passover' (1857), 'Behold, I bring you good tidings' (1857), 'Brother, thou art gone before us' (1865), and 'I heard a voice from heaven' (c.1877). In 'Behold, I bring you good tidings', for instance, there are two distinct themes, but in the exposition, the first theme modulates to the dominant, while the second begins in the tonic and has a modulatory extension to the subdominant. The recapitulation, which is considerably compressed, remains in the tonic.

A stronger claim for sonata form, or at least the more consistent operation of sonata principles, may be made for the following:

If we believe that Jesus died (1852)
Praise the Lord, O my soul (1854), second movement
O praise the Lord of heaven (1868)
O Lord, thou art my God (1868)
O Saviour of the world (1869)
The glory of the Lord (1869), second and third movements

In 'O Lord, thou art my God', a thematically independent middle section intervenes between the exposition and recapitulation, thereby producing a ternary rather than the binary structure most common in Goss's sonata anthems. Although there is no thematic development, the modulatory scheme of this middle section may be regarded as a tonal working-out. In 'O praise the Lord of heaven', the recapitulation comes in the middle of the anthem, following a passage of choral declamation intervening between it and the exposition. Tonally, the plan is more freely applied. The exposition ends not in the dominant (F) but in the mediant major (D), as in the first movement of Beethoven's 'Waldstein' Sonata. Thematically, moreover, the end of the recapitulation is only tenuously related to that of Goss's exposition. Tonally, the end of the recapitulation leans toward the dominant key (F), but an oscillation between E♮ and E♭ prevents it from settling in the dominant, while it certainly could not be heard as a strong end in the tonic. It seems likely that Goss introduces this unsettled tonal atmosphere because he proceeds to another modulatory passage, and concludes the anthem with yet another section constructed of entirely new thematic material.

In nearly all of Goss's anthems one may observe a meticulous attention to text declamation and a remarkable flexibility of phrase. He had an uncanny knack for balancing the musical and textual interests so that each seems to have full sway. His rhythms and phrasings were not enslaved to the prosody of the text; he freely indulged in word repetitions in the interest of musical proportion, but usually did so with words whose importance in context would justify the emphasis by reiteration. Goss also had a remarkable instinct for proportion in phrases of irregular length, thereby imparting to his anthems a great sense of elasticity and flow. This might seem a natural consequence of the sensitive treatment of the prose texts of most anthems, but it must be emphasised that Goss's phrasing makes musical sense. It is not a mechanical rendering of English declamation in musical notation. A simple and familiar illustration occurs in his tune for Henry Francis Lyte's hymn 'Praise, my soul, the King of heaven', obviously not a prose text. All of the phrases but the first are four bars in length, but the initial five-bar phrase effectively pre-empts any tendency to squareness in the remainder of the tune. Likewise, in the penultimate line of the tune, Goss makes a four-bar phrase by literal repetition of a two-bar melodic figure, thereby providing another variant of regular phrasing. One often encounters such short figures, either literally repeated or in sequential parallel, set in the midst of lengthier neighbours in Goss's anthems. Any number of them would serve to illustrate his characteristic phrasing. A good example is furnished by the opening section of 'I will magnify thee' (1864). The first thirty-nine bars group themselves into the following principal phrase divisions and subdivisions.

$$12 \quad + \quad 8 \quad + \quad 4 \quad + \quad 15$$
$$(5+7) \quad\quad (4+4) \quad\quad (2+2) \quad\quad (5+10)$$

An irregular but well-proportioned pair is followed by a more regular pattern. This is followed by a very short pattern of the kind described above. In this case, the treble note is held over into the following fifteen-bar group, thus linking them more closely. This is signified by the dotted slur in the diagram. Goss often concludes an anthem section like this with a substantial stretch of more nearly seamless writing than had occurred earlier, making an effective contrast with the preceding short repeated or parallel figure.

One cannot realistically speak of stylistic periods in Goss's career, but there is a significant biographical division. In 1842 he composed 'Blessed is the man', the first anthem in a projected series of 150 with texts selected from each of the psalms in turn. The piece was so badly received by the choir of St Paul's that Goss not only abandoned the rest of the series, but virtually gave up original composition for a period of ten years until, in 1852, he wrote a choral dirge ('And the King said') and anthem ('If we believe that Jesus died') for the funeral of the Duke of Wellington. The warm reception of these works appears to have revived Goss's shaken self-confidence as a composer, since they mark the beginning of his main output of church anthems, reaching a peak of productivity in the 1860s. The principal exceptions to the ten-year hiatus in original composition were the two miniatures of 1850: 'God so loved the world' and 'Let the wicked forsake his way'. Apart from his regular cathedral duties at this time, Goss devoted his energies to an editorial collaboration with the organist of Westminster Abbey, James Turle (1802–82), producing a collection of anthems and services by traditional writers, some of them published for the first time. It appeared in forty separate numbers or as three folio volumes beginning in 1843.

As a young man, Goss produced some notable secular music, including two concert overtures for the Philharmonic Society in 1825 and 1827, some incidental music for John Banim's play *The sergeant's wife*, and numerous vocal pieces. In 1826 he published *Six glees and one madrigal*, containing his most celebrated glee, 'There is beauty on the mountain'. Another of these glees, 'Hark! Heard ye not?' so impressed Edward Dannreuther that he reproduced six full pages of the score as an illustration in his volume of the *Oxford history of music*.[11] The vivid harmonic characterisation of the text and effective use of vocal textures make it a particularly noteworthy achievement.

Much of the sacred music Goss composed before 1842 was not intended for church use. Four sacred canons dating from 1823–4 appear to be primarily academic displays of contrapuntal prowess. A six-part (SATTBB) motet, 'Requiem aeternam', in memory of the Duke of York, was published in the *Harmonicon* in 1827. It has a solemnity of character and stylistic restraint that one might expect of a church anthem, but its Latin text and medium of publication suggest that it was not intended for the church service. Goss produced a similar work on the same text in 1829 on the death of the composer William Shield (b.1748).

In addition to these works, Goss composed and collected a fair number of accompanied sacred songs intended for domestic use. As a genre, such songs – mostly for solo voice with piano, but also duets and other ensembles, with or without choral refrain – account for a great deal of publication throughout the nineteenth century, in the form of sheet music, anthologies, and periodicals like William Ayrton's *Sacred Minstrelsy* (1834–5) to which, as noted before, Thomas Attwood contributed. In 1826, Goss contributed two songs ('Give praise to God' and 'Stand up and bless the Lord') to a collection edited by Alfred Pettet (c.1785–c.1845), and in 1833 brought out the first of a three-volume anthology under his own editorship entitled *The Sacred Minstrel*.

Such songs help to underscore through contrast the special character of church music proper. The pieces in *The Sacred Minstrel* are decidedly not churchly, being indistinguishable in style from serious secular ballads or operatic airs. The collection draws mainly from late eighteenth- and early nineteenth-century material. Some of the songs are adaptations. 'The Gospel is the light', for instance, is adapted from the fourth movement of Beethoven's Septet in E♭, Op. 20. Goss's own contributions to the volume are the solo songs 'They are not lost, but gone before' and 'Oh had I wings like yonder bird'. The piano introduction to the former (ex. 18) gives a good idea of the stylistic flavour. The song has an agitated middle section in C♯ minor to the

Ex. 18 John Goss: song, 'They are not lost, but gone before' (piano introduction)

words 'How many painful days on earth their fainting spirits numbered o'er', accompanied by repeated semiquaver chords in the right hand following detached bass notes on the crotchet beats. Such songs manifest Goss's gift of elegant lyricism and shapely melodic phrase. The style is well suited to the highly personal and, in a non-derogatory sense, sentimental nature of the words. Goss's ecclesiastical idiom is more restrained, with the emotion sublimated and made more formally communal. In church music he generally avoids the sinuous arabesques of the ballad style or operatic melody, and he employs less obviously colouristic harmony. Nevertheless, Goss's sense of vocal lyricism is as evident in the more reserved idiom of the anthem as in these solo songs.

Many of the features of Goss's mature anthem style are perceptible in certain of his early works. There are exceptions, of course, such as the aforementioned sacred canons and the piece which is possibly his earliest extant anthem: 'Forsake me not', which dates from the early 1820s.[12] This work is so much in the Mozartian idiom that it is difficult to think of it as the spontaneous invention of Goss at all. Such is not the case, however, with the 'Requiem aeternam' for the Duke of York (1827). The dignified restraint of language warmed by delicate passing chromaticism (ex. 19) establishes an atmosphere characteristic of the mature Goss. Even in the anthem which won the Gresham Prize of 1833, 'Have mercy upon me, O God', Goss reveals an essential contemporaneity of style and a freedom from too obvious derivation. Recall that Gresham Prize entries were expected to be in the 'true Sublime Style' as determined by William Crotch. Thus Goss's anthem may be even more restrained than usual and not highly original, but it does not sound academically bogus-antique. The concluding chorus is a canon 4 in 2, which is so fluent that it sounds remarkably spontaneous, a measure of Goss's contrapuntal mastery and essential musicality in a genre in which correctness is the most that many would expect.

In 'Blessed is the man' (1842), the anthem whose poor reception marked the beginning of a ten-year hiatus in original composition, Goss had virtually

Ex. 19   John Goss: motet, 'Requiem aeternam', for the Duke of York

achieved his mature idiom, but the work seems to fall short in exactly the
aspects in which the composer generally excels in his later compositions.
The opening, for example, promises a fluent, diatonic part-song treatment,
and is somewhat reminiscent of the beginning of 'Happy and blest are they'
from Mendelssohn's *St Paul*. Unusually for him, Goss fails to sustain the
flow, so there is sometimes an uncomfortable effect of protracting the phrase
to get in all the words. There are other minor miscalculations of phrasing,
accentuation, and harmonic flow that prevent one from classing this anthem
with the finest of Goss's works. It was not published until 1861, when it was
included in the first volume of Ouseley's *Special anthems for certain seasons*
as appropriate for St Andrew's Day.

There is no question of miscalculation in the two miniatures Goss contributed to Haycraft's *Sacred harmony* (1851). Indeed, the first of them,
'God so loved the world', is a prime example of a Goss miniature whose
musical form is closely moulded to that of the words (John 3:16–17), and
whose phraseology is flexible but perfectly balanced. The entire piece is only
twenty-six bars long in $\frac{3}{2}$ metre, falling into two sections corresponding with
the two verses of the text. The first section is thirteen bars in length, falling

into two phrases: the first in E♭ (six bars) and the second in the dominant (seven bars). These may be further subdivided as 3+3 and 3+4 respectively. The melody has a purposeful curve, beginning on B♭ with a stepwise descent in the first three bars. The next three bars answer with another descent, this time starting a tone higher. The dominant-key segment begins with a stepwise ascent to E♭, the climax being reached in the first of the concluding four-bar division with an F on the first syllable of 'perish' before the descent back to B♭. The second part of the piece consists of ten bars in two phrases, 4+6, which do not lend themselves to the kind of further subdivision observed in the first half. To these is added an 'Amen' of three bars. The second half opens in F minor, with the final phrase returning to E♭. The setting is homophonic and diatonic throughout. The only instance of word repetition is the key phrase 'through him', the second appearance of which coincides with the climax of the piece as a whole, the actual return to E♭ harmony. The 'Amen' is introduced by a D♭ appoggiatura in the bass. The other miniature, 'Let the wicked forsake his way', is organised according to a similar plan, the whole being twenty-five bars, deployed as follows:

$$12 \quad + \quad 13$$
$$(5+7) \quad (4+3+6)$$
Keys: G D e a G

The texture is more varied. The first five bars are homophonic, but the succeeding seven ('and let him return unto the Lord') are in freely imitative counterpoint, often with pairs of voices moving in parallel thirds.

These pieces provide something of a foretaste of the music for Wellington's funeral. 'If we believe that Jesus died', the anthem composed for that occasion, is justifiably celebrated. Its general shape is binary, like the two miniatures just discussed, only on a larger scale, apparently the first of Goss's anthems in sonata form. The piece falls into two roughly equal halves, an exposition and recapitulation, of forty-five and forty-three bars respectively. This aspect of structure is not derived from the text, since each half has the same words, but within each half, the natural division of the verse (I Thess. 4:14) determines the structural subdivision of each half into first and second themes: 'If we believe that Jesus died and rose again: even so them also which sleep in Jesus, will God bring with him.' The subdivisions are 21+24 and 16+28 bars respectively, to which is added a four-bar coda in triple metre, 'Wherefore comfort one another with these words.' Much of the effectiveness of the anthem comes from Goss's delicate but affective use of mode and tonality. He avoids straightforward cadences, thereby giving a sense of flow without compromising the tone of solemnity. The ambivalent feeling that comes from the tendency to hold off the completion of major-mode cadences might almost be heard as a musical symbol for the dichotomy implicit in the Christian attitude towards death: mourning of the human loss, but confidence in the better life hereafter. Consider, for example, the course of the exposition. Towards the end of the fugal opening in D minor, a crescendo leads to a somewhat surprising V_7 of F at the end of the first thematic group. The next section begins quietly in block chords, and seems to take up F major, with vi-V^6_5-I being the first three chords (ex. 20). Note, however, that the tonic

Ex. 20   John Goss: anthem, 'If we believe that Jesus died'

comes on the weak beat of the bar, and the introduction of an E♭ diverts the flow to B♭, then G minor, with a cadence in G major following a dominant pedal and affective diatonic dissonances at the words 'which sleep in Jesus'. From here there is a return to F to complete the first half of the anthem. In the second half, the first group, based on the same subject as the opening, is more compressed and in free rather than fugal counterpoint, leading to the dominant of D. Much of the final group is a literal transposition of its counterpart in the exposition, the diversion this time being to E minor, with a cadence in E major, ending finally in D major. A superficial glance at the score might lead one to suspect an exercise in the 'timeless' contrapuntal idiom, but the expressive use of harmonic function and use of tonality as a basis for the essential musical organisation of the work belie this possible first impression.

A number of Goss's mature anthems are cast in a jubilant triple-metre idiom that he made particularly his own. Possibly the earliest instance occurs in the first movement of 'Praise the Lord, O my soul', an anthem composed for the 1854 Festival of the Sons of the Clergy, on which occasion it was sung by a choir of 250 voices assembled from some of the principal cathedrals and other choral foundations of the south of England, with the accompaniment of organ and wind band.[13] The *Times* critic, almost certainly J. W. Davison, characterised the work as 'grand, broad, and massive' in its harmony, 'but free from any servile adherence to models',[14] thus giving contemporary testimony of Goss's originality.

The special triple-metre idiom of the anthem's first movement is characterised by a vigorous swinging movement and Goss's customary elasticity of phrasing, with the vigour further enhanced by dotted rhythms, syncopations, and hemiola. The idiom is reminiscent of Purcell's 'Rejoice in the Lord alway', and this may indeed be its historical antecedent. Among other Goss anthems in this idiom, either in whole or in part, are

> O praise the Lord, laud ye (1856)
> Behold, I bring you good tidings (1857)
> In Christ dwelleth (1861)
> Fear not, O land (1863)
> Stand up and bless the Lord your God (1863)
> I will magnify thee (1864)
> O Lord, thou art my God (1868)
> O praise the Lord of heaven (1868)
> The Lord is my strength (1872)

'Almighty and merciful God' (1858), while having some of the rhythmic properties of the jubilant idiom, is in a somewhat smoother style and slower tempo, and so assumes a very different character. Similarly, 'And kings shall be thy nursing fathers', the concluding movement of 'Lift up thine eyes' (1863, also for the Sons of the Clergy), is in a gentle and flowing triple metre, possibly derived from the example of Attwood.

A highly significant anthem on stylistic grounds is 'Brother, thou art gone before us', composed for the 1865 Festival of the Sons of the Clergy. The words are from *The martyr of Antioch* by Henry Hart Milman (1799–1868), Dean of St Paul's. Perhaps it is because of the unmistakably modern tone of the metrical rhyming text, but in this anthem, Goss's vein of expression is far more personal than in his previous church music. It is a vein reminiscent of his earlier sacred songs, here approaching the fully-fledged High Victorian idiom with its warmth of chromatic colour. Earlier chromatic passages had occurred in settings of a far more conservatively formal tone. This can be better illustrated than explained. The quoted passage (ex. 21) is representative

Ex. 21   John Goss: anthem, 'Brother, thou art gone before us'

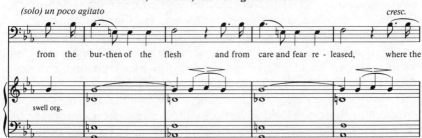

Ex. 21 *(cont.)*

wick - ed cease from troub-ling, and the wear - y are at rest.

of the general flavour of 'Brother, thou art gone before us'. The alternation of bass solo with choir in this anthem seems to underscore the personal nature of the text. In 'O taste and see' (1863) there is a passage which is strikingly similar in outward appearance (ex. 22), involving an accompaniment of alter-

Ex. 22 **John Goss: anthem, 'O taste and see'**

The li - ons do lack and suf - fer hun - ger, but they who

(basses)

seek the Lord, they who seek the Lord

who seek the Lord

nating sustained seventh harmonies, but the continuation – indeed the flavour of the anthem as a whole – is worlds removed from the atmosphere of the 1865 piece. Certainly the conclusion of 'Brother, thou art gone before us' (ex. 23) is not typical of Goss's settings of scriptural words, but a real High Victorian composer like Barnby would probably have been unable to resist flattening the first tenor's C in the fourth bar from the end.

It must be emphasised that this anthem is exceptional in Goss's output, nor can one claim any historical priority for it as a pioneering effort in the High Victorian idiom. By the mid 1860s the idiom was already in the air.

Ex. 23   John Goss: anthem, 'Brother, thou art gone before us'

What seems significant is that a composer of the elder generation, who had hitherto observed a fairly strict separation of the highly personal style of non-ecclesiastical sacred music from the communal dignity of conservative early Victorian church music, should so decisively cross this *ad hoc* boundary in an anthem intended expressly to be sung in the chief cathedral of the nation as part of a festival service redolent of some two hundred years' tradition and accumulated dignity. It would be wrong to judge this as a secularisation of church music. Rather, it may be seen as a development in the perception of stylistic propriety. During Attwood's lifetime, the enhancement of expression and softening of severities warmly commended by H. J. Gauntlett gained acceptance as a stylistic development appropriate to the dignity of English cathedral music. The growth of the High Victorian idiom after the middle of the century is a continuation of the same tendency. Goss's anthem implies something of an endorsement by a highly respected elder statesman.

Goss later adapted 'Brother, thou art gone before us' to the psalm text 'Lord, let me know mine end', so that the music would be matched to a more widely serviceable text. It is a skilful piece of adaptation, but surely Goss would not have set a psalm text this way in the first instance. Still, from 1865 onwards, Goss seemed more inclined than before to employ greater chromatic warmth and tenderness of expression in more conventional anthems on scriptural or Prayer Book texts, as in 'Hear, O Lord and have mercy' (1865), the subdued section 'This is the Lord's doing' from 'O give thanks unto the Lord' (1866), the somewhat Spohrish middle movement of 'The glory of the Lord' (1869), and perhaps most movingly of all in 'O Saviour of the world' (1869).

7

Samuel Sebastian Wesley (1810–76), a frustrated romantic

Samuel Sebastian Wesley stands apart from other Victorian cathedral musicians. His compositions, while discernibly Victorian and part of the English cathedral tradition, have an individuality and expressive power which distinguish them from the works of his contemporaries. Although critical assessments differ, twentieth-century writers generally show a higher regard for Wesley than for most other Victorians.

It is tempting to account for this by assuming that Wesley was essentially like all the other Victorian cathedral composers, doing the same sorts of things they did, only better. This would be misleading, however. While certainly not at an opposite pole from his contemporaries, Wesley did differ from them significantly in outlook and temperament. To put it briefly, Wesley was a romantic, but one set in an environment largely uncongenial to romanticism.

On the whole, Wesley was a profoundly unhappy man who seems almost deliberately to have placed himself in circumstances that would guarantee his unhappiness. He was pre-eminently a cathedral musician at a time when the state of cathedral music was anything but encouraging. There was ample scope for the trenchant criticisms he made and the reforms he so strenuously advocated in his published writings. Wesley's abrasiveness, however, virtually guaranteed a stiffening of opposition to any idea he might put forward. He was ever his own worst enemy, and if he was at times treated unfairly or his work criticised with inordinate severity, his manner would seem to have invited such treatment.

If a tempestuous character is an inherited trait, then Wesley came by his honestly. Moreover, his ancestors present a chequered pattern of religious partisanships. They include seventeenth-century Nonconformists, a great-grandfather who was a High Church Tory clergyman repeatedly embroiled in rows with his wife and his Lincolnshire parishioners, and whose sons became the founders of Methodism. Sebastian's father, Samuel Wesley (1766–1837), was the younger of two prodigiously talented musical sons of the Revd Charles Wesley, and was sometimes called 'Old Sam' to distinguish him from Sebastian. He was noted for his moodiness, eccentricity, and prolonged periods of depression, which may have been worsened by a serious head injury sustained in 1787 from a fall into a builder's excavation. He attempted suicide at least once, and evidently drank heavily in an effort to alleviate his fits of depression. Although he denied having ever joined the Church of Rome, he certainly did have a more than casual flirtation with Roman Catholicism, though his motivation was musical rather than doctrinal. His marriage in 1793 to Charlotte Louisa Martin was a disaster which must have contributed to his emotional disorders. They separated two years later, and on one occasion he was imprisoned for failure to keep up court-ordered payments. Samuel Sebastian and six other children were the result of an irregular liaison between Old Sam and his housekeeper Sarah Suter. It seems inevitable that these domestic circumstances should have had an ill effect on Sebastian's emotional development, an opinion ventured by Gerald Spink in 1937.[1] In contrast with his father, however, Sebastian was a lifelong Anglican, and wrote no church music for any other rite. He was deeply committed to the role and dignity of music in worship, but does not otherwise seem to have been noted for extraordinary piety. He was probably a believer in the routine sense.

Wesley was born and raised in London. He was a Chapel Royal chorister, sang at St Paul's Cathedral, and was among the boys who periodically travelled to Brighton to sing before King George IV at the Royal Pavilion. He later assumed several London organistships and assisted with theatrical music before receiving his first cathedral appointment in 1832, at Hereford. The state of music there was in severe decline, owing largely to the infirmity of the retiring organist, Dr John Clarke-Whitfeld (1770–1836). The organist's salary was pitiful, being less than £100 per annum, but in Wesley's case, depleted by a further £40 to provide a pension for Clarke-Whitfeld. During his Hereford years, Wesley wrote two of the anthems by which he became best known: 'The wilderness and the solitary place' and 'Blessed be the God and Father'.

'The wilderness' was composed for the re-opening of the Hereford organ in November of 1832, following extensive repairs and improvements. It was for its time and circumstances an ambitious and stylistically adventurous composition, exploiting the resources of the rebuilt organ. The anthem's subsequent history, however, provides a possible illustration of Wesley's quixotic rather than practical approach to the improvement of church music. The new anthem was well received on its first performance, and favourably noticed in the local newspaper. Wesley must have sensed that the work was an extraordinary achievement in its genre, and he decided to enter it for the prestigious Gresham Prize, established in 1831 by Maria Hackett, with a jury headed by William Crotch. Crotch was no stranger to the Wesleys. He and Old Sam were musical friends of long standing, so it is inconceivable that Sebastian Wesley was unaware of Crotch's prejudices regarding the kind of music expected for the Gresham competition: works in the ultra-conservative 'true Sublime Style', derived from the models of the sixteenth and seventeenth centuries. In short, 'The wilderness' was everything a Gresham entry was expected not to be. Wesley was too late for the 1832 competition, so his entry was retained for the following year, when the judges' verdict was painfully predictable. Crotch decorated the score with a sketch of a chorister straining to reach the top A in the concluding verse, while his colleague R. J. S. Stevens declared the anthem to be 'a clever thing, but not Cathedral music'.[2] It is hard to account for Wesley's eagerness to submit his work, unless he believed secretly that it was of such surpassing and self-evident merit as to take the stodgy adjudicators by storm and override their reactionary prejudices, putting all competition of the conventional sort in the shade.

'Blessed be the God and Father' was written at the request of Dr John Merewether, the Dean of Hereford, for Easter Day 1834. On that occasion the cathedral choir was reduced to the boy choristers and a single bass. Wesley evidently had not anticipated this lack of voices, as the earliest source for the anthem, a manuscript organ book at Hereford, gives alto and tenor parts in the choral sections.

Critical assessments of the work differ. About 1865, Wesley wrote to Alderman Dyson of Windsor, saying: 'I assure you I view it merely as a sort of shewy sketch, or a little thing just made to stop a gap, and never meant for publication. It may be something new in its style, and certainly is effective, but it does not satisfy me as to being true Church music. However, people *all* seem to like it, and perhaps it may lead people to look at better things of mine.'[3] One hardly knows when to take Wesley's remarks at face value. Other remarks of his, while not flatly contradicting this assessment, suggest that it is greatly overstated and misleading. 'Blessed be the God and Father' was first published in 1853 in Wesley's volume of *Twelve anthems*. He clearly intended this collection to represent him at his best. He wrote to a gentleman in Sheffield: 'My 12 anthems will be good and not a mere catchpenny publication.'[4] Not long before his death, he wrote to his sister Eliza: 'My published 12 anthems is my most important work. I think the style of my anthems may claim notice for the manner in which the words are expressed and for the new use made of broad massive harmony combined with serious devotional effects. What is called the Church style, in these later days, is merely a series of monotonous concords suited to the abilities of uneducated country choirs. My Church music never descends to this.'[5] If Wesley's opinion of 'Blessed be the God and Father' was really as low as his 1865 letter suggests, he would hardly have included it in a publication in which he set such store. Moreover, it seems unlikely that it could have enjoyed widespread popularity prior to publication, thus making Wesley's supposed reason for its inclusion somewhat unconvincing. His remarks to Eliza in 1876 concerning harmonic and devotional effects apply as much to this as to any of his anthems. Furthermore, Wesley took some trouble over revising the work for publication.[6] The changes can be better described as careful polishing than drastic recomposition, indicating Wesley's general satisfaction with the larger features of the anthem as originally conceived.

Two recurring themes in Wesley's letters from Hereford are his loneliness and financial straits. He evidently did not feel inclined to remain, for in spring of 1835 he was a candidate for the organistship of St George's Chapel, Windsor. Out of a formidable group of competitors, the appointment went to George Elvey (1816–93), who was only nineteen years of age. To make matters worse as far as Wesley was concerned, Elvey had won the Gresham Prize in 1834. This would have been for the competition of 1833, in which 'The wilderness' was entered. This double defeat appears to have hurt Wesley deeply, since many years later it was the apparent cause for the display of a most unattractive side to his character: a propensity to harbour ill feelings and perceive personal affronts where none were intended. The afore-mentioned letter to Alderman Dyson regarding 'Blessed be the God and Father' concludes: 'I felt much obliged to you for getting it noticed at Windsor. I viewed Windsor as a place that would never do anything for me.'[7] A more drastic incident involved Wesley's inexcusable behaviour towards an American church musician, Samuel Parkman Tuckerman (1819–90), who was making systematic tours of English cathedrals during the 1850s for the purpose of gaining familiarity with the cathedral repertory and gathering information relevant to the improvement of church music in his native land. Wesley was then organist of Winchester Cathedral. Tuckerman arrived with a letter of introduction from Elvey, with whom he was on friendly terms, but when Wesley saw it he exclaimed 'Elvey! Who is Elvey?', rang for his butler, and said, 'John, this man is an impostor. Show him the door!' Wesley soon repented of this rudeness, and a fortnight later he received Tuckerman graciously, arranged for the cathedral choir to sing 'The wilderness' at even-song, entertained the visitor as a guest in his house, and later extemporised for him on the cathedral organ for upwards of two hours.[8]

Wesley seems to have had an equally low opinion of nearly all his eminent colleagues, and of precentors in general. In 1869, for instance, he wrote to Eliza: 'I see that [John Clarke] Haden, precentor of Westminster, is dead. He has been a thorn in [James] Turle's side, but Turle [Abbey organist, 1831–82] does not deserve much better. He never ought to have been at the Abbey. I wish it were vacant.'[9]

In May of 1835, Wesley was married to Mary Anne Merewether, sister of the Dean of Hereford. The ceremony took place at a parish church, and the Dean was not present, so it would appear to have been without his approval and possibly without his knowledge. In September, Wesley resigned the Hereford organistship, having already been appointed organist of Exeter Cathedral.

Wesley may have been unhappy at Hereford, but his years at Exeter (1835–42) proved to be the most tumultuous of his career. Things appear to have gone smoothly enough until 1840, from which time there was increasing friction with the cathedral authorities. In February of 1840, an infant daughter died, and this affected Wesley deeply. Paul Chappell has speculated as to whether this may have 'eventually caused Wesley's angular relationship with the Cathedral Chapter'.[10] There is no hard evidence, of course, but it seems plausible that such a severe emotional blow could have heightened Wesley's already volatile irritability and sense of self-pity almost to the point of paranoia.

In May of 1840 he was forbidden to give lessons on the cathedral organ. In June he was admonished not to allow personal engagements to interfere with his attendance at Saturday morning chapter meetings. More serious trouble developed, however, when Wesley physically attacked two boy choristers while in a rage over their having attended a meeting of a local glee club without his permission. To compound the offence, Wesley stormed unceremoniously from the chapter meeting at which he was being reprimanded for this scandalous action. According to Gerald Spink, who does not cite a source, Wesley was asked to resign the post at Exeter 'as the result of a dispute as to who should reconstruct the Cathedral organ, then sorely in need of repair'.[11] He resigned on New Year's Day 1842, effective at the end of March, by which time he had already removed to Leeds and his new post as organist at the Parish Church of St Peter.

It was also during his Exeter period, on 21 June 1839, that Wesley received the degree of D.Mus. from Oxford University. Wesley set little store in academic degrees, but he desired a university professorship, and considered the degree a more-or-less necessary qualification. Evidently wishing to capitalise on the friendship of his father with Professor Crotch, Wesley had Old Sam make the initial approach in a letter of March 1836, enclosing several of Sebastian's compositions, including his exercise for the degree of B.Mus., the extended anthem 'O Lord, thou art my God'. It seems that Wesley wished to obtain the doctorate with as little trouble to himself as possible, and so requested and received permission to accumulate both degrees on the strength of his submitted exercise, which was duly performed in the chapel of Magdalen College, where Wesley had matriculated just a few days before.

Wesley was not so successful in his quest of a professorship. He competed for the Reid Chair at Edinburgh in 1841, but lost to Henry Rowley Bishop (1786–1855). Bishop, thinking that the chair was merely a sinecure, was asked to resign in 1843. Wesley tried again, this time losing to Henry Hugo Pierson (1815–73) in 1844, despite an impressive collection of testimonials, one of them from Louis Spohr. After the death of Crotch in 1847, Wesley presented himself for the professorship at Oxford, but lost in 1848, again to Bishop. Finally, with the death of Thomas Attwood Walmisley in 1856, Wesley entered for the Cambridge professorship, but withdrew when it became clear that William Sterndale Bennett (1816–75) was the favoured candidate.

In comparison with the conditions at Hereford and Exeter, Leeds Parish Church must have seemed an almost perfect situation for the pursuit of church music according to the cathedral ideal. The Vicar, Dr Walter Farquhar Hook (1798–1875), may have been quite unmusical himself, but he was committed to the principle that choral worship, if adopted at all, must be to the highest standard, with no expense spared. Wesley thus did not have to battle against a tight-fisted cathedral chapter with a host of entrenched interests. At Leeds, high musical standards were expected, and it appears that Wesley had a fairly free hand in the musical arrangements and the full support of the Vicar. Wesley was engaged at a salary of £200 per year, which the Vicar guaranteed for ten years, and between six and seven hundred pounds a year were spent on the professional choir.

There are no signs at Leeds of the frictions and bitter tumults that so marred Wesley's last years at Exeter. William Spark (1823–97), an articled pupil at Exeter who accompanied Wesley to Leeds, noted that his master's eccentricities occasionally had an adverse effect on the rendering of the choral service at the church, but that the standards were still so high as to attract a large congregation.[12] Wesley had never been in such happy circumstances professionally, yet as early as 1846 he seriously contemplated leaving. He resigned in 1849 to accept the lower-paying organistship of Winchester Cathedral. In sharp contrast with the hard feelings left behind at Exeter, the gentlemen of Leeds gave Wesley a testimonial dinner in February 1850, and presented him with a handsome oil portrait by the local artist William Keighley Briggs. It is now at the Royal College of Music.

It is difficult to establish adequate reasons for Wesley's wishing to leave Leeds. In a letter of 1858 to the organist of Carlisle Cathedral, Wesley declared that he had enjoyed a fine income at Exeter and had loved Devonshire, that the removal to Leeds was a great personal sacrifice, that he was 'disappointed with Dr. Hook & his powers to either aid his Church Music or me', and that consequently he 'soon bitterly repented of leaving Exeter'.[13] As noted before, Wesley cannot always be taken at face value, and here his reference to Hook is flagrantly unjust. Later in life, Wesley repeatedly expressed regret for having left Exeter, which, in view of his history there, is explicable only as a fondness for the countryside and more particularly for the trout streams of Devon, where Wesley delighted to pursue his almost obsessive pastime of fishing. He could not have liked the city of Leeds as such, but the Yorkshire dales were hardly out of reach. In fact, it was on a fishing expedition in December 1847 on the River Rye near Helmsley that Wesley suffered an accident resulting in a severe leg fracture and protracted convalescence.

There is a more plausible reason for Wesley's resignation of Leeds in favour of Winchester, but one hard to prove. A clue is provided in the tract *A few words on cathedral music* (1849), which Wesley probably began to write while recuperating at Helmsley. It is a trenchant critique of the state of cathedral music together with a scheme for its reform and improvement. In this connection, Wesley insists that cathedral organists should be distinguished professors, qualified in the higher branches of their art, not merely competent service players. They should be adequately remunerated (£500 to £800 per annum) because they are 'the *bishops* of their calling'.[14] Wesley clearly believed that the improvement of church music must emanate from the cathedrals, and in taking up his pen for the cause of cathedral music, as he had already done in the extended preface to his *Cathedral Service in E* (1845), it must have pained him to think that, however happy his circumstances in Leeds, he was no longer a cathedral organist. In the terms of his own metaphor, it was as if he had traded a diocesan episcopate for a parochial living, and had thus taken a step backwards. It seems consistent with Wesley's proclivity to discontent that under such circumstances the cachet of cathedral organist, despite the disadvantages he knew only too well, should have been enough to override the advantages he was then enjoying.

Wesley's period as organist at Winchester (1849–65) was the longest spent in one place. This may in part have been because his position gave him the privilege of educating his sons at the College. The professional circumstances and relations with the authorities were neither as good as at Leeds nor as bad as at Exeter. Chappell summarises: 'Wesley's relationship with Cathedral dignitaries was ambivalent. His changeable moods kept them at a distance, although his great genius and musical reputation gained their respect. And his unfriendly dealings with that race, called Precentors, certainly arose from his inborn belief that they were nothing less than meddlesome, amateur musicians.'[15]

The Winchester years saw the appearance of Wesley's *Twelve anthems* (1853), which he regarded as his most important publication. It is convenient to consider all of Wesley's major publications together, since they all manifest aspects of the quixotic outlook alleged in connection with the submission of 'The wilderness' for the Gresham competition in 1832. One senses from the publications themselves and from what Wesley wrote and said about them that he regarded himself as the destined saviour of English church music, whose mission was to set to rights, through precept (tracts and prefaces) and example (the compositions themselves), a church-music establishment that had been going to the dogs for as long as anyone could remember.

The *Cathedral Service in E* (1845), a product of the Leeds years, involves both aspects of the mission. As a composition it is bold and highly original; indeed, it is a landmark, representing a revival in nineteenth-century terms of the tradition of the 'great service', a liturgical setting conceived along broad lines and intended to produce the effect of grandeur. It was an idea that had been virtually defunct since the early seventeenth century.

Most of Wesley's contemporaries acknowledged his musical genius, whatever they may have thought of his personality. There were, however, some bitter criticisms of his music. One London reviewer said of the Service in E:

This is not the work of a poetical musician. Mr. Wesley may be, and indeed is a wonderfully executive organist; but he has no creative fancy beyond that of foolishly entering the ring with his betters. His work is coldly correct, and that is all... Our reverence for the ancients may have provoked us to severity; but we do not like to hear lake birds cawing at the nightingales of Elizabeth's reign.[16]

This critique is so manifestly wide of the mark that it can be plausibly explained only as a jaundiced reaction to Wesley's extended preface published with the music. The clue is found in the final sentence of the quotation. In his preface, Wesley is irreverent and disdainful towards the service settings of the sixteenth and seventeenth centuries, citing passages from Tallis, Aldrich, and Rogers to support his argument that the art of music was not then sufficiently advanced to make possible an adequate expression of the texts. He claimed the meritorious passages to be few and far between: 'the Epigrammatic was within their reach...but not so the Epic: their Te Deums were failures – A volume was beyond their powers.'[17]

Wesley's two tracts, *A few words on cathedral music* (1849) and *A reply to the inquiries of the Cathedral Commissioners* (1854) assail the existing standards of cathedral music in practice while recommending reforms. The former tract was written in response to a parliamentary bill proposing the reduction of cathedral choirs to the 'least possible state of efficiency'. Wesley points out the already inefficient state of cathedral choirs, to which further reductions were being proposed. He inveighs against the Anglo-Catholic antiquarian choral revival then in progress. He gives his version of the historical decline of cathedral music since the seventeenth century, while maintaining that the art of musical composition had by his own time reached a state of perfection, implying that the church should be appropriating this perfection for the adornment of her own service, not entertaining proposals for further decline. The suggested reforms included setting the minimum number of adult singers in a cathedral choir at twelve (i.e. two to a part, ATB, on each side of the choir) with at least an equal number of boy choristers, the adequate compensation of lay singers to enable them to devote sufficient time to their musical duties, the establishment of a college to be supported by the cathedrals for the training of their musical personnel, and the maintenance by each cathedral of a music copyist. The *Reply* of 1854 was prompted by a circular letter from the Secretary of the Royal Commission on Cathedrals, sent to the precentor and organist of every cathedral and collegiate church in England and Wales, primarily to solicit their response to the proposal that choirs might be strengthened by the admission, even if only on Sundays, of musically and devotionally qualified volunteer lay singers. The contents of Wesley's tract, ranging well beyond the scope of the commissioners' direct questions, is to a great extent a recapitulation of the critique and proposals of the earlier one. Particular emphasis is given to allowing cathedral organists greater liberty to delegate service playing to assistants so as to have more time for composition. One of Wesley's more fanciful new ideas is that the university professors of music be elected by the nation's cathedral organists.

It is of great historical interest to have Wesley's ideas so vigorously articulated in these tracts. It is also noteworthy that so many of Wesley's proposed reforms eventually found their way into practice. It would be a mistake, however, to give Wesley any significant share of the credit for bringing about these reforms. Taking a broader view of the circumstances, it seems fairly certain that these improvements would have taken place in much the same way without Wesley's efforts. The real work of reform was done by persons of a more even temper, by a growth in the musical sense of the general public in the second half of the century, and by a keener apprehension of what the life and work of a cathedral can and ought to be.

The degree of importance Wesley attached to his *Twelve anthems* has already been noted. The volume is a compendium of his work as an anthem writer from his Hereford years to the time of publication, comprising large-scale verse anthems and various shorter single-movement works. He cannot be said ever to have surpassed the finest works of this collection. The contents are:

> Ascribe unto the Lord
> Blessed be the God and Father
> Cast me not away from thy presence
> Let us lift up our heart
> Man that is born of a woman
> O give thanks unto the Lord
> O Lord, my God (King Solomon's Prayer)
> O Lord, thou art my God
> The face of the Lord
> The wilderness and the solitary place
> Thou wilt keep him in perfect peace
> Wash me throughly from my wickedness

The quoted letter to Eliza in 1876 makes clear the artistic value Wesley attributed to this publication. The flavour of Wesley's pretension becomes even sharper when regarded in the light of his belated (1861) and rather insulting reply to Sir Frederick Ouseley's request (1858) for a contribution to the first volume of his collection of *Special anthems for certain seasons* (1861):

I regret to have to submit to you that I feel opposed to taking any part in your prospected work...I fear the publication will do some harm. Your specimens ought all to be *great*...Where are you to get a *single* specimen of the finest church music? I don't know. There have been only two men in my time who could publish such a thing: my Father and Mendelssohn...It vexes me to resist your bidding thus.[18]

There is a note of false modesty in his reference to Old Sam and Mendelssohn, especially as his pupil James Kendrick Pyne (1852–1938) reports that Wesley 'was *not* a great admirer of Mendelssohn'.[19] In true romantic fashion, Wesley must surely have regarded himself as the only really worthy living practitioner of church composition, a lone hero in the midst of an uncomprehending multitude.

In 1851, still early in his Winchester period, Wesley began compiling and composing tunes for his monumental work, *The European Psalmist*. It took some twenty years before the book was finally ready for publication in 1872. Even as devoted a pupil as J. K. Pyne was of the opinion that the time Wesley spent on this work was so much time wasted, because the book was 'hopelessly old-fashioned and antiquated in form' at the time of its publication.[20] When the mainstream of Anglican hymnody was running in the direction represented by *Hymns Ancient and Modern* (1861; expanded 1868), Wesley gave the public a vast psalmody collection in the old manner, which proved to be of little use except as a reference work for hymnologists.

By 1865 it was clear that Wesley's powers as a musician were in decline. It came as a surprise to all, however, when on being asked to help adjudicate the competition for the organistship of Gloucester Cathedral following John Amott's death early in 1865, he decided to take the position himself. This was to be his last appointment, and although part of it was occupied with the final production of *The European Psalmist* and a return to an active role in the Three Choirs Festivals, his later years were spent virtually in semi-retirement, as his health gradually deteriorated and his eccentricity and absent-mindedness increased. To the end he felt that, throughout his career as a cathedral organist, he had been a victim. In a letter of November 1874 he wrote:

I have moved from cathedral to cathedral because I found *musical troubles* at each. Until Parliament interferes to put cathedrals on a totally different footing as to music, I affirm that any man of eminence will find obstacles to doing himself and his music justice which will render his life a prolonged martyrdom.[21]

Without denying that there was a great deal wrong with the state of cathedral music during Wesley's lifetime, it must be said that if his career was a 'prolonged martyrdom', it was to a great extent a martyrdom of his own making.

It is hard to escape the conviction that part of Wesley's temperament and behaviour derived from a deep and perhaps subconscious sense of inferiority for which he sought to overcompensate at every turn. In his field he was of the highest eminence, but it was a severely limited field. His repeated failures to reach beyond these limitations by securing a university professorship may well have forced on him a suspicion of inadequacy to which he could not openly admit. A. M. Wesley Martin, a nephew of the composer, characterised him as a 'disheartened man, very eccentric and absorbed in his musical world'.[22] J. Kendrick Pyne denied that Wesley was really eccentric, claiming that many of the stories about him are 'apocryphal', admitting that he was 'moody, often absent-minded, nervous, and irritable; but not more than one would expect from an artist, who is usually not accustomed to hide his feelings'.[23] Later in the same article, however, Pyne noted that in his dealings with precentors and other cathedral dignitaries, Wesley took the situation 'too seriously, instead of seeing the somewhat comical side of the relationship as he might well have done'.[24] He also relates the following anecdote, which, we may therefore assume, is not apocryphal:

There was an officious minor canon at Gloucester, who was of an amiable but meddling disposition. One afternoon after service he came up to Wesley and said: 'I think the anthem went very badly to-day. I also consider that it was taken too fast.' 'Sir,' said Wesley, drawing himself up, '*I* am at the *head* of my profession; *you*, Sir, are a nobody. I am *amazed* at your audacity. *Good afternoon, Sir.*'[25]

Surely this is not how the most eminent cathedral organist in England would be expected to respond to criticism. It seems rather the embittered reaction of a man haunted by a sense of failure, insecurity, and wounded vanity.

Anthems and services are the genres demanded by the Anglican liturgy. Since Wesley's most enduring and most characteristic compositions are in these genres and designed expressly for Anglican choral worship, they are part of a traditional and conservative repertory. Through his romantic temperament, however, Wesley gave voice to a striking individuality of concept and utterance in his cathedral music, pouring new wine, as it were, into the old bottles of anthem and service. This freshness of conception is especially evident in his larger-scale anthems, the multi-movement verse anthem being the genre with possibly the greatest potential for imaginative development. Apart from the distinctive features of Wesley's harmonic and melodic diction – which have been treated in some detail by other writers and will be briefly considered later – there are two aspects of his work which account for much of its individuality and represent Wesley's special contribution to the genre. These are (1) his approach to text-setting, and (2) his means of securing large-scale coherence.

The text of a Wesley anthem is often drawn from two or three passages of scripture, but even in those cases where the text is taken from a single passage, as in 'The wilderness' (Isaiah, chapter 35) or 'Blessed be the God and Father' (I Peter, chapter 1), it is clear that Wesley does not regard his source as a ready-made anthem text to be set to music straightforwardly. Instead, the source text serves as a mine from which to extract individual verses and verse fragments, which the composer treats very freely as to order and recombination. Wesley's texts are not incongruous, but their congruity is seldom inevitable. This is often true of the psalter itself, since so many psalms consist of numerous more-or-less self-contained, even aphoristic verses elaborating or illustrating a common theme. Thus they lend themselves extremely well to selection and recombination, and Wesley extends this treatment to psalm-like passages from other parts of the Old and New Testaments.

Wesley's textual method is well represented by one of the largest of his anthems, 'O Lord, thou art my God' (1836). The text is from the Book of Isaiah, Psalm 33, the Wisdom of Solomon, and the First Epistle to the Corinthians. The verses appear in the following order:

Isaiah 25:1a, 1c, 1b, 4a and a free recombination of these
Psalm 33:21, 22
Isaiah 25:8 with minor elisions
I Corinthians 15:53b, 34a
Wisdom of Solomon 3:9a
I Corinthians 15:51b, 52a
Isaiah 25:9

The verses from Psalm 33 are selected from the Authorised Version of the

Bible. Wesley does not automatically choose the more customary text of the Prayer Book psalter, though he does frequently use it. His anthem in honour of the marriage of the Prince of Wales in 1863, 'Give the king thy judgments', draws its text from Psalms 72 and 128 in free combination, choosing some verses from the Bible and some from the Prayer Book.

As noted before, 'The wilderness' and 'Blessed be the God and Father' are unusual among Wesley's larger anthems in that each takes its text from a single passage of scripture. The selection for 'The wilderness' is as follows:

> Isaiah 35: 1, 2a, 4, 6, 8a, 9b, 10

Circumstances make this particularly noteworthy, since in 1861, John Goss composed a verse anthem on a text from the same chapter. The temptation to compare the two is irresistible. In contrast with Wesley's concentrated selection from the ten verses which comprise the chapter, Goss omits only verse 7, setting all the rest in order and without elision. Thus Goss and Wesley adopt markedly different attitudes in their treatment of the source, Goss's being the more customary and classical, regarding the text as a given entity, subject only to discreet abridgement. Goss resorts to conventional recitative to cover much of the text. Wesley favours a more melodious style of declamation, as at the beginning of the anthem, where Goss writes essentially a secco recitative. It is noteworthy that Wesley, in setting a much shorter text, produced a far lengthier but less diffuse anthem than Goss.

Despite the care taken over the selection and manipulation of the texts, the words and subject of a Wesley anthem hardly ever stand out as a memorable entity in their own right. This contrasts not only with classic anthems – including those of Goss and Ouseley among the Victorians – but also with such works as Walmisley's 'Hear, O thou shepherd of Israel' (1836), where the text forms a spiritual progress or drama which the composer illuminates through his setting. Wesley's approach also contrasts with that of Stainer, who frequently assembled widely scattered verses for the purpose of presenting a definite theological or devotional lesson. Wesley's approach is essentially lyrical. That is, he treats his text as lyric poetry, not to tell a story or preach a lesson, but to present a sequence of almost abstract devotional affects, whose meaning is hardly separable from their musical setting. Wesley seems to transcend the words of the text, and although we have virtually no documentary evidence of his step-by-step working methods, one may reasonably conjecture that the musical and textual conceptions developed simultaneously in the composer's mind. If so, it is an essentially subjective, and arguably a romantic approach to anthem composition.

Wesley's larger anthems have a remarkable coherence, for which a satisfactory explanation is elusive. The character of the text, while playing a part, does not adequately account for it. Neither does it seem to be explained on grounds of pure musical structure, such as an over-arching plan of tonal relations, thematic development, or symphonic argumentation. The answer seems to lie more in the large-scale aesthetic gesture than in such conventional focuses of analytical attention.

Some mention has been made of possible analogies between verse anthems and other musical genres, without necessarily implying historical derivation. Thus it has been observed that the classic verse anthem from the Restoration onwards is like a Corellian concerto or sonata, with a succession of relatively short, contrasting movements in related keys, sometimes with connecting material, giving an effect that is elegantly balanced but essentially static. Similarly, the dynamic, dramatic progress of Walmisley's larger anthems has been compared with the traditional oratorio, especially as practised by Mendelssohn. Wesley's larger anthems are not like either of these types. If any other genre furnishes a useful analogy to the Wesley anthem, a strong candidate must be the concert aria.

Nineteenth-century concert arias, while derived from the dramatic genre of the *bel canto* operatic scene, are not themselves essentially dramatic. They present a formal sequence of affects which, in an operatic setting, would have arisen from the dramatic scenario, but as a concert piece, might be said to exist almost in the abstract. Consider, for example, Mendelssohn's concert aria 'Infelice', Op. 94 (1834). We infer from the text that it is sung by a jilted woman. There is no clue as to time or place, let alone the identity of the protagonist; she is jilted woman in the abstract. She first inveighs against the fiancé who has deserted her. She then thinks longingly of the time when they were still together. Finally she concludes that there is no happiness in love without torment, mitigated only by fond memories. The hint of a dramatic plot is at most a pretext for expression of the affects themselves. In this respect the nineteenth-century concert aria had a counterpart in the baroque chamber cantata.

In a concert aria or operatic scene there are three distinguishable categories of material: declamatory (the recitative), lyrical (the cavatina or cantabile), and vigorous (the cabaletta). Coherence comes in large part from the complementary nature of the affects associated with these contrasting musical idioms. The material of Wesley's anthems is divisible into the same three categories, and it seems that their complementary nature produces fundamentally the same sort of coherence. In Wesley's anthems, however, the ingredients are often treated with considerable freedom, whereas in secular concert arias the recitative–cavatina–cabaletta sequence is virtually invariable.

Wesley's declamatory writing can take several forms: choral recitative, stately choral or solo declamation, declamatory arioso, and the chorale as derived from traditional psalmody and J. S. Bach. Conventional solo recitative is relatively rare in Wesley. Sections that are functionally declamatory may nevertheless be highly melodious. More often than not, Wesley will use more than one of the aforementioned declamatory idioms to produce what may be called a declamatory group rather than a single movement. The lyrical material may also be either choral or solo. One may note a distinction in Wesley between sections of anthems which, while melodious in style, are organised discursively, and those which have a greater sense of formal definition through recapitulation or a refrain, though Wesley's recapitulations are rarely literal. This discursiveness, which does not preclude local phrase repetition, is a chief indicator of the declamatory function. Indeed, the single-movement anthem 'Cast me not away from thy presence' is in this sense discursive and declamatory throughout, moving as it does from one idea to the next without recapitulation or refrain. In larger anthems, Wesley may have more than one lyrical movement, sometimes closing in this idiom, as in 'The wilderness', 'Praise the Lord, my soul', and 'Ascribe unto the Lord'. Vigorous material is most often choral, and sometimes fugal, or imitative without being strictly fugal.

The Wesley anthem which most closely approximates the customary pattern of the concert aria is 'Blessed be the God and Father'. There is a threefold declamatory group, beginning with a stately four-part choral declamation that starts quietly, but gradually rises in pitch and dynamic intensity to a climax at the key words 'the resurrection of Jesus Christ from the dead', as befits an Easter anthem. The second phase of the declamation is in unison for altos, tenors, and basses ('To an inheritance incorruptible and undefiled'). Wesley evidently expected the altos to sing with full voice in the baritone register as well as in falsetto in the upper alto range. The third phase of the opening declamatory group is a treble solo ('But as he which hath called you is holy'), which ends on a diminished seventh. A brief organ interlude connects this with the anthem's 'cavatina' ('Love one another with a pure heart fervently') for treble solo alternating with trebles in unison. This is not in a conventional aria form, but Wesley gives some signals that distinguish it from the preceding melodious declamation. The flowing quaver motion in the accompaniment immediately establishes a different order of movement from the basic chordal support earlier in the anthem, though Wesley does anticipate this quaver motion in the brief organ interlude between the second and third phases of the declamatory group. Furthermore, 'Love one another' begins with an antecedent–consequent phrase group in which the identical solo phrase is answered by the choral trebles first with a straightforward half cadence, and afterwards with a tonic close that avoids a strong cadential feeling by means of a feminine ending involving a chromatic rise from the second to the third degree of the scale (ex. 24). This phrase with its inconclusive tonic arrival recurs literally twice as a kind of refrain, and the movement itself concludes with an adaptation in two parts of its final two bars, thus effecting a close in the tonic while leading onwards. There follows a choral recitative for altos, tenors, and basses in unison ('Being born again, not of corruptible seed') forming a link with the concluding vigorous chorus ('But the word of the Lord endureth for ever'), the 'cabaletta' of this anthem. After a pair of fanfare-like homophonic statements by the choir, the movement becomes imitative, but not fugal.

Ex. 24   S. S. Wesley: anthem, 'Blessed be the God and Father'

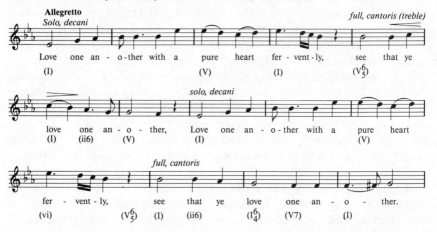

While it cannot be proved that Wesley had the concert aria form in mind when composing 'Blessed be the God and Father' or any of his other larger-scale anthems, it was characteristic of early nineteenth-century romanticism for genres to overflow their customary bounds, and in particular for theatrical idioms to appear in non-theatrical genres. Spohr's Violin Concerto No. 8 in A minor, Op. 47 (1816) is a well-known instance. In Wesley's case, the supposed influence of the concert aria becomes more convincing when one considers a remarkable unpublished work: the sacred song for solo baritone and orchestra 'I have been young and now am old', first performed at the Hereford Festival of 1834. This piece could be described as a solo anthem with orchestral accompaniment, but just as accurately as a concert aria with a scriptural text. There is a vigorous and operatic-sounding introduction which prepares an opening declamatory arioso. The second movement ('He hath shewed thee, O man, what is good') is slow and lyrical, while the third ('I will sing to the Lord as long as I live') forms a vigorous conclusion to a very substantial work. The association here of the concert aria format with a sacred text seems significant, especially in a composition dating from the same time as 'Blessed be the God and Father'.

'The wilderness' is a slightly earlier work, and in it the shape of the concert aria is not so pronounced. Nevertheless, it is possible to hear as the heart of the work a pair of chorus-with-verse movements: the smoothly lyrical (despite its unpromising opening melody) 'For in the wilderness shall waters break out', followed by the energetic and climactic 'And the ransomed of the Lord'. It may be more or less obligatory that a concert aria have a rousing conclusion, but this is certainly not so with an anthem. Indeed, there is much to be said for reaching a climax of volume and energy in an inner movement and allowing the conclusion to relax gracefully towards a resumption of the spoken portion of the service. This is the effect of the verse 'And sorrow and sighing shall flee away' which concludes 'The wilderness'. While it is in a fully-closed ABA form, the movement's brevity, as well as its tonal and textual continuity with the previous movement, cause it to be heard as a pendant to what has gone before rather than as a fully independent movement. This leaves the opening of the anthem, which, for all its melodiousness and recurrence of the opening thematic idea, may still be heard as essentially a declamatory group. This is even arguable for the substantial bass solo 'Say to them of a fearful heart', whose tonal structure is ternary (a–F–a), but whose thematic form is binary (AA'BB). Thus there is no conspicuous vocal recapitulation to impart a sense of closed return, though the organ postlude does recapitulate the introduction, which is the basis of the voice's A material.

In his later multi-movement anthems, Wesley departs even further from the outward shape of the concert aria, but in so far as the principle of coherence depends on a complementary sequence of affects, these anthems remain true in spirit to the proposed analogy, even if they diverge in letter. Of the categories of material, the vigorous assumes less prominence. In 'Let us lift up our heart', for instance, the principal vigorous chorus is an episode, 'O that thou wouldest rend the heavens', coming at the end of the declamatory group, out of which it subtly emerges. The remainder of the anthem is largely an exploration of several facets of lyricism appropriate to the selected text: 'Be not very sore' is quiet and placid, its opening melody serving as a recurring refrain; in the magnificent bass solo 'Thou, O Lord God, art the thing that I long for', placidness is replaced with an impassioned agitation; the concluding chorus joins an imposing chorale ('Thou judge of quick and dead') to a lyrical fugue ('O may we thus insure a lot among the blest') whose calm and confident subject is smoothly conjunct, admirably suiting the Charles Wesley hymn verse to which it is set. Similar kinds of adaptation may be noted in 'Ascribe unto the Lord' (c.1852) and 'Praise the Lord, my soul' (1861). 'Give the king thy judgments' (1863) is noteworthy among the later works for a closer resemblance to the outward format of the concert aria.

A fair amount has been written about the influences on Wesley's musical style, particularly the influence of Spohr. Wesley certainly admired Spohr, especially his oratorio *The Last Judgment* (1826) and his most famous opera *Jessonda* (1823). Like so many nineteenth-century organists, Wesley included a transcription of that opera's overture as a favoured item in his recital repertory. Paul Chappell has very cleverly traced and illustrated striking similarities between brief passages from Wesley's anthems and moments in *Jessonda*,[26] alleging that 'he freely borrowed ideas from Spohr's opera'.[27] Chappell goes on to note similarities to snatches from other composers' works.[28]

With regard to such snippets, it must be replied that however striking the similarities may be on this minute scale, the fact remains that Wesley is perhaps the most thoroughly individual of all nineteenth-century English composers. Indeed, one would be hard-pressed to find ten consecutive bars of

Wesley that could have been written by anyone else, and most critics agree that Wesley's musical declamation of the English language is in a class by itself, worthy to be compared with Purcell. While there are undoubtedly Spohrish moments in the earlier anthems, as in the recitative preceding the final chorus of 'Blessed be the God and Father' (ex. 25), these become rarer in

Ex. 25 S. S. Wesley: anthem, 'Blessed be the God and Father'

the later works, and at no time do Wesley's compositions sound on the whole like Spohr. Watkins Shaw disagrees with the contention that Wesley's chromaticism is derived from Spohr, noting that in Spohr, chromaticism is far more pervasive.[29] Indeed, much of the characteristic Wesley sound comes from the management of diatonic suspended dissonances, as in the opening phrases of 'Thou wilt keep him in perfect peace', or from the pursuit of a rich sequential path, whatever discords may lie in the way, to its musically logical conclusion, as in the closing pages of 'Let us lift up our heart'. Wesley must have derived this practice from J. S. Bach. Shaw does observe, however, that 'what Wesley may have got from Spohr was a feeling for enharmonic change'.[30] Much of Spohr's chromaticism arises not from a fundamental tonal complexity of the kind found in Wagner, but rather from the rich elaboration of an essentially straightforward, even conventional tonal plan. The unexpected harmonic digressions and enharmonic excursions have a way of returning fairly soon to the point of departure. Much the same can be said of the striking tonal juxtapositions in Wesley, especially in the Service in E, or in such progressions as the celebrated tonal parenthesis which occurs at the climax of 'The wilderness' (ex. 26).

While Wesley's indebtedness to other composers has sometimes been exaggerated, it is indisputable that he frequently repeats himself. Characteristic turns of phrase, melodic figures, and harmonic progressions recur in the choral works and organ pieces, constituting the most conspicuous fingerprints of Wesley's style. Kenneth Long gives a considerable list of examples.[31] A specimen not on Long's list is a striking progression in the opening chorus of the 1836 anthem 'O Lord, thou art my God' (ex. 27a) that finds an echo at the climax of the Andante in G (1849) for organ (ex. 27b).

Ex. 26   S. S. Wesley: anthem, 'The wilderness and the solitary place'

Ex. 27a   S. S. Wesley: anthem, 'O Lord, thou art my God'

Ex. 27b   S. S. Wesley: Andante in G major, for organ

Watkins Shaw concludes his brief Wesley Centenary article of 1976 with the observation that Wesley's chief contributions to cathedral music were, first, that he restored to it a sense of breadth and grandeur, and secondly, that 'by his solitary efforts he moved it forward bodily by some 75 years, placing it once more in touch with the progress of musical composition and, by so doing, furnished an aspect of the Romantic movement. That he was, nevertheless, able to write so little, and that no worthy school grew up around him, is a sorry reflection on the conditions under which he laboured.'[32] Such an assessment comes dangerously close to the absurd statement that Anglican Christianity, in so far as it was embodied and represented by the nation's cathedrals, is impeachable for not having adapted itself to Wesley's aesthetic vision. The conflicts that plagued Wesley ran much deeper than merely 'the conditions under which he laboured'. His career illustrates the irreconcilable tensions between a volatile romantic temperament and a corporate Christian body, whatever its temporal flaws. It is to the credit of Wesley's contemporaries that during the greater part of his career he was almost universally acknowledged to be the finest organist and cathedral composer in England. Nonetheless, he could never have been the founder of a school, for his temperament ran counter to a living tradition of greater standing than himself. In true romantic fashion, he was an impassioned individualist, and was thus, virtually by definition, unrepresentative.

8

Sir Frederick Ouseley (1825–89): the timeless idiom and beyond

Sir Frederick Ouseley was a musician of enormous native talent and technical expertise. His precocity was on a par with Mozart's. He was a voluminous composer, producing more cathedral music than any one of the composers thus far discussed, and a good deal of it was highly elaborate technically, including a complete service and numerous anthems with full orchestra. In many ways, Ouseley epitomised the early-to-mid-Victorian conception of the church composer as 'gentleman musician', scholar, and antiquary. Nevertheless, even his greatest admirers did not consider him a great composer. Being a model Victorian church musician, in a way that a finer composer like S. S. Wesley was not, Ouseley's limitations are to some extent the limitations of the ideals of Victorian church music itself.

England in the eighteenth and nineteenth centuries seems to present more than her fair share of musical prodigies whose later careers failed to keep pace with their dazzling native ability. Charles Wesley (1757–1834), his brother Samuel Wesley (1766–1837), and William Crotch (1775–1847), whatever attractive things one may find in their works, are prime examples from among the most precocious. Likewise, William Sterndale Bennett (1816–75) showed great youthful promise and was hailed as an equal by Mendelssohn and Schumann, but historical perspective reveals that he produced his finest work before the age of thirty, then settled down to a career of pedagogical drudgery, frequently failing to complete compositional projects. Nicholas Temperley claims that the depressed state of English musical culture had much to do with smothering Bennett's creativity, enthusiasm, and self-confidence.[1] This may be alleged of the other composers mentioned, but in Ouseley's case it does not adequately explain his limits as a composer.

Numerous anecdotes and reports attest to Ouseley's childhood exploits.[2] He had perfect pitch and an extraordinarily retentive musical memory. His understanding of abstruse harmonic progressions reveals a virtually complete intuitive grasp of harmonic principles. Before the age of four, he was able to play tunes at the piano and compose short pieces, several hundred of which were notated by his mother and by his older sister Mary Jane. His compositions, vocal and keyboard improvisations, and feats of aural harmonic identification won the admiration and wonder of those who witnessed them, including members of the royal family, the nobility, and eminent professional musicians.

Ouseley was born into an exalted social circle. His father was the distinguished diplomat and amateur orientalist Sir Gore Ouseley, Bt (1770–1844). His godfathers were no less than the Dukes of York and Wellington. Even so, he had a very sheltered childhood. He was born in London, but the greater part of his childhood was spent at the family residence of Woolmers, near Hertingfordbury, Hertfordshire, and after 1832 at the newly purchased estate of Hall Barn Park, near Beaconsfield, Buckinghamshire. While not exactly a sickly child, Ouseley had a delicate constitution, with a nervous disposition that remained throughout his life. He was educated at home by a governess and a Latin tutor, music having no place in the formal curriculum. His only instruction in the art was a mere smattering from his sister and answers to his direct questions about chords. His parents feared that more than this would induce too much harmful excitement, as was then the general belief. The Duchess of Hamilton had advised: 'I hope they don't excite his musical feelings too much. I know something about that, and certainly few things produce such an electric effect on the nerves as some combinations of harmony. I have often made myself ill by listening to certain chords.'[3] Ouseley's musical predilections were never actually discouraged, but they seem not to have been taken very seriously. This was not owing to any antimusical prejudice. On the contrary, Sir Gore Ouseley was a founder of the Royal Academy of Music in 1822 and an amateur instrumentalist in his own right. Still, as G. R. Sinclair observed, it probably had never occurred to anyone that music would be a suitable profession for someone of Ouseley's standing.[4]

To what extent, however, were Ouseley's limitations as a composer a consequence of his social, educational, and cultural environment, and his lack of early training? Was his artistic temperament decisively moulded by these influences, or was its character inherent and prior to them? Might he have become an outstanding composer in a different national setting or a less exalted social position? The case of Sterndale Bennett, if Temperley is right, illustrates that environment can stifle a lively creative imagination, but was Ouseley's imagination, as distinct from his indisputable musical ability, in the same class with Bennett's?

As for temperament, it is conspicuous that Ouseley was nearly always at ease in the gentlemanly ecclesiastical ethos of the Victorian era. He was dissatisfied with the low standards of piety and technical accomplishment in musical worship, but his goal was to attempt a realisation of what was ostensibly the existing ideal. S. S. Wesley, in contrast, was generally at odds with the ethos of the cathedral close, and his tracts on musical reform seem to urge that the system be turned upside down. According to Sinclair, Ouseley regarded church music as 'the handmaid of religion, and no longer an art which soared free, breathing alike the joys and sorrows of men, but an art which sought to shadow forth that heavenly calm which exists beyond the fever and fret of human life'.[5] It is arguable that there was no place for unbounded, romantic creative genius within the established ideals of worship music, and that Ouseley accepted this condition, not with resignation, but with pious fervour. Could it be that Ouseley's pious acquiescence is itself evidence of a less lively creative drive than that of Wesley or Bennett, especially in a century when a romantic view of creativity was more or less taken for granted?

While such questions probably do not admit of completely satisfactory answers, one must incline to the conclusion that Ouseley's creative imagination was probably not of the highest order. As for his lack of early training, Henry C. Colles has observed that genuine creative genius, like that of Berlioz, Wagner, or Elgar, will invariably secure the necessary technical knowledge to remedy insufficient formal instruction. Ouseley did acquire a technical proficiency of the highest order, but in the absence of creative genius, this could not make him a great composer.[6] Sinclair notes that Ouseley's childhood exploits 'bear witness to the acuteness of his faculties rather than to the sensitiveness of his imagination', being evidence of the 'mathematical sense' which 'grew with years, and may be said to have predominated the genius of the musician'.[7]

Such observations are borne out even by some of Ouseley's childhood compositions. A march in C major (1832), for example, which was published in the *Harmonicon* in 1833, has a middle section displaying some remarkable modulations. From the tonic minor, it proceeds to the flat submediant, which becomes enharmonically the third of the mediant major. This is flattened to E minor, and proceeds to the dominant seventh of C before the *da capo*. The little piece is satisfactorily proportioned, but it displays harmonic ingenuity rather than inspiration.

Ouseley's youthful compositions (preserved in Tenbury MSS 660, 759, 1087a, and 1146) are mostly in the fashionable, conservative idioms of the day, and are probably a good indication of the kinds of music he knew as a boy. There are lightweight piano dance pieces with waltzes predominating; piano nocturnes in the style of John Field; solo piano sonatas, a piano duet sonata, and chamber music for piano and strings in the elegant and florid post-Mozartian idiom of composers like Hummel and Spohr; and numerous solo art songs, mostly to Italian texts. Perhaps the most remarkable of Ouseley's juvenile compositions is the Metastasian opera *L'isola disabitata*, dated 1833, when he was eight years old. William Ayrton (1777–1858), editor of the *Harmonicon*, professed to like it better than Haydn's setting of the same libretto. The opera is in twelve scenes, the manuscript (Tenbury MS 1087a) comprising 115 pages of vocal score with piano accompaniment. It is noteworthy that, even at this stage, Ouseley was unable to read musical notation. The following description, probably written by Ayrton, accompanied the publication of Ouseley's March in C in the *Harmonicon*.

He improvises entire scenes, singing to his own accompaniment, the latter often exhibiting harmony the most recherchée, chords that an experienced musician only uses with caution; but these are always introduced and resolved in a strictly regular manner, not by rule, for he has learnt no rules, but by the aid of a very surprising ear, and of some faculty, which, for want of a better term, we will call intuition.[8]

This corresponds with the characteristics of *L'isola disabitata*, which captures unequivocally the flavour of contemporary *bel canto* opera, as an excerpt from one of the bass arias illustrates (ex. 28). While other arias are more

Ex. 28   Ouseley: opera, *L'isola disabitata*, bass aria

florid, this displays many stylistic features of the idiom: colouristic flattening of the sixth degree, an essentially ornamental vocal line, upward-resolving appoggiaturas on the downbeat, and a deceptive cadence on the flat sub-mediant. The score abounds with enharmonic twists and unexpected modulations, revealing an apparent special fondness for augmented-sixth harmony.

The only liturgical music in these early manuscripts is a Te Deum in F, dated March 1840, and a Jubilate Deo in D (both in Tenbury MS 759). These are in short score and display the perfunctory idiom of the Georgian short service. It is a reasonable conjecture that when a service was sung at the local parish church, it was probably the ubiquitous Jackson in F or something like it. It seems that Ouseley took this to be the appropriate churchly style, different as it is from his youthful secular music.

Instead of attending a public school, Ouseley was tutored privately, in preparation for his university education, at the home of the Revd James Joyce, Vicar of Dorking, beginning in 1840. It was largely because of his influence and example, as well as the friendship of his son and curate, the

Revd James Wayland Joyce, that Ouseley resolved upon a career in Holy Orders.[9] In 1843 he entered Christ Church, Oxford, as a gentleman commoner. In November of the following year, Sir Gore Ouseley died at the age of seventy-four, and his son succeeded to the baronetcy.

It was during his undergraduate years that Ouseley had his only formal instruction in music, in the form of lessons in theory and composition from Stephen Elvey (1805–60), Choragus in the university and organist of New College. It was probably around this time that Ouseley first came under the reactionary influence of William Crotch, whose *Lectures* had been published in 1831. Stainer claimed that Crotch's influence tended to stifle such creative imagination as Ouseley then possessed.[10] Sinclair disagreed, however, claiming that Ouseley's musical ideas and predilections were more the product of his personal temperament and convictions than 'the passing influence of a few Oxford lectures', and that his compositional style 'was almost, one might say, a part of his creed'.[11]

It is worth noting that Ouseley probably never heard Crotch deliver a lecture at Oxford. Although he remained professor until his death in 1847, Crotch ceased giving professorial lectures around 1807, and indeed, was seldom in Oxford at all. Ouseley did uphold Crotch's doctrine of the three styles to the end of his life, and his early church music adheres closely in style and technique to the approved historical models of the Sublime Style. From the later 1860s onwards, however, much of Ouseley's music has a flavour well outside Crotch's conception of Sublimity. Perhaps Ouseley had a wider conception of the Sublime than did Crotch, but in some works he more than merely touches upon the High Victorian idiom. His style is not as uniform as some of Sinclair's remarks might suggest.

Unlike so many other eminent Victorian church musicians, Ouseley was never a boy chorister in a cathedral or collegiate choral foundation. Indeed, it would appear that he had no sustained exposure to the English cathedral repertory before coming to Oxford. Judging from reports by correspondents to the *Parish Choir* in 1847, the year after Ouseley received the BA, the state of music at Christ Church Cathedral was deplorable. The choir was possibly the worst in England, with too few singers and most of them 'engaged in business'.[12] Furthermore, the Dean (Thomas Gaisford) and canons were entirely unmusical. It is hard to imagine how Ouseley could derive musical or devotional inspiration under such circumstances, but the state of affairs certainly dramatised the need for reform. The experience of daily services at Christ Church must have had a part in convincing Ouseley that a model institution, like St Michael's, Tenbury, was necessary if the choral tradition were to be restored to integrity.

A number of service settings date from Ouseley's undergraduate years or shortly thereafter. There were at least four unpublished services, and two published complete services – in G and A (the latter with the alternative evening canticles, Cantate Domino and Deus Misereatur) – which appeared in a series of cathedral services edited by William Marshall (1806-75), organist of Christ Church from 1825 to 1846. The series came out between 1841 and 1849. To these may be added three further complete services – in E (1847), E♭, and B minor – which Ouseley published in a collection of his *Cathedral music* in 1853, also including reissues of the two services from the Marshall series.

For the most part, these works adhere strictly to the idiom of the eighteenth-century short service. It is tempting to regard them not as original compositions, but rather as student exercises undertaken to gain mastery of the idiom. Surely this is why Stainer expressed regret that the 1853 volume was ever published.[13] It is noteworthy that Marshall's series consists mostly of seventeenth- and eighteenth-century services. Ouseley in G is the first work by a living composer to appear in the series, and stylistically it is not out of place in its company, bearing some stylistic similarity to the Service in D of Benjamin Rogers (1614-98). Nevertheless, the fact that Ouseley singled out five of his early services for publication indicates that he at least regarded them as legitimate original compositions, even if originality as such had not been his principal aim. There is a distinct gain in fluency with the passage of time. A characteristic passage from the Te Deum of the unpublished Service in D of 1846 (ex. 29) displays squareness of phrase, constricted part-writing,

Ex. 29   Ouseley: Service in D, Te Deum

and a dull, plodding texture with almost no rhythmic variety. Since Ouseley's youthful secular music displays far greater fluency than this, it is conceivable that here he was trying too hard in imposing stylistic strictures he thought appropriate to the true church style, deliberately banishing the harmonic adventurousness that so delighted him as a child. In the A major service of the following year, however, he was able to produce a passage (ex. 30) which, within the inherited idiom, is as fluent and lively as the foregoing is awkward

Ex. 30   Ouseley: Service in A, Te Deum

[doubled by organ]

and dull. Such textural intricacy is not maintained throughout, but the Service in A does tend to have a propulsion and flow absent from the one in D, due, one may reasonably suppose, to the confidence of a year's additional experience in the idiom.

These early services of Ouseley and many of his other church compositions lead naturally to consideration of a stylistic principle which, for convenience, may be termed the 'timeless idiom'. Ouseley embodied it as fully as anyone. It is important to note that this is intended as a term of stylistic description, not a congratulatory expression of aesthetic worth. Masterpieces may be timeless in the sense that their intrinsic value is so high that they remain vital long after the period of their composition. This, however, is not the sense in which the term 'timeless' is intended here.

A piece of music may be considered stylistically timeless to the extent that it does not obviously proclaim the period in which it was written. This does not necessarily imply the conscious and strict imitation of a stylistic model from the past, but rather an adherence to fundamental usages in harmony, counterpoint, melody, and rhythm, that belong to no single style period. It is an important part of Crotch's notion of the Sublime. The prevailing conservatism of church music tends to promote timelessness, favouring gradual change and much continuity rather than abrupt novelty. In English church music, this has generally been the rule in the evolution of style. Abrupt changes, like the music of the Restoration Chapel Royal, are exceptions which can be accounted for by specific and extraordinary historical circumstances. Even the more progressive Victorians, whose church music tends not to be timeless in this stylistic sense, were far more conservative than radical on the broader scale of nineteenth-century European music.

The category 'timeless idiom' may not have been present as such in the composer's mind. Nevertheless, it is not claiming too much to allege that the more conservative Victorian church composers consciously held that stylistic propriety entailed the avoidance in sacred music of features suggesting recent and possibly ephemeral trends in secular or popular music. Thus the concept of a timeless idiom does represent a tendency which may be discerned in the music and which corresponds with a verifiable aspect of the composer's outlook. If it is regarded as a tendency, something which may be present to a greater or lesser extent in specific pieces, rather than a minutely defined set of technical conditions which may correspond with no existing work, it can be a helpful indicator of stylistic complexion. Most fugues by Mendelssohn, for instance, would not be mistaken for Bach, but they are more timeless than a typical Mendelssohn 'song without words'.

Ouseley was unquestionably a conservative among Victorian church composers. In his early services, he seems to be striving for fluency in the inherited idiom, quickly achieving it to an eminent degree, until it becomes a normal musical dialect. Having reached this stage, he begins to introduce elements which, while conservative to the extent of being consonant with the inherited idiom, are still the technical products of a subsequent age. If the strict imitation of the historical idiom is timeless, then the latter development may be considered the timeless idiom *par excellence*, in so far as it retains the inherited spirit while admitting a certain freedom in the letter.

There are occasional passages in the services of the 1853 collection which, on such grounds as dissonance treatment and tonal fluidity, look beyond the normal idiom of the eighteenth-century short service, but it is with the Service in C major (1856) for double choir and organ that Ouseley may be said to achieve the timeless idiom *par excellence*. It may be the most complete setting of the Anglican service ever written. It includes a Venite based on the eighth psalm tone, which appears in both tenor parts throughout, and settings of all the regular and alternative canticles for Morning and Evening Prayer, as well as the 1662 Communion Service. The work was never published, but copies of the Cantate Domino and Deus Misereatur were lithographed for the use of King's College, Cambridge, and for the reopening of Hereford Cathedral in 1863. Around the turn of the century, Bumpus noted that portions of the service had been in regular use at Durham, York, Norwich, and Lichfield.[14]

The years 1855–6, when the Service in C was composed, were a momentous time for Ouseley. In 1855 he was ordained priest, appointed precentor of Hereford Cathedral, and elected professor of music at Oxford University on the death of Sir Henry Bishop. In 1856, Ouseley's dream of an institution dedicated to the perpetuation of the English choral service became a reality with the opening of St Michael's, Tenbury. One may conjecture that the

Service in C was deliberately conceived as a monument appropriate to coincide with such an occasion.

The work was evidently intended to be Sublime. The style is broad, yet practical liturgical proportion is never exceeded. The spirit is still that of the eighteenth-century service, but with a greater sense of grandeur. The great difference between the C major service and Ouseley's earlier settings is that the idiom, despite being ultra-conservative, no longer sounds like a student's imitation of music from another century. If the sense of Ouseley's timeless idiom *par excellence* may be conveyed by a short excerpt, perhaps the opening of the Magnificat illustrates it best (ex. 31).

Ex. 31   Ouseley: Service in C, Magnificat

Occasionally in the Service in C, there are passages whose harmony and dissonance treatment generate a flavour quite unlike that of the eighteenth century (ex. 32). Moreover, in melodic character and 'choral orchestration', Ouseley sometimes expands on the conventions of the inherited idiom, as in

Ex. 32   Ouseley: Service in C, Te Deum

Ex. 32 (*cont.*)

didst not ab - hor the Vir - gin's womb.

the unison siciliano-like melody in G minor from the Creed, set to the words 'Who for us men', and sung by Choir I to a chordal accompaniment in Choir II. In contrast with such passages, Ouseley elsewhere secures timelessness by the most reliable of means: contrapuntal artifice, especially formal canon. The Gloria Patri of the Venite is set as a canon 6 in 3 at the fourth to the psalm tone as *cantus firmus* in the two tenor parts. The Benedictus and Nunc Dimittis have different settings of the Gloria Patri in canon 8 in 4. There are numerous other instance of extended contrapuntal, though not canonic writing, such as the Amen from the Gloria in excelsis.

Ouseley's 1853 collection also contains three sets of short anthems – five dedicated to the Revd Henry Fyffe, six to A. T. Crispin, and six to E. J. Ottley – and one moderately large-scale anthem for double choir, 'I will magnify thee', dedicated to the Revd Sir W. H. Cope, Bt. Ouseley wrote all of these in 1851, during the European tour he made after resigning his tumultuous London curacy, while in a state of spiritual anxiety and with his confidence in the Church of England shaken in the wake of the Gorham controversy.

When John Henry Newman and Richard Hurrell Froude toured the south of Europe in 1832–3, they recorded their thoughts and meditations in verses which were published in the *British Magazine* under the title *Lyra Apostolica*. One may surmise that Ouseley had a similar intention in writing the anthems of 1851. In one case, an autobiographical reference is well established: 'How goodly are thy tents' (Numbers 24:5–6), from the anthems dedicated to Henry Fyffe, was inspired by the sight of Milan Cathedral in moonlight.[15] Other autobiographical references may reasonably be inferred. The anthems dedicated to E. J. Ottley were composed in Rome. Ouseley, like Newman and Froude, became disillusioned upon first-hand acquaintance with the Roman Church. For Ouseley, this was probably an important factor in quelling the serious ecclesiastical doubts of the previous year and in his deciding to proceed to priest's orders. It seems noteworthy, then, that five of the six anthems in the set have texts which are either penitential or supplicatory from a state of distress:

> O Lord, we beseech thee (collect for Trinity 16)
> Save me, O God (Ps. 54:1–3)
> Be merciful unto me (Ps. 56:1, 3, 4)

Unto thee, O Lord (Ps. 25:1)
To the Lord our God (Daniel 9:9–10)

The first of these is particularly to the point, with its petition to 'let thy continual pity cleanse and defend thy Church...because it cannot continue in safety without thy succour'.

An even more striking case of autobiographical significance may be inferred from one of the anthems from the set dedicated to A. T. Crispin: 'O almighty and most merciful God' (collect for Trinity 20). The anthems of this set were composed at Cologne. A letter to Wayland Joyce, dated from Berlin, 28 October 1851,[16] is full of Ouseley's thoughts about the school and choral foundation he was planning to establish on his return to England, evidently the subject uppermost in his mind at the time. Toward the end of the letter, he speaks of plans to travel to Cologne on Thursday (30 October), intending to spend a week there before proceeding to Holland. This implies that he was in that city on 2 November, the Twentieth Sunday after Trinity in 1851. Surely the collect of the day must have had a special personal significance:

O almighty and most merciful God, of thy bountiful goodness keep us, we beseech thee, from all things that may hurt us; that we, being ready both in body and soul, may cheerfully accomplish those things that thou wouldest have done; through Jesus Christ our Lord. Amen.

His choosing this as an anthem text can hardly have been mere coincidence.

It is helpful to remember that, in the opinion of many, greater stylistic freedom was acceptable in anthems than in service canticles. Thus, while remaining largely timeless, there is a greater sense of personal expression in these early anthems than in the early services, and Ouseley more readily admits the Beautiful style. For instance, one often encounters a lilting triple-metre idiom. It is quite different from Goss's jubilant idiom, and seems to derive less from Attwood or even Handel than from certain movements in the Psalms of Benedetto Marcello (1686–1739), which were once better known in England than they are at present. 'Blessed is the man' from the Ottley set is a specimen of this style. As with many of Ouseley's early anthems, it begins homophonically, then introduces points of imitation. There are gentle diatonic dissonances leading to a hemiola at the cadence, with an understated but Italianate elegance (ex. 33). Compare this with a characteristic passage from the final movement of Marcello's Fourth Psalm (ex. 34). In 'How goodly are thy tents' from the Henry Fyffe set, this idiom is joined with what may be perceived as an attempt to evoke the sense of shimmering stillness of Milan Cathedral in moonlight. This is done by an initial point consisting of long notes in close imitation, with little sense of regular pulse until all the voices have entered, whereupon the anthem proceeds in graceful triple metre.

Most of these early anthems, indeed all of the Ottley set, are miniatures deriving their musical form directly from that of the text. They are not conspicuous for a purely musical sense of form and proportion such as that dis-

Ex. 33   Ouseley: anthem, 'Blessed is the man'

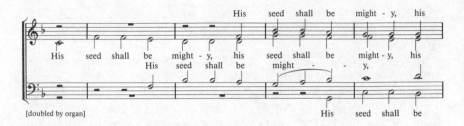

Ex. 34   B. Marcello: *Psalms of David*, **No. 4, soprano–alto duet**

played in Goss's 'God so loved the world', an anthem similar in dimension and compositional technique. The principal exceptions to this format are four multi-movement anthems: 'I will give thanks' from the Henry Fyffe set, 'O how beautiful is thy goodness' and 'O love the Lord' from the A. T. Crispin set, and 'I will magnify thee', the separate anthem dedicated to W. H. Cope. Ouseley later scored the first and last of these for full orchestra, most likely for use at St Michael's, Tenbury, where orchestral forces were sometimes employed for festive occasions.

Most of the anthems dating from the mid 1850s to the early 1860s have stylistic traits consistent with those of the Service in C. The style is well represented by the original works Ouseley included in his anthology of *Special anthems for certain seasons*, published in 1861:

From the rising of the sun (1855)
Thus saith the Lord (1855)

The Lord is King (1857) – scored for orchestra in Tenbury MS 1495
Is it nothing to you? (1859)
Awake thou that sleepest – scored for orchestra in Tenbury MS 1188
Christ is risen from the dead – scored for orchestra in Tenbury MS 1188
Why standest thou so far off?
Unto thee will I cry

On the whole, these anthems show a keener sense of musical form than do most of those of 1851.

Ouseley begins to make much use of recapitulating ternary form (ABA′) with greater or lesser leanings toward sonata procedure. The opening A section usually modulates to the dominant, while the concluding A′ often adapts the closing material of A in the tonic key. Whereas Goss's sonata-form anthem movements are essentially binary, Ouseley generally supplies a contrasting middle section, not a thematic development. This can weaken the sense of sonata procedure, because a substantial portion of the movement, the middle section itself, has little or no direct relationship to the sonata principle operating in the outer sections. A concise example is furnished by 'From the rising of the sun', a full anthem only forty-eight bars in length, with a thematically independent middle section of twelve bars. In contrast, the first movement, of 'Behold now, praise the Lord' (1863) is a sonata movement more along the lines of Goss, with no real middle section. The first movement of 'The Lord is King' (1857) is a noteworthy case. The middle section is contrasting rather than developmental, but the exposition, which is actually repeated, has a distinct imitative second subject over a dominant pedal, whose return in the recapitulation is unmistakable. Yet another pattern occurs in the first movement of 'It came even to pass', an anthem composed for the reopening of Lichfield Cathedral on 22 October 1861, on which occasion it was performed by a choir of 980 voices plus orchestra. The opening chorus is essentially a monothematic sonata movement. A very short middle section – only six bars, excluding orchestral interludes before and after – consists of choral sequential treatment of the opening of the theme, and in a limited way might be considered developmental.

This enhanced sense of musical form is not confined to anthems in more-or-less standard patterns. The Good Friday anthem, 'Is it nothing to you?' (1859), for instance, is a miniature which sets the text clause by clause. Roughly the first two thirds of the piece, however, consists of perfectly balanced phrase pairs with repetitions of the text in the following symmetrical pattern of bars:

$$(6+6)+(1\tfrac{1}{2}+1\tfrac{1}{2})+(6+6)$$

This gives the work a sense of formal purpose sometimes wanting in the 1851 anthems, yet without adhering to a set mould.

In Ouseley's multi-movement anthems, like 'Awake thou that sleepest' and

'Christ is risen from the dead' in the 1861 publication, imposing choruses in the Sublime Style most often frame verse movements in a lighter, more Beautiful vein. In the 1850s and early 60s, these inner movements still owe much to stylistic models from the past. In addition to the aforementioned Marcello-like idiom, one finds in Ouseley a triple-metre style somewhat reminiscent of Attwood and tending to move in regular phrases. A good specimen is the opening movement of 'Why standest thou so far off?' (ex. 35).

Ex. 35 Ouseley: anthem, 'Why standest thou so far off'

[doubled by organ]

The quartet verse 'For he is good' from 'It came even to pass' (ex. 36) seems at first glance to be in the same Attwood-like idiom, but the chromaticism has a distinctly different flavour. The colouristic use of secondary diminished and dominant seventh chords may help to account for the specifically Victorian sound of this passage. In many of Ouseley's later anthems, internal verse movements increasingly assume the character of a High Victorian part song rather than the Marcello-like or Attwood-like flavour of the works from the 1850s and 60s. The verse from 'It came even to pass' seems to point in this direction.

Ex. 36 Ouseley: anthem, 'It came even to pass'

[doubled by organ]

Ex. 36   (*cont.*)

Bumpus speaks of a change of style in Ouseley's music, noting that his later church compositions, 'without the sacrifice of dignity and religious repose, became, to a certain extent, tinctured with emotion and modern feeling',[17] as compared with the obvious historical roots and discipline of his earlier works. Bumpus seems to suggest that Ouseley's striving after timeless Sublimity in his early church works had a stabilising effect on his later, more characteristically Victorian works, preserving a traditional sense of dignity and devotional feeling. He singles out the set of eight anthems dedicated to Thomas Helmore in 1868 as the turning point in this process, claiming that they 'show a decided advance on the composer's ideas, both as regards melody and harmony, as exhibited in those pieces of a similar character published in his volume of 1853 – a change altogether beneficial to Church music'.[18] Such emphasis is misleading, however, since the change in Ouseley's style may be detected as proceeding gradually through the course of the 1860s, with perhaps an even more significant landmark reached in the Morning, Communion, and Evening Service in F of 1867 and the Evening Service in B♭ of the same year.

In this connection, it is important to consider a still earlier work which, for its stylistic freedom, stands out among the pieces Ouseley was producing around the same time. It is the large-scale anthem 'And there was a pure river' (1853), composed for the baptism of the daughter of Henry Fyffe. Sinclair remarks that Ouseley was initially reluctant to publish the work, and that it took considerable persuasion from friends and associates before he consented to include it in the second volume of *Special anthems* in 1866.[19] The anthem appears to have held a high place in Ouseley's affection, however, as scores and parts, including a version for full orchestra, survive in no fewer than five sets of Tenbury manuscripts. The piece begins with a verse movement (SSATB), opening with a passage for the upper voices alone, prolonging the chord of E major and moving from it very slowly, thus evoking a sense of motionlessness not unlike that of the opening of 'How goodly are thy tents'. As the verse proceeds, the harmony and texture become richer (ex. 37).

Ex. 37   Ouseley: anthem, 'And there was a pure river'

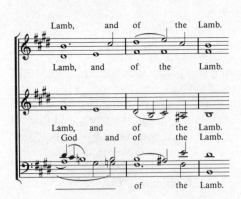

A choral recitative, sung by all voices in unison and punctuated by chords for full organ, prepares the first of two fugal movements, 'But the throne of God'. This is more formal and timeless than the preceding, though there are chromatic touches at the cadences, imparting a characteristic Victorian flavour. This is followed by another verse, 'And his servants shall serve him', in triple metre and similar in style to ex. 36 above. Another unison choral recitative leads to the concluding fugal chorus. As ex. 37 might suggest, the stylistic language of the anthem as a whole is akin to that of S. S. Wesley, but without that composer's highly distinctive harmonic and melodic fingerprints.

Several anthems of the mid 1860s continue this enrichment of the traditional style, with occasional similarity to the styles of Goss or Wesley. Among the works in the second volume of *Special anthems* (1866) is 'Who shall ascend into the hill of the Lord?', a verse anthem for treble and tenor with four-part choir, much of it in the Italianate baroque manner of Marcello. Some elegant canonic writing in the opening movement, first at the seventh below (ex. 38) and later at the ninth, is worthy of note. The short but im-

Ex. 38   Ouseley: anthem, 'Who shall ascend into the hill of the Lord'

posing anthem for unaccompanied double choir, 'O Saviour of the world' (1865), may be regarded as a specimen of the timeless idiom *par excellence*. Ouseley's setting of this text, while highly expressive and closely moulded to the words, is formal and solemn in contrast with the tenderness of Goss's setting of 1869.

Considering the formality with which traditionalists approached the service canticles, as compared with the degree of subjective latitude admitted in anthems, the freedom, even the sense of drama, that Ouseley brings to his Service in F makes it a landmark in his output. The simple designation 'Service in F' is misleading, because there are two interrelated services in F. The first is a complete morning (Benedicite and Benedictus), communion, and evening service with organ accompaniment. In Tenbury MS 1513 this is dated 1867. The other is a morning (Te Deum and Benedictus), communion, and evening service with full orchestra. An autograph manuscript (Tenbury MS 1511) is dated 1880, but a fair manuscript copy of the communion service (Tenbury MS 1192) is dated 1873, while a similar fair copy of the morning and evening service (Tenbury MS 1186) is dated 1880. Apart from the scoring of the accompaniment, the Kyrie, Creed, and Sanctus are the same in both services, and in the first part of the Gloria Patri to the Magnificats there are only minor differences. Presumably the organ service of 1867 is the earlier, but it is possible that the orchestral service dates from very nearly the same time. The dates on the manuscript copies are not necessarily those of composition, and Bumpus dates the orchestral service 1867, without mentioning the organ service.[20]

These services might almost be regarded as a compendium of Ouseley's compositional technique, from the timeless and historical to more modern idioms, with moments of imposing grandeur, high drama, and tender repose. The Benedicite is a chain of short movements, mostly timeless or historical, for various combinations of voices. Some of them are canons. Most of the remainder of the service is more modern in style. Even a brief excerpt from the Benedictus of the organ service (ex. 39) may serve to illustrate this newer

Ex. 39   Ouseley: Service in F (organ), Benedictus

Ex. 39 *(cont.)*

[organ tacet]

stylistic atmosphere as compared with the more timeless productions of the 1850s and 60s. Ouseley's most dramatic writing is in the Magnificat of the orchestral service. The climax at 'He hath scattered the proud' is particularly exuberant. A brief passage from later in the same setting (ex. 40) may give

Ex. 40 Ouseley: Service in F (orchestra), Magnificat

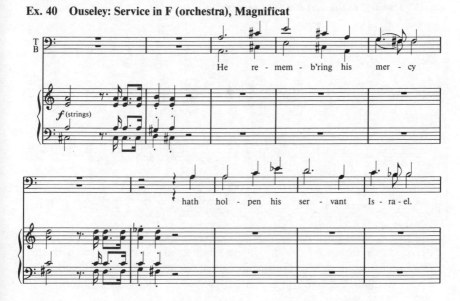

some indication of the nearly theatrical gestures Ouseley was willing to admit in this work. In passages of lower emotional temperature and more tender expression, Ouseley's enriched harmonic diction approaches the idiom of the Victorian part-song.

While not lacking in moments of tenderness and delicacy, the Services in F are characterised by massiveness and grandeur, as one might expect from such monumental works. This impression is generated immediately by the orchestral introduction to the Te Deum, which sounds almost suspiciously like the opening of S. S. Wesley's Magnificat in E, with arpeggiated crotchet chords in the upper strings over a stepwise descending bass line. The Gloria Patri of the organ Magnificat is extraordinarily expansive, culminating in an eight-part fugue of fifty bars. In the Gloria Patri of the organ Nunc Dimittis, Ouseley obtains a richness of choral sound by beginning in ten parts (SSSSAATTBB), prolonging an A major chord, which proves to be the dominant of D minor. He reduces to eight parts at 'As it was in the beginning', starting immediately in F for a much more concise conclusion than its fugal counterpart in the Magnificat. Many of the stylistic features noted in the Services in F are also found in Ouseley's 'Short and Easy Evening Service in B♭', which also dates from 1867.

In his later anthems, Ouseley continues in the course indicated by the works of the mid 1860s. While preserving the traditional formats of single- and multi-movement anthems, he displays a greater readiness to adopt a modern style, even the High Victorian idiom in all its tenderness and harmonic colour. A particularly poignant and affective chromaticism is found in a short full anthem of 1869, 'Love not the world' (ex. 41). The text (I John 2:15–17) is

Ex. 41   Ouseley: anthem, 'Love not the world'

a stern admonition, and one might have expected Ouseley to set it in the solemn and formal style of his 'O Saviour of the world'. Instead he chooses the way of understatement, in a gentle triple metre, and if the harmonic diction is not as poignant as that of S. S. Wesley's 'Wash me throughly', it is not in a totally different world.

Reminiscences of Mendelssohn occasionally appear in Ouseley's later works. 'The Lord shall roar out of Zion' (1871) includes writing which might be traced to the sterner passages of Mendelssohn's oratorios, but on the whole, Ouseley tends to incline toward the Mendelssohn of the gentler part-songs or such oratorio numbers as 'O rest in the Lord' (*Elijah*) and 'Be thou faithful unto death' (*St Paul*). Examples from Ouseley's anthems include the opening tenor solo of 'I waited patiently' (c.1870), the quartet verse 'Blessed is the man' from the same anthem, the quartet verse 'But the Lord will be the hope of his people' from 'The Lord shall roar', and the opening tenor solo of 'O send out thy light' (1876). When Ouseley requires sterner stuff, he generally resorts to a more timeless idiom, the dramatic passages from the Services in F notwithstanding. Furthermore, timeless or historical writing is found even in the latest of the anthems, especially in imposing outer choral movements.

Ouseley's last anthem, 'It is a good thing to give thanks', was composed for the Salisbury Choral Union Festival held in June 1889, on which occasion it was performed by full orchestra and a choir of 3,000. It contains a quartet verse which, while not one of his strongest conceptions, is indicative of the stylistic distance Ouseley had travelled with respect to what he deemed appropriate for use in church (ex. 42). Such writing in an anthem would have been inconceivable for Ouseley in the early 1850s.

Many of the anthems which Ouseley either composed with full orchestra or rescored from versions with organ accompaniment are preserved in a series of bound manuscripts (Tenbury MSS 1187, 1188, and 1495) dating from the mid to late 1880s. Since Ouseley occasionally employed orchestral forces at Tenbury from the time of its foundation, it seems unlikely that these works and rescorings actually date from so late in the composer's life. Judging from their condition, the manuscripts were clearly never used as conducting scores in performance. The paper is as clean and crisp today as it was nearly a

Ex. 42   Ouseley: anthem, 'It is a good thing to give thanks'

Ex. 42 *(cont.)*

hundred years ago. The folio volumes are so tightly bound that they do not readily stay open on a library table, let alone a conductor's desk. Ouseley, with his astounding musical memory, would certainly not have needed a score when conducting the works himself.

It would appear, then, that Ouseley prepared these fair copies of some of his most ambitious works primarily for the purpose of preserving them. He possibly knew by the mid 1880s that his health was in a poorer state than he was willing to have generally known. On the afternoon of Saturday, 6 April 1889, Ouseley was standing on the Broad Street, Hereford, in conversation with Prebendary E. B. Hawkshaw, when he suddenly collapsed from a heart spasm. Mr Kenrick, the manager of the nearby office of the Birmingham, Dudley and District Bank, assisted in moving Ouseley into a private room in the bank building, and a physician was sent for. Ouseley seemed to recover from the attack, but was then suddenly convulsed by a seizure from which he died. He is buried in the churchyard of St Michael's, Tenbury, directly beneath the east window of the church.

It is undeniable that most of Ouseley's style and technique may be comprehended by reference to the works of other composers, both early and contemporaneous, and to existing stylistic stereotypes. To fault his works for lack of originality, however, would entail a fundamental misunderstanding. Henry C. Colles observed:

Ouseley's anthems are thoroughly in keeping with his character and particularly with his preoccupation with the act of worship, in which he, whether as priest, composer or singer, rejoiced to take his part. Originality and external attractiveness are not of primary importance to him. He is content that the music should be as good as he can make it, thorough in workmanship, sincere in expression and meet for the service of God.[21]

In view of such an understanding, it is highly significant that Colles should say a few pages further on in the same essay, 'He was an innate conservative, and of such great artists are never made.'[22] Whether or not the artistic careers of, say, Palestrina or J. S. Bach effectively refute the plain sense of his statement, Colles does seem implicitly to reject – and clearly not out of ignorance – the ideal of church music held by Ouseley, and not by him alone: the ideal of an art set apart for a special purpose and assessed according to special criteria. It is possible to admit that Ouseley's compositions fall short of immortality without rejecting his ideal, though it might be plausibly argued that it would require the genius of a Palestrina or a Bach to achieve artistic immortality within the strict terms of this ideal. Nevertheless, it is inescapable that the general tendency of British musical culture, from the 'Renaissance' of the 1880s onward, sounded a note alien to the spirit of that thoroughly ecclesiastical and devotional art which occupied the talents, the energy, and the affection of Sir Frederick Ouseley.

9

John Stainer (1840–1901) and Joseph Barnby (1838–96): the High Victorian idiom

The term 'High Victorian' may not be a standard part of the musicological vocabulary, but it is useful in designating a stylistic flavour in English music from the second half of the nineteenth century, epitomised in the church compositions of Stainer and Barnby. The flavour is readily detected, though difficult to account for adequately in technical terms. A most conspicuous though not solely definitive feature is a richness of chromatic harmony, often merely decorative or colouristic, but sometimes having structural signifi- cance. To this may be added a predominance of homophonic texture, a trait shared with the Victorian part-song, though certainly not to the complete exclusion of counterpoint. A prevailing regularity of phrase length, a fre- quent employment of harmonic motion over a static bass with the conse- quent production of gentle dissonance, and a predilection to state important triads and seventh chords in inversion rather than root position, thereby softening their character, may be noted as some other conspicuous features of the idiom.

The enumeration of such technicalities may furnish a general impression of the idiom, but not a full explanation of its important finer shades. For example, it is often maintained that the chromaticism of the High Victorians derives largely from the model of Spohr, and indeed, a good technical case can be made. Very little high Victorian church music, however, could really be mistaken for the distinctly early-nineteenth-century flavour of Spohr. The Spohr idiom is essentially restless. His chromatic harmony, while faultlessly fluent and polished, is constantly churning, with a surprising harmonic twist or enharmonic modulation never far away. High Victorian chromaticism, in contrast, tends to be more relaxed and leisurely, giving an impression of tender and meditative reflectiveness.

Acquiring a sympathetic understanding of High Victorian church music is made difficult by the prevailingly hostile tone of post-Victorian critical fashion, amounting at times to apparently wilful misrepresentation. Two chief characteristics most liable to misapprehension are those of tenderness and understatement. No two terms could come closer to summarising the essential atmosphere of the High Victorian idiom. While tenderness is frequently taken for weakness or sentimentality by hostile critics, understate- ment often goes unacknowledged, although it is a manifestation of the con- servative restraint central to the character of English church music in general.

Sometimes it is amazingly misread for its opposite by critics who deplore allegedly theatrical or 'blood-curdling' effects in High Victorian church music, on the assumption that it is false emotion. Stainer's *Crucifixion* is a prime target, but comparison with works like the Rossini *Stabat Mater*, Berlioz *Te Deum* or Verdi *Requiem* immediately reveals the fallacy. Genuinely dramatic or theatrical music bears the same relation to Victorian anthems as the acting of a part does to the reading of the lessons at Morning and Evening Prayer. Unless a detached intonation is employed in the public reading of the scriptures, the alternative to histrionics is a reading that is expressive, but with dignified restraint. This corresponds nicely with the expressive understatement of most Victorian church music.

It is too often assumed that the characteristics of High Victorian church music result from ignorance or insensitivity on the part of the composer. In the case of Stainer, at least, this is disproved by his thoughtful essays on musical aesthetics and criticism in general, and in particular, the remarks on church music from his Oxford inaugural lecture, *The present state of music in England*, delivered in the Sheldonian Theatre on 13 November 1889 and published the same year.

Stainer recognised the issues on which opinions were then, and would long continue to be, divided.

Any review of the present state of Church music would be incomplete unless it pointed out that we are passing through a crisis. About three centuries ago the Church was thoroughly disturbed by the excessive employment of contrapuntal devices in its ritual music. In these days there is no danger of fanciful counterpoint getting the supremacy, but there is cause for fear lest a too plentiful use of that descriptive and sentimental colouring which we derive from the modern 'romantic style' should tempt our church composers into a striving after picturesque and dramatic effects not consistent with the dignity or repose of worship. Three centuries ago the musician, quite regardless of the meaning of the words, revelled in the intricacies of counterpoint: now, our church composers watch narrowly every shade of meaning in the words in order to represent it in a tone-picture. Is this a legitimate form of Church music?[1]

The question is not merely rhetorical, nor does Stainer imply a simple or obvious answer. He proceeds to cite remarks attributed to a clergyman who urges a restrained and dispassionate style.

'When I listen to a musical setting of the *Te Deum* or Nicene Creed, I do not want a series of illustrations in sound, or tone-pictures; these, though they may add to my appreciation of the power and force of your art, do not strengthen my grasp on the ancient truths of my religion...What I really want...is a colourless dignified vehicle of the words, which will enforce their deeper meaning without tempting my thoughts aside by its artistic attractions.'[2]

Stainer continues with a hypothetical conversation between the clergyman and a musician who maintains that the fault lies not in the music itself but in the failure of the listener to acquire an instinctive appreciation of the expressive resources of modern music. Granting this condition, the characteristics of the music would not be a distracting novelty requiring an analytical exercise extraneous to the act of worship, but rather a medium of expression which the mind could grasp as readily as a mirror reflects the image exposed to it. The clergyman replies that the degree of musical training needed to accomplish this cannot be expected of every worshipper. The musician responds that this is not sufficient reason to exclude a form of high art from the service of the church, to which the clergyman retorts that if the musician wants to exercise the latest developments of his art, he should confine his efforts to the concert room or opera house.[3] Stainer obviously recognises the pitfalls on each side of the controversy: the danger of irreverent theatricality on the one hand, and frigid antiquarianism on the other. The tenderness and expressive understatement of the High Victorian idiom may be seen as a possible solution, avoiding the extremes of secular theatricality and dispassionate coldness. Stainer's own church music is thus an attempt to put into practice deeply considered issues and theories exhibited in this and other essays. His compositions are not a contradiction of his principles, as some later critics have suggested, but a confirmation of them.

Stainer's appointment to St Paul's Cathedral in 1872 marks a convenient dividing point in his output as a composer. Most of the anthems composed before then are recognisably in the tradition of the English cathedral repertory as he would have known it as a boy chorister and as an organist in his teens. As a chorister at St Paul's, he naturally came under the influence of Goss, and one may reasonably suppose that the anthems and services of Attwood continued to hold a respectable place in the repertory there. Another branch of influence joined these when, as organist of St Michael's, Tenbury (1857–60), Stainer was associated with Sir Frederick Ouseley, whose devotion to the traditional school of English cathedral music and passion for musical antiquities left a strong impression. Stainer acknowledged Ouseley's role in introducing him to extensive portions of the early polyphonic repertory during sessions of exploration and score reading among the manuscripts of Ouseley's library at Tenbury.[4] Ouseley, already professor of music at Oxford, urged Stainer to compete for the organistship of Magdalen College in 1859, and his example may well have induced Stainer to read for an arts degree. Without this sort of influence, Stainer's intellectual horizons might have been circumscribed by the immediate duties of a practising professional musician, and without the breadth of mind and sense of scholarship he acquired, he might still have made a great cathedral organist, but hardly a great professor. At the same time, Ouseley's influence was not taken uncritically, as their respectful disagreement on the teachings of Crotch demonstrates. Stainer's years at Magdalen (1860–72) may be taken to mark his full maturing as a musician.

Most of the anthems from Stainer's Tenbury and Magdalen period are moderate- to large-scale works in multi-movement format, written with the resources of a trained cathedral choir or its equivalent in mind:

The morning stars sang together (1858)

*The righteous live for evermore (1858)
*They were lovely and pleasant in their lives (by 1866)
*Drop down, ye heavens (by 1866)
 Sing a song of praise (1866)
 Awake, awake; put on the strength, O Zion (1871)

These follow much the same pattern as the larger anthems of Goss and Ouseley; those marked with an asterisk have fugal concluding movements. Unlike the typical Ouseley fugue, which can be relied upon to reach an extended dominant pedal and conclude with a broad statement of the subject, sometimes in augmentation and often followed by a neo-Handelian closing cadence, Stainer's fugues generally depart from strictly fugal technique well before the end of the movement to make a freer and far less timeless finale. Also, Stainer's freedom of tonal movement, encompassing a wider range of keys than either Goss or Ouseley, distinguishes his early works from theirs, even though there is great similarity of style.

Of the other anthems from this period, 'The Lord is in his holy temple', published in the first volume of Ouseley's *Special anthems* (1861) is an energetic and generally timeless fugue in five parts, though the exposition is in four parts with the trebles dividing immediately thereafter and remaining independent. It is a notable feature of this and nearly all of Stainer's fugal expositions that the successive voices enter at exactly the same time interval. When the material is not as propulsively energetic as it is here, the result can often seem mechanical, when a slight extension before the third entry would have imparted the needed sense of elasticity. Also from this early period, 'For a small moment have I forsaken thee' (1862) and 'What are these that are arrayed in white robes?' (1871) are smaller-scale anthems in the traditional vein. The two anthems which stand most apart from the traditional style and format are 'I saw the Lord' (1858) and 'Lead, kindly light' (1868). While both of these require highly proficient choirs for successful performance, they anticipate some features which characterise a great many of Stainer's later and less technically formidable anthems.

Notwithstanding an anthem like 'The Lord is in his holy temple', the timeless idiom plays but a small part in Stainer's style, even at this early period. The opening of 'The morning stars sang together' (1858) could almost be regarded as the homophonic variety of the timeless idiom, with phrases repeated across the choir, except for the tonal ground covered and the trait of harmonic movement over a static bass. 'What are these that are arrayed in white robes?' (1871), because of its harmonic restraint, cannot be considered High Victorian on grounds of extreme chromaticism, yet it is essentially High Victorian on other stylistic grounds. The few decorative chromatic touches confirm the part-song flavour of certain passages (ex. 43), as does the warm expressiveness of a passage like 'They shall hunger no more', with its static bass line. The dotted rhythms found in the opening 'Hallelujahs' and other parts of the more energetic portions of this anthem were very much a High

Ex. 43   Stainer: anthem, 'What are these that are arrayed in white robes?'

[doubled by organ]

Victorian mannerism, sometimes overworked by Stainer himself, and too easily adopted by less competent composers, appearing inevitably in march-like choruses and organ voluntaries.

The influence of Mendelssohn is very strong in early Stainer, and nowhere more so than in his oratorio *Gideon*, composed for the Oxford D.Mus. in 1865. Both the energetic and the gently lyrical sides of Mendelssohn are reflected by Stainer. Among the anthems, 'They were lovely and pleasant in their lives', published in the second volume (1866) of Ouseley's *Special anthems*, begins with a quartet verse reminiscent of a gentle Mendelssohn part-song. The same anthem also contains a *furioso* duet for two basses, 'As gold in the furnace' (ex. 44), inviting comparison with 'Is not his word like a fire?' from *Elijah*. Also in the 1866 volume is 'Drop down, ye heavens', which contains a fugal chorus, 'Thou art fairer than the children of men', with a singularly Mendelssohnian subject. Before the final adagio statement

Ex. 44   Stainer: anthem, 'They were lovely and pleasant in their lives'

Ex. 44 (*cont.*)

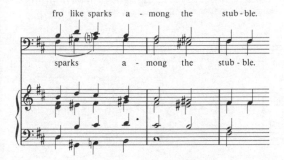

of the subject which concludes the movement, there occurs a passage (ex. 45) which seems to recall S. S. Wesley, specifically the final line of 'And the ransomed of the Lord', which precedes the concluding verse 'And sorrow and sighing' from 'The wilderness' (see ex. 26 above, p. 145). Passages like these, as well as many which seem to suggest Attwood or Goss as antecedents, help to demonstrate continuity in the works of Stainer with the sacred music of previous generations.

Ex. 45   Stainer: anthem, 'Drop down, ye heavens'

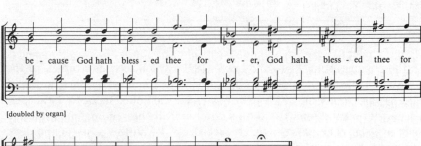

A general feature of Stainer's work, apparent in *Gideon* and these early anthems, is that he is most successful in lyrical set pieces and most likely to misfire when attempting dramatic or narrative depiction. At one point in *Gideon*, for instance, he attempts to generate dramatic excitement by the repetition in the various chorus parts of what is really a rather square dotted figure over chromatic harmonies (ex. 46). This, of course, is strikingly similar

Ex. 46   **Stainer:** *Gideon*

to the passage from 'I saw the Lord' (1858) which sets the words 'and the house was filled with smoke'. In the earlier anthem, however, there are eight chorus parts, not four, which give out an identical dotted figure to the accompaniment of harmonies based on a chromatically descending line projected over a pedal. The passage which precedes it ('And the posts of the door moved at the voice of him that cried') seems almost cheap in its all too obvious effort of musical depiction, especially when compared with the brilliantly atmospheric *tableau* and angelic 'Holy, Holy, Holy' earlier in the anthem. This underscores the difference between the evocation of a mood through musical resources and the imitation of a physical action by musical analogy.

It is noteworthy that Stainer, unlike Goss and Ouseley, seldom employs sonata principles in his anthem movements. The nearest he comes is in the first movement of 'Sing a song of praise' (1866), a recapitulating binary structure involving the exposition of two 'themes' and a modulation to the dominant, the tonic prevailing in the recapitulation. The 'first theme' ends with a dominant chord, but it is a genuine dominant, not the goal of modulation, and it recurs literally in the recapitulation. All real modulation is confined to the 'second theme', which, in a classical sonata movement, would confirm a preceding modulation. In general, Stainer's tonal organisation is often not according to classical principles based on the closeness of relationship between keys a fifth apart.

Fluid chromaticism is conducive to keeping the tonality in a state of flux and allowing a wide variety of almost equally probable routes of tonal motion. The implications of major/minor equivalence are more fully developed in Stainer than in the composers hitherto discussed. This allows rapid passage to distant keys while still following a classical grammar of harmonic resolution. Hence, for example, C major can pass to its relative minor, which is equivalent to A major, which may pass to its relative minor, which is equivalent to F♯ major. Thus, given an atmosphere of sufficient chromatic colour as not to make the progression seem forced, one may modulate rapidly to a key a tritone away from the tonic. Stainer also makes much of harmonic progressions involving the relation of a tonic with its flat submediant, with or without the augmented sixth coming into play. In many of his later works, he bases tonal organisation on the polarity of keys a major third apart. In the morning and evening canticles of the Service in B♭ (1877, 1884), for example, the principal secondary key is D major. Such tonal relations and the readiness to pursue chromatic tangents were certainly not novel in the absolute sense, but their admission as part of the normal diction of conservative English cathedral music is noteworthy. In Stainer and other High Victorians, this chromatic diction becomes so normal that it tends to lose the restless or languishing flavour it often has in S. S. Wesley.

In Ouseley and Goss, whatever chromatic colour they may impart to their harmony, the clarity of function is rarely in doubt. Stainer, however, makes a much freer use of roving chromaticism, departure on enharmonic tangents, and chains of secondary dominants regularly and irregularly resolved, to the extent that tonal and harmonic function within such passages seems sometimes secondary to the sense of tonal flux itself. The passage from 'I saw the Lord' beginning 'Each one had six wings' is a good example. The goal of the passage is modulation from G minor to the dominant of D. After a clear establishment of G minor, a rising chromatic line leads through a chain of secondary seventh relations whose functions could be analysed, as they behave according to grammatical rule, but their tonal implications are so evanescent as to exist hardly at all. The internal logic of the passage seems not to be determined by a functional succession of chords but by the provision of

colourful harmonic clothing to a rising scale in the bass. This may be illustrated by the organ accompaniment alone (ex. 47). A passage which behaves
similarly comes from the duet in 'They were lovely and pleasant' (ex. 44
above), in which a chromatic 'parenthesis' of the sort often associated with

Ex. 47   Stainer: anthem, 'I saw the Lord' (organ part)

Chopin transpires entirely within a B minor context, and has really nothing to
do with the immediately ensuing modulation to F♯ minor. Again the internal
logic of the passage lies in the linear progress of the bass. Such passages seem
to have the earmarks of an experienced keyboard player 'thinking through his
fingers', and surely it is more than coincidental that Stainer was renowned in
his day for organ improvisation.

Accounts of Ouseley's improvisations[5] seem agreed that they had an
animation and spontaneity generally lacking in his written compositions.
Stainer observed, for example, that Ouseley's 'real gifts were shown when he
extemporised, quite privately to a friend or two, on the pianoforte...Yet when
this talented man took up his pen to *write* a composition it seemed as if some
evil genius stood by to damp his invention and wreck his originality.'[6] Even if
one allows for the almost inevitable tendency for admiring hearers to overrate
the artistic merit of such performances, it might reasonably be conjectured
that Ouseley, when engaged in written composition, deliberately suppressed
this tendency to think through his fingers in favour of greater formality. This
may account for the alleged difference in style and effect. Although it has also
been alleged that Stainer's improvisations outstripped many of his written
works,[7] he was apparently less inhibited than Ouseley about the admission of
an improvisatory freedom to his church compositions.

One of the most chromatically fluid of Stainer's early anthems is 'Lead,
kindly light' (1868), a setting of Newman's famous lyric of 1833. It departs
from the structural format of the traditional multi-movement or short-and-
full anthem, largely through accommodating the stanzaic structure of a
rhyming metrical text rather than the traditional prose of the Psalter or
Bible.[8] It invites comparison with Goss's 'Brother, thou art gone before us'

(1865), which Stainer most likely knew. Although it begins with a tonic chord, the very opening of the anthem provides a good illustration of Stainer's predilection for making an oblique approach to the main tonality (ex. 48). Stainer sometimes uses this technique at the beginning of an internal move-

Ex. 48 Stainer: anthem, 'Lead, kindly light'

ment, to make a link with the key of the movement preceding it. He some-times makes a connection between two fairly remote keys by means of a single note common to both. In 'Lead, kindly light', the E♭ of the first movement is respelt D♯ to become the third of B major, the key of the solo middle move-ment. It is noteworthy that one of the principal goals of modulation in the first movement is C♭ major ('The night is dark'), the flat submediant of E♭ and the enharmonic equivalent of B♮. The work is full of harmonic excursions and unexpected juxtapositions, at one point (ex. 49) seeming to lean in the

Ex. 49 Stainer: anthem, 'Lead, kindly light'

Ex. 49 *(cont.)*

direction of French or Italian opera. In spite of such things, the piece is not theatrical in character. The contrapuntal intricacy of much of the part writing is unusual in a work of its predominantly tender character.

Tenderness as a characteristic of the High Victorian idiom is well established in these early anthems of Stainer. It can possibly claim ancestry in what Crotch called the Beautiful Style of the eighteenth century, and a form of it was certainly present in Attwood and the early Victorian generation. Stainer clearly associated a tender and often chromatic idiom with words of comfort. A quartet verse (ex. 50) from 'For a small moment have I forsaken

Ex. 50   Stainer: anthem, 'For a small moment have I forsaken thee'

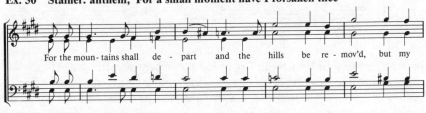

thee' (1862) illustrates this nicely. Some critics might prefer a more fearsome treatment of the mountains departing and the hills being removed, but Stainer perceived that the real message of the text is comfort and reassurance, and he set it accordingly. Note also the static bass in the first bars, and the gentle dissonances produced against it.

Hardly anyone considers Stainer a great composer, and he appears to have been under no self-delusion as to his imaginative powers. Still, there are works in which the creative flame leaps high: pieces of striking originality, standing out against the background of works which, if not extraordinarily inspired, are at least put together with workmanlike competence and integrity. One of the precious few is also one of his earliest extant works, 'I saw the Lord' (1858). The opening movement has won the respect of many twentieth-century critics for its evocation of numinous awe in the *tableau* of Isaiah's vision. This is sometimes achieved by the simplest of means, as at the very beginning, where the elemental major triadic motif, given out by the full choir in unison, is repeated in the minor. The use of chromatically induced tonal flux in this anthem has been noted. The passage cited (ex. 47 above) ends with a strong dominant of D, followed immediately in F♯ minor by the angels' 'Holy, Holy, Holy'. It is noteworthy that Stainer generally resorts to just such a juxtaposition of keys without modulation at the corresponding place in his settings of the Te Deum, seeming to lift the praise of the angels to another tonal plane. The second movement, 'O Trinity! O Unity!', has been criticised by those who praise the first.[9] It is not likely, however, that the change of style at this point is the result of faulty judgment or poverty of invention. The double bar which separates it from the first movement represents a change of scene, as it were. We are no longer standing in the Temple with Isaiah, but brought into the present and gathered for worship in a contemporary church. The words of the hymn make this explicit:

> O Trinity! O Unity!
> Be present as we worship thee,
> And with the songs that angels sing
> Unite the hymns of praise we bring.

The tune is simple and regular in metre, subjected to contrapuntal elaboration, yet as in answer to the supplication of the words, it goes in counterpoint with a major-mode adaptation of the angels' 'Holy, Holy, Holy' from the first movement. Thus Stainer dramatises the united praise of the Church Militant with that of the heavenly host before the same majesty of the Holy Trinity.

Another early work with moments of striking originality is 'Drop down, ye heavens', which first appeared in the second volume of Ouseley's *Special anthems* (1866). In the opening movement, against a gentle undulating line of crotchets in the midst of the organ part, the various voices enter in imitation with a descriptive melodic motif (ex. 51). Stainer again seems to approach the

Ex. 51   Stainer: anthem, 'Drop down, ye heavens'

Drop   down,   ye heav'ns   from   a - bove.

tonality obliquely, as this leading motif carefully avoids the tonic note. The second movement is a recitative for soprano solo ('Hail, thou that art highly favoured') with later entry of the full choir in unison. Stainer again gives a special musical treatment to the angelic words by keeping the quiet accompaniment high on the organ manual, avoiding straightforward resolution of secondary dominants. Changes of colour and function are often obtained by letting a single voice or two move unobtrusively by semitone. The angelic words seem to be enveloped in an aural halo.

After his appointment to St Paul's Cathedral in 1872, an ever greater proportion of Stainer's anthems were designed not specifically for the professional forces of cathedral and collegiate choirs, but were more modest in their technical demands, in many cases intended for volunteer choirs. Some critics have adduced this as part of a case virtually to discredit Stainer as a composer. The prosecution's chief evidence comes from the report of a conversation between Stainer and E. H. Fellowes not long before Stainer's death. Fellowes wrote: 'He suddenly stopped me in the Magdalen walks and said he wanted me to know that he regretted ever having published most of his compositions; that he knew well they were "rubbish" and feared that when he was gone his reputation might suffer because of their inferiority.'[10] Fellowes goes on to note that many of them were written at the request of clergymen who wanted something tuneful but not too difficult for their parish choirs, and that Stainer, presumably against his better judgment, gave way to pressure. Elsewhere Fellowes remarks that Stainer 'did in fact know that he had written most of his earlier anthems too easily', and he cites W. H. Hadow to the effect that 'this music was deplorably easy to write'.[11]

The authenticity of Stainer's statement to Fellowes is not in doubt, but some insupportable conclusions have been drawn from it. To regard it as a general artistic recantation is to go far beyond the substance of the statement. Fellowes admitted that it is impossible to determine exactly what scope Stainer intended the statement to have, so it cannot be taken as a definitive judgment on any work in particular. Stainer was generally humble about his abilities as a composer, as documented in numerous personal recollections of those who knew him. Furthermore, as Peter Charlton has pointed out, Stainer was unwell and tired when he had his conversation with Fellowes,[12] and indeed, the statement does have the ring of one in whom depression has cast a shadow of doubt over the value of a large and conspicuous portion of his life's work. Even under the best of circumstances, a composer is not always the best judge of the ultimate value of his own work. Finally, whatever Stainer may have thought of his church music in 1901, this cannot be used to impugn his integrity at the time of composition.

Fellowes gives the impression that Stainer dashed off a quantity of cheap anthems without a thought in order to placate the parsons who were constantly pestering him for compositions. This simply does not accord with what is known of Stainer's character. In fact, it is very difficult to tell what Fellowes means by Stainer's 'earlier anthems' which were allegedly written 'too easily'. This surely cannot be said of 'I saw the Lord', 'Drop down, ye heavens', or the other larger-scale cathedral anthems which constitute the greater part of his work from before 1872. If Fellowes means earlier as opposed to later anthems from 1872 onward, it is difficult to tell where the critical turning point occurs. On consideration, Fellowes's statement seems careless and misleading.

Unfortunately, this is not the only instance of a careless and misleading statement by Fellowes about Stainer. In his article of 1951, Fellowes observed: 'The total loss of an eye through an accident at the age of five was also a severe handicap throughout his life, and his sight was indeed one of the urgent reasons which made his doctors recommend him to resign St Paul's for the lighter tasks involved in the Professorship at Oxford University.'[13] Stainer suffered an injury to his good eye through being struck in the face by a ball during a game of fives at Tenbury in 1875. Failing eyesight was given as the principal reason for his resignation from St Paul's, communicated in January 1888 to take effect the following June. The Oxford professorship could hardly have been a consideration, however, as it did not fall vacant until Ouseley's death in April of 1889, and Stainer certainly did not take his professorial tasks to be light ones.

In his inaugural Oxford professorial lecture in 1889, Stainer provides some real evidence on his attitude towards the composition of church music intended for amateurs. He comments in general on the problems even to the cathedral composer of the *de facto* limit imposed on the duration of anthems and canticles, and takes a good-natured swipe at the *Musical Times*, perhaps the most prolific disseminator of anthems especially designed for the capacity of amateurs.

Our Church composers are compelled...to get the largest amount of musical and religious effect from the smallest quantity of music, and some of our best services and anthems may be better described as running comments on the character of the words, than as artistically constructed movements. Owing to this desire or necessity for shortness it is probable that the most widely used and popular Anthems are those selected from a well-known monthly series, each of which is guaranteed to last for three minutes only, and is sold for three-halfpence.[14]

The remarks must have been good-natured, inasmuch as Stainer had by then contributed his own share of anthems to the *Musical Times*, and would continue to do so in the 1890s.

Later in the same lecture, he addressed the issue in a more serious vein. He acknowledged the fact that there was then a great and growing stimulus to the production of elaborate church music, including festival service settings and anthems with orchestral accompaniment, and the performance in large churches and cathedrals of oratorios and cantatas, both of the traditional repertory and new compositions. Indeed, Stainer, as organist of St Paul's and *ex officio* director of music for the annual Festival of the Sons of the Clergy, had been responsible for commissioning many such pieces, one of the more enduring being Stanford's Evening Service in A, composed for the Festival of 1880. Stainer was also responsible for instituting regular oratorio services at St Paul's, the devotional aspect being stressed and the entire orchestra clothed in surplices, with Bach's *St Matthew Passion* figuring annually in the repertory.

With characteristic modesty, Stainer makes no mention of his own role in bringing about the improved state of affairs in more elaborate church music, but he speaks from his own experience about parochial composition.

Whilst advocating the production of the higher branches of sacred music, I should like to make an appeal to our young rising composers for easy and simple contributions for the use of our ordinary parish churches. Settings of the Canticles, especially of the *Te Deum*, which are somewhat more varied and interesting than a mere string of chants, but sufficiently simple to be mastered by a whole congregation, are very much needed. I know by experience that the composition of simple music is a thankless task, there is little scope for originality in the composer, and a wide scope for ridicule from the critic. But as the Church of England is at the present time giving the greatest encouragement to our composers by providing them with ample resources at special services, she has a right to demand, I think, some effort on their behalf to supply the daily wants of her parish churches.[15]

These remarks contain the germ of several fallacies, though it is difficult to tell how far Stainer recognised them as such. He was undoubtedly sincere in his exhortation to young composers, and was not urging them to an endeavour he had not already undertaken conscientiously himself. It is just possible, however, to infer from his exhortation that easy church music is necessarily inferior and so can be written to order, that it is always a burden to the imagination, and that composers have a duty to undertake this disagreeable task. Still, it may be rejected as inconsistent with his character that Stainer was urging his colleagues to premeditated hack-work or, as some have suggested, that he himself deliberately wrote music which he knew at the time to be bad, however admirable his motives.[16]

Turning to Stainer's anthems from after 1872, the following are relatively large-scale works for cathedral use or festivals:

    O clap your hands (1873)
    *I desired wisdom (1876)
    Let the peace of God rule in your hearts (c.1882)
    *And all the people saw the thunderings (1883)
    *Lord, thou art God (1887)
    *Lo! Summer comes again (c.1888)
    Honour the Lord with thy substance (1892)
    *And Jacob was left alone (1894)

The anthems marked with an asterisk take all or part of their text from a source other than the Psalter or Bible, in most instances a verse from a hymn used in conjunction with scriptural words. 'Let the peace of God', while it does not involve any extra-scriptural text, implies one by introducing the chorale tune 'Nun danket alle Gott' as a *cantus firmus* in the organ accompaniment. Of these anthems, the ones which seem to adhere closest to the traditional mould of the multi-movement anthem with verses are 'O clap your hands', 'Let the peace of God', 'Lord, thou art God', and 'Honour the Lord'.

The following anthems are generally smaller in dimension and less technically demanding than those just named. Those published in the *Musical Times* are indicated. All are within the capacities of a reasonably good volunteer parish choir, though most could do respectable service in the cathedral.

*O Zion, that bringest good tidings (*MT* 381, Nov. 1874)
They have taken away my Lord (1874 – *MT* 384, Feb. 1875)
*Hosanna in the highest (*MT* 392, Oct. 1875)
Leave us not, neither forsake us (*MT* 410, Apr. 1877)
*Ye shall dwell in the land (*MT* 414, Aug. 1877)
*I am Alpha and Omega (*MT* 423, May 1878)
*Thus speaketh the Lord of Hosts (*MT* 453, Nov. 1880)
Grieve not the Holy Spirit (1880)
*There was a marriage in Cana of Galilee (1883)
*Let every soul be subject unto the higher powers (*MT* 527, Jan. 1887)
*The hallowed day hath shined upon us (*MT* 550, Dec. 1888)
*Let not thine hand be stretched out (Additional supplement to *MT* 628, June 1895)
*Mercy and truth are met together (Additional supplement to *MT* 633, Nov. 1895)
*Behold, two blind men sitting by the way side (1895)
*It came upon the midnight clear (*MT* 681, Nov. 1899)
*O bountiful Jesu (*MT* 684, Feb. 1900)
Blessed is the nation (1901)

As before, anthems incorporating hymn texts or other extra-scriptural words are marked with an asterisk. In addition to these, Stainer wrote numerous short anthems or introits, successors to such miniatures as Goss's 'God so loved the world' or Ouseley's 'Is it nothing to you?'.

Stainer's approach to anthem composition, especially in these later works, suggests a special emphasis on the anthem's role as a sermon in music. Critics have remarked on the breadth of thought and care reflected in Stainer's choice of anthem words. He ranged well beyond the confines of the Psalter, often taking words from the New Testament, the Prophets, and the Apocrypha. Stainer not only ranges widely over the resources of the Bible; within an individual work, he often combines widely separated texts and then frequently includes a hymn verse. It would seem, then, that he is not merely taking an attractive and devotional text and setting it to music, but rather building up a homiletic structure through the careful bringing together of texts and setting them to music so as to illuminate their relationships.

In doing this, Stainer often employs the methods of oratorio or cantata, and indeed, it is not far-fetched to see in the cantatas and Passions of J. S. Bach a model for Stainer's employment of hymn texts, and occasionally hymn tunes, in his anthems. Often a passage of narrative or dialogue – sometimes treated in recitative, sometimes in a semi-lyrical declamation, sometimes alternating recitative with more lyrical material – forms the central theme or lesson on which the anthem is based. This is often given out at the beginning and followed by lyrical commentary – a pattern followed repeatedly in the shorter anthems – or it is set in the midst of such commentary, with the hymn verse usually coming at the end. 'I desired wisdom' (1876), an anthem for the feast of the Epiphany, is a good specimen among the larger works. The opening chorus is from chapter 51 of Ecclesiasticus, beginning 'I desired wisdom openly in my prayer. I prayed for her before the temple, and will seek her out even to the end.' The next movement is a trio for trebles, setting part of the narration of the visit of the Wise Men from chapter 2 of St Matthew's gospel. Such passages of narration or dialogue in Stainer's anthems are rarely very extended. They give enough of the context to make it clear to the listener, and always the heart of the passage in question. Here it is confined to four verses (1, 2, 9, and 10), but this is sufficient to establish the link between the Son of Sirach's prayer for wisdom, and the Wise Men's quest for the Holy Child. Musically, Stainer provides articulation for the most telling parts of the text. The trio, for example, is largely unaccompanied, in F major. The organ enters at 'Where is he', which is sung by the voices in unison, and there is a sudden shift to A major for 'and are come to worship him', sung pianissimo and *Più lento*. Stainer often sets apart such special words by sudden changes of key, tempo, and dynamics. In this case, the intention to worship the Christ Child expresses the wisdom which prompted the quest. After a return to the key of F, the full choir enters with 'Hallelujahs' leading to a verse in A major of *Adeste fideles* ('Sing, choirs of angels'), punctuated with reiterated 'Hallelujahs'. Note that the key of the hymn verse is the same as that of the specially pointed words of the Wise Men in the trio.

One of Stainer's most powerful musical sermons is the Advent anthem 'Hosanna in the highest', which appeared in the *Musical Times* of October 1875. The theological profundity of the work is belied by the deliberate lightness of its opening. The organ introduction presents a rather precious-sounding tune which is then sung by the choir trebles (ex. 52). This is a refrain

Ex. 52   Stainer: anthem, 'Hosanna in the highest'

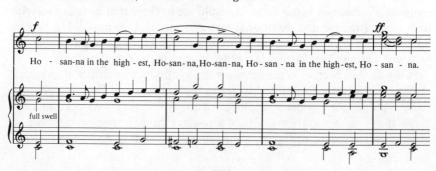

which recurs to punctuate the various short sections of the first part of the anthem. Stainer frequently uses a refrain or motto, which imparts a structural unity to a movement without imposing a large-scale tonal plan like that of sonata form. After the treble refrain, the tenors and basses in unison have the first part of the main anthem text, taken from chapter 63 of Isaiah: 'Who is this that cometh from Edom?' This is in A minor, but retains the light character established by the opening. The words are delivered as a series of short statements with dotted rhythms over a carillon-like figure in the organ left-hand part, and this is followed by the refrain, again in C major, this time sung by trebles with altos in parts. The tenors and basses return with the next segment of the prophetic text: 'Who is this with dyed garments from Bozrah? This that is glorious in his apparel, travelling in the greatness of his strength?' This begins in C, but moves to A minor, finishing on the dominant. The refrain follows in A major, in a richer version than before. The trebles have the tune, while the other parts of the full choir have a loose texture of accompanimental 'Hosannas', all over a dominant pedal in the organ and a carillon figure in the right-hand part. Tenors and basses then answer broadly: 'I that speak in righteousness, mighty to save', moving to D major, which serves as a dominant for the refrain in G major, beginning quietly with the tune in the alto, 'Hosannas' in the other parts, and an organ accompaniment similar to the one in the previous refrain. A brief organ interlude modulates to B minor for the troubled statement by the trebles: 'Wherefore art thou red in thine apparel, and thy garments like him that treadeth in the winefat?' sung quietly. This proves to be the turning point of the anthem. After a general pause, the tenors and basses answer, fortissimo in C major: 'I have trodden the wine-press alone', then pianissimo at a slower tempo, 'and of the people there was none with me', a phrase in E minor with major chord to finish. The next section, still for tenors and basses in unison, is faster and fortissimo, accompanied with vehement chromatic harmonies: 'I will tread them in mine anger, and trample them in my fury; (*fff*) for the day of vengeance is in mine heart, (*p*) and the year of my redeemed (*pp*, slow) is come.' This ends on the dominent of C via a German sixth. The anthem concludes with a four-part chorale setting of the following hymn verse:

> And when as judge thou drawest nigh,
> The secrets of all hearts to try;
> When sinners meet their awful doom,
> And saints attain their heavenly home;
> O let us not for evil past
> Be driven from thy face at last;
> But with the blessed evermore
> Behold and love thee and adore.

The style might be described as that of a Bach chorale seen through Victorian spectacles. Stainer thus projects the essential ambivalence of the Advent season. There is a sense of joyful anticipation of the Incarnation, and Christmas bells seem to ring through the refrain, but 'Hosanna' was what the people of Jerusalem sang as Jesus entered the city to meet his Passion, and indeed, in Isaiah's vision, the one who is coming wears bloodstained garments, the Passion being a consequence of the Incarnation. Advent is, after all, a penitential season, a time when the Church traditionally contemplates the Last Things, among them the Second Coming and Judgment. The apparent preciosity of the opening of the anthem is clearly not a failure of Stainer to devise an adequate setting for beautiful words; it is an essential part of the gesture of the anthem as a whole, and it is the anthem as a whole which reveals Stainer's secure grasp of the theme and his capacity to project it vividly within the confines of six pages of octavo vocal score, without exceeding the technical capacity of a volunteer parish choir.

Among the anthems using oratorio techniques to present narrative or dialogue is 'They have taken away my Lord' (1874), which gives a choral setting of the dialogue between St Mary Magdalen (sopranos) and the risen Christ (tenors and basses) followed by a jubilant triple-metre chorus, 'O death, where is thy sting'. The dialogue is in a semi-lyrical declamation rather than *recitativo secco*. 'And Jacob was left alone' (1894) is cast as a series of narrations and dialogues from chapter 32 of Genesis, set for solo voices (Narrator, bass; Angel, bass; Jacob, tenor) alternating with choral settings of verses from Charles Wesley's 'Come, O thou traveller unknown'. 'Behold, two blind men' (1895) is also set as a scene in narration for a solo soprano, and dialogue in which the blind men are sung by tenor and bass soloists and the words of Jesus by three sopranos. In England, during the nineteenth century, there was great reluctance, even in oratorio, to suggest the impersonation of Jesus by an actor or vocal soloist, hence the three voices. Consistent with his practice in setting angelic or other special words, Stainer here places the Dominical utterances in a foreign key (A♭), linked to its surrounding (B major) by an enharmonic respelling (D♯ = E♭).

In the context of his anthems, it is appropriate to consider what is indisputably Stainer's best-known composition, *The Crucifixion* (1887). Its enormous popularity, obviating the need for detailed description here, has undoubtedly stimulated disproportionate critical abuse. It has been assailed as a weakly sentimental, wholly inadequate attempt at musical depiction of the events of the Passion, when it really is a mistake to regard it as a *depiction* at all. It most emphatically is not an oratorio. The work's subtitle describes it as 'A Meditation on the Sacred Passion of the Holy Redeemer'. This should naturally lead one to expect a more contemplative and intimate, even a more subjective treatment of the theme than a straightforward setting to music of the Passion story. The intentional warmth, tenderness, and understatement of the work have caused it to be mistaken as weak and superficial, even insincere.

The compositional procedure employed by Stainer in *The Crucifixion* is essentially the same on the larger scale as that of his mature anthems on the smaller. Without actually being an oratorio, it makes use of oratorio technique to present in recitative just enough narration and dialogue to establish the context for the lyrical commentary. The greater part of the work is, indeed, lyrical. Robin Legge, in a review of a 1930 recording of the work, observed: 'It has never been claimed for it that it ranks with the great "passions" or Handel's oratorios. It is direct, sincere and simple music, which seeks not to be dramatic in a modern sense.'[17] Peter Charlton comments that 'perhaps more than others, this work needs a beautiful performance from accomplished singers to draw beauty from it'.[18] The same could be said for many of Stainer's anthems, and herein lies the ironic problem of the work. Its limited technical demands are such as to put it within the reach of choirs and soloists who lack the artistry needed to do it full justice. Consequently *The Crucifixion* is a work more often performed badly than well. It might be claimed that a truly great work can shine through an inadequate reading, but no such claim is made for it. Nevertheless, it is unjust to confound the caricature of the work with its considerable intrinsic merits, or make the inadequate performance a measure of the composer's intention or achievement.

In Stainer's services, the High Victorian flavour of the anthems is not as prominent. This accords with the general attitude of greater formality respecting the canticles and communion office. This may even be why Fellowes regarded the services as the best of Stainer's output.[19]

At the summit of Stainer's service settings are the three complete cathedral services: No. 1 in E♭ (Evening, 1870; Morning and Communion, 1874), No. 2 in A and D (Evening service with orchestra for the Festival of the Sons of the Clergy, 1873; Morning and Communion, 1876), and No. 3 in B♭ and F (Evening, 1877; Morning and Communion, c.1884). Apart from tonal mobility and occasional chromatic touches, the Morning and Evening Services in E♭ are reserved in style, almost timeless in places, or reminiscent of Goss, though there are some more florid touches, notably a Gounod-like tenor solo in the Creed.

The Service No. 2 in A and D is, on the whole, more florid than the morning and evening canticles in E♭. Though somewhat less theatrical than in the E♭ Communion Service, the Creed in D also has a Gounod-like tenor solo which is very active tonally, in one passage modulating from D to C♯ minor to A♭ major within eight bars. The Sanctus recapitulates the corresponding portion of the Te Deum from the same service.

The Service No. 3 in B♭ combines passages of great sturdiness and vigour, like the opening of the Magnificat, with others of gentler character and more chromatic colour. A notable characteristic is its tonal organisation around the polar keys of B♭ and D. This relationship of keys a major third apart, though prevalent throughout Stainer's mature works, seems to be carried out here in a more systematic and deliberate manner than usual. The Benedictus of the morning service is actually set in D. The communion office, however, is in F, but the central portions of the Creed and Gloria are in D, while the Sanctus is in A.

In keeping with the exhortation in his Oxford inaugural lecture in 1889, Stainer furnished several settings of the canticles for parish use. Some are written-out chant settings, in some cases with varied accompaniments and vocal dispositions. The Magnificat and Nunc Dimittis in F major and D minor, not a chant setting, is noteworthy for its use of the strophic principle. In the Magnificat, for example, the first twelve bars form the basis for all that follows, with adaptations, expansions, shortenings, rhythmic alterations, etc. to suit the contingencies of the text. It is essentially a composed setting that makes very economical use of material. The Te Deum in C is like an extended hymn tune. The Evening Service in E is a relatively easy but fully composed setting.

A work unique in style for Stainer is his Communion Service in C for unaccompanied choir in six parts (SSATBB), dating from 1899. The harmonic diction is spare for him, with very little decorative chromaticism, almost timeless apart from diatonic dissonance treatment and harmonic inversions where an earlier composer might have been more likely to use root position chords. On the other hand, there is no sense of antiquarian imitation or severe austerity. It is an idiom which might not have been possible without the experience of a more luxurious harmonic diction. Furthermore, Stainer here abandons his customary tonal fluidity, making few decisive modulations even to closely related keys. In one passage from the Creed, for instance (ex. 53),

Ex. 53   Stainer: Communion Service in C, Creed

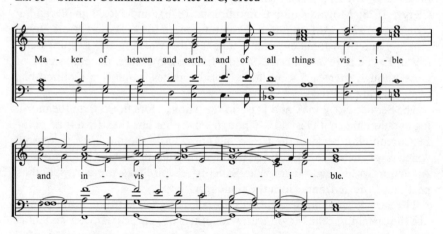

there is a very brief leaning towards D minor, and a quick return to C with a short dominant pedal. The passage also gives some idea of the stylistic flavour of the whole. Unlike Walmisley's turn to a more diatonic idiom in most of his later works, the Communion Service in C stands alone in Stainer's output. Some of the anthems he was writing around the same time may be somewhat less florid than those of a slightly earlier period, but none of them depart so decisively from the distinctive flavour of the High Victorian idiom.

Joseph Barnby has fared even worse than Stainer at the hands of twentieth-century critics. While most of the general points made with reference to Stainer apply equally to Barnby and to virtually all exponents of the High Victorian idiom, there are respects in which Stainer and Barnby differ significantly in background, temperament, and practice. He thus represents an instructive variant of essentially the same artistic orientation.

Both Stainer and Barnby were boy choristers – Stainer at St Paul's and Barnby at the Minster in his native city of York – and so had a similar exposure to the traditional repertory of English cathedral music. After this early and impressionable period, however, the directions of their careers diverged slightly. In comparison with Stainer's academic and scholarly grounding acquired at Tenbury and Oxford, Barnby was a professional musician in the narrower sense. In 1854, at roughly the same age that Stainer was appointed to Tenbury, Barnby entered the Royal Academy of Music. After a brief period in York, where he consolidated his formidable skills as a choral conductor, he returned to London, where he held several minor organistships before being appointed to St Andrew's, Wells Street, in 1863.

Barnby was not noted as a High Churchman, as Stainer was, but St Andrew's (consecrated 1847) was one of the chief centres of Anglo-Catholic worship in London. It was at first a stronghold of the ecclesiological Gregorian ideal of the choral service. Around 1850, however, the orientation began to turn in the direction of the cathedral ideal, which was firmly in place by the time Barnby was appointed. Under Barnby's direction, music at St Andrew's achieved great distinction. Adaptations of masses by continental composers were employed to adorn the Sung Eucharist. The liturgical performance of Gounod's *Messe solennelle de Ste Cécile* in 1866, for which a harp was used for the first time in Anglican worship, was a landmark of this tendency.

In 1871 Barnby resigned from St Andrew's for the non-Tractarian parish of St Anne's, Soho, and here he worked an even more dramatic transformation, making the church a veritable Mecca for those who delighted in the most elaborate musical adornments of the liturgy, attracting large congregations from various parts of London to a rather plain church in an unsavoury neighbourhood. The church became a centre for performances of the works of J. S. Bach, especially the *St John Passion*, of which Barnby conducted the first British performance in March 1872 at the Hanover Square Rooms, in aid of the St Anne's Church Restoration Fund.

Barnby was a musical advisor to Novello's from 1861, and under their auspices he founded in 1867 a professional choir which gave many distinguished performances at St James's Hall. In 1872 this choir was amalgamated under Barnby's direction with the Royal Albert Hall Choral Society.

This group had been founded a year before and had given several financially unsuccessful concerts conducted by Gounod. With patronage granted in 1888, the choir was renamed the Royal Choral Society. In 1875 Barnby was appointed Precentor of Eton College, a post he held until 1892, concurrently with St Anne's until 1886. In 1892 he was knighted and appointed principal of the Guildhall School of Music, a position he retained until his sudden and unexpected death in January 1896.

Barnby was recognised during his lifetime as a thoroughly High Victorian composer. Joseph Bennett, for instance, writing a few months after Barnby's death, said of him:

The composer showed himself in sympathy with the musical feeling of his day rather than with the austere scholasticism of an earlier time. The fact might easily have been different, since Barnby's most impressionable years belonged to a time in which the older school of Church composers flourished and the era of free effects and what was then looked upon as operatic sentiment had only just begun to dawn. Barnby, however, had few tastes in common with the contrapuntists. He was essentially, if not assertively, a man of his own era. While shunning frivolity and the undignified, he did not at all see why the Church should be closed against musical developments in the direction of ornate or even pretty effects. To this he gave practical expression in his works, but always with the prudence and self-restraint which were conspicuous in his musical career. Hence the popularity of his compositions as having in them the modern spirit yet not offensive to older tastes. We cannot forestall the judgments of the future, and it remains to be seen whether Barnby's anthems, &c., will win for him a lasting place among the finest masters of Church song; but one would fain believe, and can scarcely resist prophesying, that not a few of them will go down to far distant posterity, and to that extent assure the fame of their author.[20]

Bennett thus accepts the very characteristics of Barnby's style that have elicited the severest castigations from later critics. Other Victorians found these characteristics not merely acceptable, but the chief virtue in Barnby's work. This is the judgment in a leading article from the *Lute* of January 1891, probably written by that journal's editor, Lewis Thomas, who characterises Barnby as a bold innovator, bringing a much-needed freshness and vitality to the stuffy and backward-looking cathedral-music scene.[21]

Barnby's earliest extant anthems, dating from 1857 to 1866, are not High Victorian, however, but similar to works of the earlier generation. An imitative contrapuntal texture characterises the outer choral sections of 'I will lift up mine eyes' (1857). Between them is a quartet movement in the relative minor, giving an early illustration of Barnby's predilection for song forms beginning with a balanced phrase pair. His short full anthems 'Let the words of my mouth' (published in the *Musical Times* of June 1863) and 'As we have borne the image of the earthy' (published in the *Musical Times* of March 1865), might pass for the work of Goss. An anthem which is relatively timeless and contrapuntally active throughout is 'I bow my knee' (1863). A moderate-scale multi-movement anthem along traditional lines is 'The grace of God', which appeared in the *Musical Times* of December 1864. It has a substantial solo verse, 'Blessed be he that cometh', which is tender, but more Mendelssohnian than High Victorian. The final chorus, 'Hosanna in the highest', is in a jubilant triple-metre style, somewhat reminiscent of Goss, but with stronger colouristic leanings. 'O Lord God to whom vengeance belongeth' is a short anthem for double choir published in the second volume of Ouseley's *Special anthems* (1866). Its opening section is fugal, progressing to a section in which vehement seventh chords to the text 'shew thyself', set in dotted rhythms, alternate with unison passages for fewer voices to 'arise thou judge of the earth'. The conclusion is quiet and homophonic. Again the idiom, both in contrapuntal and homophonic textures, recalls Mendelssohn.

These anthems, taken alone, might give a misleading impression of Barnby's stylistic development. They are preceded by a highly significant work, the complete Service in E major, in which all the resources of the High Victorian idiom are found. The work was widely advertised as having been composed when Barnby was seventeen years old. This would be in 1855, when he was still a student at the Royal Academy of Music. A folio edition was published in 1864 and dedicated to the Revd Benjamin Webb, incumbent of St Andrew's, Wells Street. The octavo edition of 1874 adds a Benedictus to the Te Deum and Jubilate of the morning service, suggesting that it may have been composed after the initial publication. The sextet verse 'For the Lord is gracious' from the Jubilate is well known from having been cited by Ernest Walker and some critics after him as a prime example of all that is depraved in the High Victorian idiom.[22] Recalling what has been observed of Stainer, it is apparent that Barnby here adopts a tender idiom in response to two key words in the text: 'gracious' and 'mercy'. Apart from such a justification, it seems noteworthy that a passage in this style should appear in a service as early as Barnby in E, which was, after all, composed around the same time as Walmisley in D minor and anticipates by more than ten years Henry Smart in F. The noteworthiness lies not in absolute stylistic novelty but in the employment of this style in the most conservative genre of a highly conservative repertory at a time when High Victorian characteristics were by no means universally accepted. Furthermore, it is misleading to isolate this movement, as if it were a pallid effusion by one incapable of more vigour. On the whole, the Service in E is a remarkably bold and energetic composition.

The Te Deum, like the other lengthier texts, is set as a series of short movements, with tender passages occurring in the expected places: 'When thou tookest' (with *più animato* at 'Thou didst open') and 'Vouchsafe, O Lord', both for quartet in $\frac{3}{2}$ metre. In general, chromatic colour is richly used, though not usually for the purpose of modulation. A characteristic passage from the Te Deum (ex. 54) illustrates how Barnby stays close to the home key – in this case B major – and uses chromaticism mainly for local inflection and colour.

The Benedictus text is treated more expansively. For example, Barnby writes a fugato in B major for the words 'To perform the mercy', one of

Ex. 54 Barnby: Service in E, Te Deum

Thou sit - test at the right hand of God in the

[doubled by organ]

glo - ry of the Fa - - ther.

several examples of sustained contrapuntal writing in the service. Another is the fugue in the Gloria Patri of the Jubilate Deo, which is repeated for the Gloria Patri of the Nunc Dimittis. There is some remarkably vigorous word-setting, as a brief excerpt from the Benedictus may illustrate (ex. 55). In the Creed, there is a passage of seemingly experimental word-setting (ex. 56). It

Ex. 55 Barnby: Service in E, Benedictus

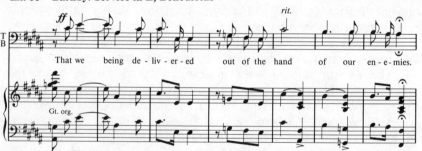

That we being de - liv - er - ed out of the hand of our en - e - mies.

Ex. 56 Barnby: Service in E, Creed

God of God, Light of Light, ve - ry God of ve - ry God.

would appear that Barnby is counting on the natural accentuation of the words to make a syncopation against the prevailing metre, which is reinforced in the organ part.

Barnby sets three of the offertory sentences as part of his setting of the communion office. They are like an anthem in three short movements, and indeed, they were later so published, but in the key of E♭, in which key they appear in the octavo edition of the complete service. The folio edition gives them in E. The Sanctus is short, with a rich choral texture, the voices dividing into as many as seven parts. In the Magnificat, rich with chromatic accompanimental embellishment, vigorous unison passages – 'He hath shewed strength' (tenors) and 'He hath put down' (basses) – give way to a tender quartet at 'He hath filled'. There is a sudden switch to the flat submediant at 'He remembering', which is brought back to the home key in the Gloria Patri by means of a German sixth, a tonal manoeuvre common enough in Walmisley and Stainer, but not often encountered in Barnby. While not without its faults, the Service in E is an estimable piece of work, especially in consideration of its composition date and the youthfulness of the composer.

After these early works, Barnby's church compositions quickly assumed the characteristics that prevailed throughout the remainder of his career. In comparison with Stainer, Barnby's technique, on nearly all grounds, is less sophisticated and more straightforward. His anthems are not theologically profound musical sermons like Stainer's. Barnby seems rather to have approached the genre in the traditional sense of text-setting. The shape of Barnby's anthems in not always traditional, though he did produce his share of moderate- to large-scale anthems with verse movements, as for example:

> The grace of God (1864)
> Drop down, ye heavens (1869)
> I will give thanks unto thee (1871)
> It is a good thing to give thanks (1877)
> Blessed be the Lord God of Israel (1887)
> Ye shall go forth with joy (1890)
> All thy works praise thee, O God (1894)

There are also numerous works of smaller dimension, continuous with the tradition of the short full anthem, but like Stainer, a large number of his works are short anthems alternating full choir with solo voices or semichorus, often within the technical capacity of amateur choirs. Also like Stainer, Barnby makes frequent use of texts from hymns and other extrascriptural sources.

Beyond these anthem categories, Barnby cultivated a genre of choir piece which owes much to the style and shape of the Victorian part-song and hymn tune. Writers frequently note that the character of Victorian hymn tunes arises largely from their similarity to the part-song. In the second half of the century, it is nearly impossible to establish reliable distinctions in the border area where the genres of anthem, part-song, and hymn tune meet. This is especially true of the increasing number of anthems set to metrical texts rather than selections from the Psalter or Bible. Some choir part-songs, like Barnby's through-composed setting of Tennyson's 'Crossing the bar' (1895) and Dykes's 'Ecce panis', actually found their way into hymnals. Barnby's 'Sweet is thy mercy' (1873) alternates treble solo with full choir in a hymn-like setting after the manner of Attwood's 'Come, Holy Ghost'. Barnby composed 'O perfect love' for the marriage of Princess Louise of Wales to the Earl of Fife (27 July 1889). It is very much a part-song with optional organ accompaniment. Its main melody has been adapted as a strophic hymn tune and is often used as such with the same words. 'The first Christmas' (1893) is a cycle of carol-anthems, essentially choir part-songs. 'Hail to the Christ!' (1895) is also a carol-anthem. Each strophe of the text is set to different music, but the stanzaic structure is clearly perceptible. This is not true of all of Barnby's anthem settings of metrical texts. 'Like silver lamps' (1889) consists of a series of unison sections for individual voice parts of the choir, culminating in a concluding full choral section. 'While shepherds watched their flocks' (1895) borrows some oratorio techniques, as the words of the angel are given to a solo soprano, and the choir at times takes the part of the shepherds, with 'All glory be to God on high' set as a grand concluding chorus. The musical format, in this case, is not bound to the stanzaic structure of the text.

On the whole, Barnby is less adventurous than Stainer in tonal relations. It has been noted that Stainer delights in a highly chromatic harmonic diction which allows him free movement among keys which are only remotely related according to classical notions of tonal proximity, often using the flat submediant relation as a primary ground of structure. Barnby's chromatic diction is as florid as Stainer's, but he relies more on classical tonal relations. Chromaticism serves the purpose of decoration and local inflection rather than manoeuvring for larger-scale tonal structure. Barnby's chromaticism is not so much complicated as elaborate. Nowhere is he more elaborate than in his cantata setting with orchestra of Psalm 97, *The Lord is King*, composed for the Leeds Festival of 1883. The opening chorus makes much use of chords of equivocal function (mostly diminished sevenths), irregular resolutions, and evanescent local tonics to keep the tonality in suspense. Where it does settle down to a clear cadence, however, it is generally either in the home key of D major or a closely related key. By contrast, in a comparable Stainer work like *St Mary Magdalen* (Gloucester Festival, 1883), one is almost equally likely to alight in any key whatever.

Barnby shows an overwhelming predilection for ternary (ABA) form in his anthem movements. He seems to think most comfortably in the miniature forms of the song or hymn tune. In such movements the 'A' section often takes the form of a matched phrase pair. In some cases the phrases will be in a formal antecedent–consequent relationship: the first moving to the dominant, the second beginning like the first but ending in the tonic. This pattern is found, for instance, in 'O how amiable' (1876) and 'Break forth into joy' (1882). More often, the second phrase will lead onwards tonally rather than drawing to a tonic close. Middle sections are often modulatory rather than thematic in their own right. Short motives are often subjected to sequential repetition. Recapitulations are rarely literal. Sometimes they are curtailed, as in the second movement of 'I will give thanks unto thee' (1871), which leads to a chorale finale. In other cases, as in the first movement of 'Blessed be the Lord God of Israel' (1887), the recapitulation is extended. Most often, the recapitulation is only partial, sometimes extending no farther than a few bars or a mere head motif, thereafter developing freely as a concluding section. The possible variants within the basic ternary scheme are numerous. Where a larger-scale single-movement form is required, Barnby sometimes produces ternary forms within ternary forms. 'O praise the Lord' (1876), for instance, is a substantial single-movement full anthem, the greater part of which is in ternary ABA form with a literal recapitulation. Each 'A', moreover, is itself a miniature ternary form. The intervening 'B' section has a structure which might be rendered schematically as AA'BB'B''. The first movement of the large-scale anthem, 'I will give thanks unto thee', composed for the ninth annual festival of the Richmond and Kingston District Church Choral Association in 1871, also has an elaborate ternary-within-ternary structure. Such procedures seem consistent with a predilection for the fundamentally simple and straightforward.

While it is true that the characteristic harmonic diction of the High Victorian idiom is especially well suited to the expression of tenderness, it must be noted that in the latter part of the nineteenth century it had become a normal mode of discourse. One repeatedly finds passages in the works of Barnby and others in which the full resources of the idiom are employed without any serious possibility of alleging sentimental affectation. An excerpt from Barnby's 'Blessed be the Lord God of Israel' (1887), an anthem which incorporates part of the Benedictus canticle text, furnishes a good illustration (ex. 57).

One of Barnby's most impressive pieces is the Evening Service in E♭, composed with orchestral accompaniment for the 1881 Festival of the Sons of the Clergy, and thoroughly infused with a sense of occasion. It is worth noting that Barnby's compositional energies in church music, apart from

Ex. 57   Barnby: anthem, 'Blessed be the Lord God of Israel'

197

Ex. 57 *(cont.)*

hymn tunes – of which he wrote approximately 250 – were almost entirely devoted to anthems rather than service settings. The complete Service in E and the Evening Service in E♭ are the only works of this kind intended for the cathedral and festival repertory. His other canticle settings were contributed to Novello's Parish Choir Book, and consist of unison and chant settings. Perhaps the most striking moment in the E♭ service comes in the Magnificat. The reviewer from the *Musical Times* said of it: 'At the words "He hath shewed strength with his arm", occurs a passage of much dramatic power; and although the modulations at first sight appear to be rather abrupt and unexpected, we feel convinced that on closer acquaintance this passage will be found both effective and fine.'[23] In the passage in question, emphatic statements from the choir are punctuated by orchestral commentary notable for sweeping figures in the bass line. It bears some resemblance to a passage from the second main section of Liszt's Second Piano Concerto (published 1863), though perhaps toned down by several degrees. The Nunc Dimittis, contrary to the usual practice even in festival services, is treated expansively, so that this canticle nearly matches in length the setting of the Magnificat.

It is often observed that Gounod had an influence on later Victorian church composers. Perhaps too much has been made of this. In Barnby's case, the composition most often produced in evidence of stylistic imitation is the motet 'King all glorious' (1868), which is possibly the best known of his sacred vocal works apart from some hymn tunes and psalm chants. The piece does push emulation almost to the point of caricature, but it must be emphasised that 'King all glorious' is hardly a typical work. While Barnby would have been the last person to fault the propriety of the Gounod style for use in church, it is noteworthy that 'King all glorious' was first performed in a concert by Barnby's Choir at St James's Hall on 11 March 1868. The accompaniment, far from being a characteristic specimen of inept organ writing, as at least one modern critic has suggested,[24] was for full orchestra. The *Musical Times* gave the first performance a highly favourable notice, remarking especially on the composer's 'bold and vigorous style, based upon the highest models in sacred writing, and an intimate knowledge of orchestral resources', and noting that the final movement was encored.[25] In other Barnby works, the Gounod flavour is never so obtrusive, though certainly his influence may be suspected in some passages. In such cases, however, it is extremely difficult to distinguish between actual emulation by one composer of another and the case of contemporaries employing a shared musical language. This is not, of course, to deny the influence of Gounod on Barnby altogether.

A final aspect of Barnby's sacred vocal music worthy of notice is the introduction of a lighter style. The most remarkable instance comes not from the church compositions but in *Rebekah* (1870). It is misleading to call the work an oratorio if, by that designation, one invokes the sense of high seriousness the Victorians normally attached to the genre. This was recognised at the time, as the *Musical Times* review indicates:

The title [a Sacred Idyll], style and length of this work, alike point out the fact that it is not brought before the public as something great. Bearing this in mind, it is not difficult to award it the praise it justly deserves. The music throughout is most pleasing, and from its thoroughly modern texture, will offer to Choral Societies which are longing, after repeated musical solids, for some musical sweets, a source of real gratification. It is moderately long, moderately difficult, and perhaps we ought to add, moderately sacred.[26]

Lightness is certainly the characteristic of such numbers as the chorus of damsels with solo, 'Who shall be fleetest', or the love duet, 'Oh flow'r of the verdant lea'. Thoughts immediately turn to Sullivan's operettas, but it is instructive to remember tht Barnby here precedes *Trial by Jury* by about five years. Chronologically and stylistically, *Rebekah* stands midway between Sterndale Bennett's the *May Queen* (1858) and Alexander Campbell Mackenzie's the *Rose of Sharon* (1884).

Barnby does not generally bring quite the same degree of lightness to his church compositions, but one does occasionally encounter in anthems passages suggestive of lighter, unecclesiastical genres. The semichorus movement from 'Lord of the harvest' (1892) will serve as a specimen (ex. 58). Indeed, this lighter touch is most likely in the popular genre of harvest anthems. Evidently Barnby did not make as rigid a separation of styles as did

Ex. 58 Barnby: anthem, 'Lord of the harvest'

some of his contemporaries and predecessors, while many perceived the conflict as between modernity and reaction. It cannot automatically be assumed that innovations of this sort were perceived as intrusions of secularity. The partisans of the antiquarian choral ideal would have perceived them so, but it is worth reiterating that there were many others who thought the High Victorian idiom and the style of Gounod to be dignified and exemplary modes of religious expression. A dignified lightness of touch, such as Barnby brought to several of his numerous Christmas and harvest anthems, would not have seemed inappropriate to many who favoured the modern style of worship music, while those who disapproved of the idiom itself acknowledged little mitigation in the more consistent seriousness of Stainer.

The generation of Stainer, Barnby, and Sullivan was the last, and perhaps the only one, in which the leaders of British musical life were exponents of the fully-fledged High Victorian idiom. Beginning in the 1880s, the generation of Parry and Stanford marks the beginning of a change in stylistic orientation and professional temperament that provided the distinctive background for British music in the first half of the twentieth century. The High Victorian idiom certainly did not disappear in the twentieth century, but it tended to be cultivated by composers of considerably less than the first rank. John Henry Maunder and Caleb Simper are among the best known of these neo-Victorians, whose considerable popularity among churchgoers and amateur choirs lent some strength to the verdict of early twentieth-century writers like

D. F. Tovey, W. H. Hadow, E. H. Fellowes, and Ernest Walker, who were brashly confident not only that they knew what they liked and why, but that they knew in seemingly absolute terms what is good, and that High Victorian music is not.

The present-day musicological atmosphere, in contrast, seems increasingly tolerant of categories of nineteenth-century music which, until relatively recently, tended to be dismissed without much thought as unworthy of investigation. Without expecting to discover long-lost masterpieces, scholars are turning with interest to aspects of popular music making and composition which were an integral part of the culture from which sprang the masterworks of the standard repertory. Victorian cathedral music, while not exactly 'popular' in the same sense as the brass band or the music-hall ballad, is still one class of music that has long been denied such consideration, yet which amply repays the effort to acquire a sympathetic historical understanding. Perhaps it should not be surprising that the music's intrinsic value seems greater now, when it can be regarded as legitimately historic, than it did earlier in our century, when it was merely old-fashioned.

Notes

Introduction

1 See also G. Faber, *Oxford apostles* (London, 1933), pp. 72–81.
2 See I. C. Bradley, *The call to seriousness* (London and New York, 1976) for a detailed modern account of the influence of the Evangelicals in Victorian society and in the moulding of characteristic social and moral attitudes.
3 F. Warre-Cornish, *The English Church in the nineteenth century*, 2 vols. (London, 1910), ii:1

1 The malaise of neo-puritanism

1 H. R. Haweis, *Music and morals* (London, 1871), pp. 124–5
2 F. J. Crowest, *Phases of musical England* (London, 1881), p. 6
3 Essay republished in W. Spark, *Musical reminiscences* (London and Leeds, 1892), pp. 37–8
4 *MT* 484 (June 1883), xxiv:310
5 Cited in C. L. Graves, *The life and letters of Sir George Grove* (London and New York, 1903), p. 299
6 E. J. Dent, 'Early Victorian music', in *Early Victorian England*, ed. G. M. Young (London, 1934), pp. 253–4
7 J. R. Sterndale Bennett, *The life of William Sterndale Bennett* (Cambridge, 1907), pp. 55ff, 85ff
8 'Amateur music as it should be', *MT* 493 (March 1884), xxv:144. Published anonymously; attribution to Wakefield according to E. D. Mackerness, *A social history of English music* (London and Toronto, 1964), p. 205
9 Crowest (1881), pp. 7–8
10 For a detailed history of musical education in England between 1800 and 1860, see B. Rainbow, *The land without music* (London, 1967).
11 P. A. Scholes, *The Puritans and music* (London 1934), *passim*
12 Letter of 19 April (O.S.) 1749
13 See Rainbow (1967), pp. 22–3.
14 W. Weber, 'The muddle of the middle classes', *Nineteenth-century music* (November 1979), iii(2):175
15 *ibid.*, pp. 176–82
16 See, e.g., Élie Halévy, *England in 1815* (Orig. 1913, trans. London, 1924; rev. edn: London, 1949), pp. 424–5, 436, 450–5; A. Briggs, *The age of improvement* (London, 1959), p. 72; G. Himmelfarb, *Victorian minds* (New York, 1968), pp. 278–80.
17 E. Routley, *The musical Wesleys* (London, 1968), pp. 48–9
18 See, e.g., J. A. Latrobe, *The music of the church* (London, 1831), p. 336, where this point is made with respect to anthems.
19 *CC* (Newcastle 1881), p. 329

20 E. Hodges, *An apology for church music* (London, 1834), p. 7
21 *ibid.*, p. 9
22 According to Owen Chadwick, this line of thought was a pre-eminent feature of the Tractarian outlook. See the introduction to his anthology *The mind of the Oxford Movement* (London, 1960; rev. 1963), especially pp. 11–12, 26–30, 44–5.
23 Latrobe (1831), pp. 10, 152–7, 387–9
24 *ibid.*, pp. 36ff
25 *ibid.*, pp. 424–9
26 *ibid.*, pp. 267–8
27 *ibid.*, p. 298. Cf. Hodges (1834), pp. 17–18, who cites the *Three treatises* (1744) of James Harris to the effect that words and music combined strengthen the effect of each other because affections and ideas stand in a reciprocal relationship. Hodges also cites Richard Hooker, *Ecclesiastical polity* (1594), book V, ch. 38, para. 1, on the capacity of music to arouse the affections, including the spiritual, independently of words. Latrobe's use (p. 298) of the distinctive phrase 'native puissance', with similar reference to the power of music, is almost certainly derived from the cited passage in Hooker.
28 Latrobe (1831), pp. 323–4, 333–5
29 R. Druitt, *Conversations on the choral service* (London, edn of 1853), pp. 21–4. Cf. the similar argument advanced by John Hullah, *The duty and advantage of learning to sing* (London, 1846), pp. 4–5.
30 Cited in H. B. Cox and C. L. E. Cox, *Leaves from the journals of Sir George Smart* (London, 1907), p. 294
31 Druitt (1853), p. 103
32 *ibid.*, p. 105
33 *ibid.*, p. 25
34 *CC* (Newcastle 1881), p. 350
35 *CC* (Portsmouth 1885), pp. 199–200
36 *ibid.*, pp. 201, 203, 205 respectively
37 S. A. Pears, *Remarks on the Protestant theory of church music* (London, 1852), p. 25
38 E. Young, *The harp of God* (London, 1861), pp. 174–6
39 *ibid.*, pp. 79–80
40 J. Otter, *Nathaniel Woodard, a memoir of his life* (London, 1925), p. 178, citing a letter of 1865 to the Revd Edward Low, headmaster of Hurstpierpoint College
41 *CC* (Nottingham 1871), pp. 377–8
42 Crowest (1881), p. 106
43 *CC* (Carlisle 1884), pp. 310–11
44 *ibid.*, pp. 316–17
45 *ibid.*, pp. 319–20
46 Latrobe (1831), pp. 299–300
47 F. D. Wackerbarth, *Music and the Anglo-Saxons* (London, 1837), p. 43
48 J. Jebb, *The choral service* (London, 1843), p. 20
49 *ibid.*, pp. 18–19
50 J. Jebb, *Three lectures on the cathedral service* (2nd edn, with additions: Leeds and London, 1845), p. 107
51 *CC* (Wolverhampton 1867), p. 342
52 *ibid.*, p. 335
53 Haweis (1871), pp. 119ff
54 *CC* (Rhyl 1891), p. 281
55 *CC* (Exeter 1894), pp. 531–5
56 J. S. Curwen, *Studies in worship music, first series* (2nd edn, enlarged and rev.: London, 1888), p. 331; or (1st edn: London, 1880), p. 157

57 J. S. Curwen, *Studies in worship music, second series* (London, 1885), p. 79
58 W. R. W. Stephens, *The life and letters of Walter Farquhar Hook*, 2 vols. (London, 1878), ii:133

2 Morality, singing, and church music

1 P. A. Scholes, *The mirror of music* (London, 1947), pp. 162–3
2 See, e.g., William Mullinger Higgins, *The philosophy of sound and musical composition* (London, 1838), a layman's guide to acoustical physics together with some musical history; and William Pole, *The philosophy of music* (London, 1879; 6th edn, 1924), which originated as a course of lectures in 1877 presenting the findings of Helmholtz in a form comprehensible to the English-speaking musician.
3 See, e.g., Herbert Spencer, 'On the origin and function of music' (originally published in *Frasers Magazine*, October 1857), an essay which traces the origin of music to human speech; and James Sully, *Sensation and intuition: studies in psychology and aesthetics* (London, 1874), a volume including essays which attempt to relate musical experience to aspects of human anatomy and psychology.
4 H. R. Haweis, *Music and morals* (London, 1871), p. 42
5 *ibid.*, p. 116
6 H. R. Haweis, *My musical life* (London, 1884), p. 127
7 C. Avison, *An essay on musical expression* (London, 1752; 3rd edn, with alterations and large additions: London, 1775), pp. 4–5
8 See, e.g., 'Early shop closing', *MT* 6 (November 1844), i:41–2; Vernon, 'The influence of music on the public', *MT* 100 (September 1852), v:59–60.
9 Haweis (1871), p. 40. Cf. 'Objects of music', *MT* 25 (June 1846), ii:7.
10 A. B. Marx, *General music instruction*, trans. G. Macirone (London, 1854), p. 59
11 W. Holman-Hunt, *Pre-Raphaelitism and the Pre-Raphaelite Brotherhood*, 2 vols. (London, 1905; 2nd edn, rev.: London, 1913), ii:372
12 Ruskin's principal writings on music and morality are the Sir Robert Rede *Lecture on the relation of national ethics to national arts* (1867), *The queen of the air* (1869), *Fors Clavigera* nos. 82 and 83 (1877), the preface to *Rock honeycomb* (1877), and *The pleasures of England* (1884). See also Augusta Mary Wakefield, *Ruskin on music* (Orpington and London, 1894).
13 See *The works of John Ruskin*, library edn, ed. E. T. Cook and Alexander Wedderburn, 39 vols. (London, 1903–12), xxxi(1907):513–21, for one specimen in music type and several facsimiles of manuscripts.
14 E. Gurney, *The power of sound* (London, 1880), pp. 376–7
15 *ibid.*, pp. 378–9
16 Scholes (1947), p. 3
17 Hansard, 3rd ser., lxv(12 July – 12 August 1842):8
18 J. Mainzer, *Music and education* (London and Edinburgh, 1848), pp. 101–2
19 F. Hullah, *Life of John Hullah* (London, 1886), pp. 5–6. N.B. This is quoted from an autobiographical fragment which Frances Hullah incorporated in the early chapters of the biography of her husband.
20 *ibid.*, p. 6
21 J. Hullah, *The duty and advantage of learning to sing* (London, 1846), p. 11
22 *ibid.*, p. 17
23 *ibid.*, p. 19
24 *CC* (Bristol 1864), pp. 296–303
25 J. Jebb, *The choral service* (London, 1843), pp. 544–5
26 R. Druitt, *A popular tract on church music* (London, 1845), pp. 31–2
27 R. Druitt, *Conversations on the choral service* (London, edn of 1853), p. 95
28 *CC* (Leeds 1872), p. 334

3 Orthodoxy and the composer

1 J. A. Latrobe, *The music of the church* (London, 1831), pp. 114–36
2 J. Jebb, *The choral service* (London, 1843), pp. 113–17
3 T. Helmore, 'On church music', *CC* (Wolverhampton 1867), p. 343. Cf. remarks by Canon Walsham How following a paper by Joseph Barnby, *CC* (Bath 1873), p. 460; also a paper by the Revd C. H. Hylton Stewart, *CC* (Carlisle 1884), p. 332.
4 F. W. Joyce, *Life of Sir F. A. G. Ouseley* (London, 1896), pp. 131–7. Joyce reproduces full texts of two sermons by Ouseley.
5 *CC* (Carlisle 1884), p. 310
6 A generous selection of spiritual letters is given in J. T. Fowler, *Life and letters of John Bacchus Dykes* (London, 1897), pp. 237–301.
7 See, e.g., a sermon of 9 December 1860 at St Peter's Church, Derby, published with one of Ouseley's as *The choral worship of the church* (London, Derby, Oxford, and Durham, 1861); also a 'Lecture on church music', *CC* (Norwich 1865), pp. 290–310.
8 F. A. G. Ouseley, 'The education of choristers in cathedrals', in *Essays on cathedrals by various writers*, ed. J. S. Howson (London, 1872), especially p. 212
9 For the text of the surviving letters, see Joyce (1896), pp. 52–63. The last letter dated is of 8 March 1850. The one following is undated, but appears to be the only one written after the Gorham decision was rendered by the Committee of Privy Council. The bulk of the correspondence took place while the decision was pending. N.B. Ouseley does not mention the Gorham case directly in any of these letters, but the timing and subject matter strongly suggest the connection.
10 See letters to J. W. Joyce reproduced in F. W. Joyce (1896), pp. 69ff.
11 *ibid.*, p. 75
12 T. A. Walmisley, preface to his edition of Attwood's *Cathedral music* (London, 1851)
13 From a letter of condolence to Attwood's second son, the Revd George Attwood, Rector of Framlingham, cited in J. S. Bumpus, *A history of English cathedral music* (London, 1908), p. 412
14 *MT* 448 (June 1880), xxi:271
15 M. Elvey, *Life and reminiscences of George J. Elvey* (London, 1894), p. 51
16 *ibid.*, p. 139
17 Cited in F. G. Edwards, 'John Stainer', *MT* 699 (May 1901), xlii:303, 308
18 C. S. Lewis, 'Christianity and literature', in *Rehabilitations and other essays* (London, 1939), pp. 185–92; also in *Christian reflections*, ed. Walter Hooper (London, 1967), pp. 3–7, and (Glasgow, 1981), pp. 17–22
19 C. M. Bowra, *The romantic imagination* (Cambridge, Mass., 1949), pp. 1–10
20 Lewis (1939), pp. 192–6; or (1967), pp. 7–10; or (1981), pp. 23–6
21 See, e.g., remarks on originality in J. Stainer, 'The principles of musical criticism' (3 January 1881), *PMA* (1880–1), vii:38–42. Stainer's ideas are akin to romantic lines of thought, but the predominant character is of dispassionate balance of thought and common sense, the very opposite of fiery romantic propaganda.
22 Bowra (1949), pp. 4–10
23 S. S. Wesley, *A reply to the inquiries of the Cathedral Commissioners* (London, 1854), pp. 15–16
24 E. Routley, *Church music and the Christian faith* (Carol Stream, Illinois, 1978; and London, 1980), especially p. 45
25 F. Blume, 'Klassik', *Die Musik in Geschichte und Gegenwart*, vii(1958):1032, 1035; or Blume, *Classic and romantic music*, trans. M. D. Herter Norton (New York, 1970), pp. 11, 15. Cf. Blume, 'Romantik', *Die Musik in Geschichte und Gegenwart*, xi(1963):821; or Blume (1970), p. 155.

26 J. Jebb, *Three lectures on the cathedral service* (2nd edn, with additions: Leeds and London, 1845), p. 138

27 H. Heussner, 'Das Biedermeier in der Musik', *Die Musikforschung* (October–December 1959), xii(4):422ff. C. Dahlhaus, 'Romantik und Biedermeier', *Archiv für Musikwissenschaft* (1974), xxxi:25 *et passim*

28 Dahlhaus (1974), pp. 39–41

29 See, e.g., K. R. Long, *The music of the English Church* (London, 1971), p. 360; H. Watkins Shaw, 'Church music in England from the Reformation to the present day', in F. Blume, *Protestant church music* (New York, 1974), p. 728; C. H. Phillips, *The singing church* (London, 1945; with new material by Arthur Hutchings, rev. Ivor Keys: London, 1979), pp. 245–6.

30 Heussner (1959), pp. 427–8; Dahlhaus (1974), p. 37

31 N. Temperley, 'Mozart's influence on English music', *Music and Letters* (October 1961), xlii(4):311–18, esp. 313–15

32 O. Chadwick, *The mind of the Oxford Movement*, introduction (London, 1960; rev. 1963), p. 55

33 Long (1971), p. 306

34 E. Walker, 'Free thought and the musician', *Music and Letters* (July 1921), iii(3):254; also in *Free thought and the musician and other essays* (London, 1946), pp. 9–10

35 J. H. Newman, *Apologia pro vita sua*, Pt VII (London, 1864), p. 402; critical edn by M. Svaglic (London, 1967), pp. 233–4. Cf. Pt VI (1864), pp. 329–30; (1967), pp. 184–5.

36 C. Dahlhaus, 'Neo-romanticism', trans. Mary Whittall, *Nineteenth-century music* (November 1979), iii(2):101; or Dahlhaus, *Between romanticism and modernism*, trans. Mary Whittall (Berkeley, Los Angeles and London, 1980), p. 8

37 See O. Chadwick, *The secularization of the European mind in the nineteenth century* (Cambridge, 1975), for a detailed staking out of the conceptual territory, and in the process a demonstration of the complexity of the issue.

38 Dahlhaus (1979), p. 100; or (1980), p. 7

39 *ibid.*, (1979), p. 99; or (1980), p. 5

40 E. Gurney, *The power of sound* (London, 1880), p. 368

41 *CC* (Carlisle 1884), p. 324

42 M. Arnold, general introduction to *The English poets* (London, 1880), p. xvii; cited in *CC* (Portsmouth 1885), p. 193

43 Walker (1921), p. 255; (1946), pp. 10–11

44 R. Wagner, *My life* (1865–80; trans. New York, 1911), pp. 634–5. Cf. *Mein Leben*, complete critical edn by Martin Gregor-Dellin (Munich, 1976), p. 539.

45 Walker (1921), pp. 255–6; or (1946), p. 11

46 *ibid.*, (1921), pp. 256–7; or (1946), pp. 12–13

47 O. Chadwick, *The Victorian church*, 2 vols. (London, 1966 and 1970), i:363–9

48 Ouseley (1872), p. 212

49 M. B. Foster, *Anthems and anthem composers* (London and New York, 1901), p. 23

4 Proprieties and constraints

1 Cited in M. Elvey, *Life and reminiscences of George J. Elvey* (London, 1894), p. 320

2 C. Avison, *An essay on musical expression* (London, 1752), pp. 74–5; W. Jones, *A treatise on the art of music* (Colchester, 1784), introduction, p. ii; W. Mason, *Essays on English church music* (York and London, 1795), *passim*

3 J. A. Latrobe, *The music of the church* (London, 1831), p. 134, citing Deuteronomy 23:18

4 See O. Chadwick, *The Victorian church*, 2 vols. (London, 1966 and 1970), i:277–8, 281–3, 293.

5 E. Holmes, *A ramble among the musicians of Germany* (London, 1828), pp. 5–6

6 J. Jebb, *Three lectures on the cathedral service* (2nd edn, with additions: Leeds and London, 1845), pp. 115–16

7 *MT* 108 (May 1853), v:189

8 M. Elvey (1894), p. 244

9 R. Druitt, *A popular tract on church music* (London, 1845), pp. 34–6

10 *CC* (Wolverhampton 1867), p. 338

11 *ibid.*, p. 337, citing *Ecclesiastical polity* (1594), book V, ch. 38, para. 3

12 See, e.g., preface to the folio edn of his *Service in E* (London, 1845).

13 S. S. Wesley, *A few words on cathedral music* (London and Leeds, 1849), pp. 44–5

14 *ibid.*, p. 37

15 J. Jebb, *The choral service* (London, 1843), p. 341

16 *ibid.*, p. 391

17 *ibid.*, p. 387

18 Jebb (1845), p. 137

19 Jebb (1843), p. 380

20 G. A. Macfarren, 'The music of the English church', pt 2, *MT* 288 (February 1867), xii:471

21 *ibid.*, pt 12, *MT* 300 (February 1868), xiii:280

22 *CC* (Bristol 1864), p. 306

23 F. A. G. Ouseley, 'Considerations on the history of ecclesiastical music of western Europe' (3 January 1876), *PMA* (1875–6), ii:36

24 M. Elvey (1894), p. 244

25 *CC* (Carlisle 1884), pp. 326–7

26 W. Crotch, *Lectures on music* (London, 1831), p. 28, citing Reynolds, Discourse IV. N.B. Here and elsewhere in this study, the terms Sublime, Beautiful, and Ornamental are capitalised when denoting Crotch's categories.

27 *ibid.*, p. 83

28 See N. Temperley, 'Crotch', *NG*, v:66

29 Letter of 4 March 1833, cited in J. S. Bumpus, *A history of English cathedral music* (London, 1908), p. 370

30 H. J. Gauntlett, 'The ecclesiastical music of this country', *MW* 17 (8 July 1836), ii:49–52; 'The Gresham Prize', *MW* 19 and 20 (22 and 29 July 1836), ii:81–6, 97–101; 'English ecclesiastical composers of the present age', *MW* 21 (5 August 1836), ii:113–20

31 *MW* 19 (22 July 1836), ii:83–4

32 *ibid.*, p. 84

33 *MW* 21 (5 August 1836), ii:113

34 W. Crotch, *Elements of musical composition* (London, 1812), pp. 19–24

35 *MW* 21 (5 August 1836), ii:114–15

36 Wesley (1845), p. v

37 'On cathedral services in general, and one by Mr Henry Smart in particular', *MT* 301 (March 1868), xiii:311. A strong conjectural candidate for authorship is William Spark, Smart's friend, most ardent admirer, and subsequent biographer. They became acquainted in 1852. See Spark, *Henry Smart: his life and works* (London, 1881), p. 288.

38 Jebb (1843), pp. 377–9

39 Macfarren (1867–8), pt 1, *MT* 287 (January 1867), xii:445

40 Jebb (1845), pp. 144–5. Cf. Helmore and Druitt above.
41 Reprinted in *MT* 65 (October 1849), iii:212, 219
42 J. Otter, *Nathaniel Woodard, a memoir of his life* (London, 1925), p. 178
43 Wesley (1849), pp. 49–50
44 Spark (1881), pp. 294–5
45 G. A. Macfarren, *Six lectures on harmony* (London, 1867), p. 10. N.B. This passage was substantially revised in subsequent editions. Cf. Macfarren (1867–8), pts 5 and 7, *MT* 291 and 293 (May and July 1867), xiii:50–1, 95.
46 See, e.g., *CC* (Manchester 1863), pp. 161–72; *CC* (Leeds 1872), pp. 326–34; and an unpublished professorial lecture, 'The art of musical criticism' (1881), Tenbury MS 1456/2.
47 *CC* (Leeds 1872), p. 335
48 See J. Stainer, 'The character and influence of the late Sir Frederick Ouseley' (2 December 1889), *PMA* (1889–90), xvi:25–39.
49 *CC* (Brighton 1874), p. 536
50 *ibid.*, p. 537
51 See F. Liszt, 'Über zukünftige Kirchenmusik', a fragment (1834), in *Gesammelte Schriften*, ed. and trans. Lina Ramann, 6 vols., (Leipzig, 1880–3), ii(1881):55–7.
52 *MW* 21 (5 August 1836), ii:113
53 Jebb (1843), pp. 289–90
54 *CC* (Bath 1873), p. 447; reprinted in *MT* 369 (November 1873), xvi:269
55 W. A. Barrett, 'Music in cathedrals' (3 April 1877), *PMA* (1876–7), iii:90
56 W. A. Barrett, *English church composers* (London, 1882), p. 178
57 J. Bennett, 'Victorian music', pt 4, *MT* 650 (April 1897), xxxviii:225
58 *ibid.*
59 *ibid.*, pt 5, *MT* 651 (May 1897), xxxviii:301
60 K. R. Long, *The music of the English Church* (London, 1971), p. 363
61 *ibid.*, p. 360
62 Bennett (1897), pt 5, *MT* 651 (May 1897), xxxviii:301
63 *ibid.*, p. 300
64 Long (1971), pp. 364–5
65 N. Temperley, *The music of the English parish church*, 2 vols. (Cambridge, London, New York and Melbourne, 1979), pp. 304ff
66 *CC* (Bath 1873), pp. 454–5; reprinted in *MT* 370 (December 1873), xvi:312; abridged reprint in P. A. Scholes, *The mirror of music* (London, 1947), pp. 543–4
67 *MT* 371 (January 1874), xvi:365
68 *ibid.*
69 *ibid.*
70 J. Barnby, preface to *Original tunes to popular hymns* (London, 1869); reprinted in his collected *Hymn tunes* (London, 1897)
71 Jebb (1845), p. 137; previously in the *Christian's Miscellany* (1841), i:23
72 *CC* (Manchester 1863), p. 174
73 See A. Hutchings, 'In praise of John Bacchus Dykes', offprint of an article in the *Durham University Journal* (March 1950), p. 2.
74 *CC* (Leeds 1872), p. 333
75 See Hutchings (1950), p. 1, citing an essay by Constant Lambert from *Life and letters* (July 1928); cf. Lambert, *Music Ho!* (London, 1934; 3rd edn with introduction by Hutchings, 1966), p. 179.
76 Hutchings (1950), *passim*; Hutchings, *Church music in the nineteenth century* (London, 1967), especially pp. 152–6; Hutchings with W. G. Roe, *J. B. Dykes (1823–1876): priest and musician* (Durham, 1976), *passim*
77 *CC* (Nottingham 1871), p. 379
78 Spark (1881), p. 280

79 *ibid.*
80 Bennett (1897), pt 4, *MT* 650 (April 1897), xxxviii:226–7
81 *ibid.*, p. 227
82 Barrett (1882), p. 172
83 Bumpus (1908), pp. 496–501
84 *CC* (Newcastle 1881), p. 338. Cf. W. H. Monk, 'The cultivation of church music' (5 December 1881), *PMA* (1881–2), viii:45.
85 ibid., *CC* p. 335; or *PMA* p. 42
86 Hutchings (1950), p. 7

5 Thomas Attwood (1765–1838), forefather of Victorian cathedral music

1 M. Kelly, *Reminiscences*, 2 vols. (London, 1826), i:228
2 N. Temperley, 'Mozart's influence on English music', *Music and Letters* (October 1961), xlii(4):307–9
3 *ibid.*, p. 313
4 *CC* (Dublin 1868), p. 418
5 Temperley (1961), pp. 313–15
6 J. S. Bumpus, *A history of English cathedral music* (London, 1908), pp. 415–16. Cf. Bumpus, *The organists and composers of S. Paul's Cathedral* (London, 1891), pp. 124–5.
7 W. M. Higgins, *The philosophy of sound* (London, 1838), pp. 248–9. The book is primarily a disquisition on acoustical physics for the scientific and musical dilettante, but also contains a brief survey of musical history. Higgins was a scientist who wrote several volumes on geology for the general reader.
8 *ibid.*, p. 249
9 J. Bennett, 'Victorian music', pt 3, *MT* 649 (March 1897), xxxviii:154
10 Bumpus (1891), p. 129
11 *CC* (Leeds 1872), p. 338, citing the Service in A (1825) as an example. The same opinion was expressed by the anonymous author of 'On cathedral services in general and one by Mr. Henry Smart in particular', *MT* 301 (March 1868), xiii:311
12 W. A. Mozart, *Neue Ausgabe sämtlicher Werke*, series X, supplement, division 30, vol. 1: *Thomas Attwoods Theorie- und Kompositionsstudien bei Mozart* (Kassel, 1965)
13 See W. A. Barrett, *English glee and madrigal writers* (London, 1877), and *English glees and part-songs* (London, 1886), *passim.*
14 Bumpus (1908), pp. 407–8. Bumpus notes that the anecdote was communicated to him directly by Boardman, shortly before his death in July 1898.
15 N.B. 'Sailor' William's anthem of 1831 had an introduction based on 'Rule, Britannia'.
16 W. A. Barrett, *English church composers* (London, 1882), p. 152
17 Bumpus (1908), p. 367
18 M. B. Foster, *Anthems and anthem composers* (London and New York, 1901), p. 101
19 J. Jebb, *The choral service* (London, 1843), p. 389
20 F. G. Edwards, 'Thomas Attwood', *MT* 694 (December 1900), xli:793
21 Bumpus (1891), p. 117; Bumpus (1908), pp. 414–15
22 *MW* 108 (N.S. 14)(5 April 1838), viii(N.S. i):227–8
23 Bennett (1897), pt 3, *MT* 649 (March 1897), xxxviii:154

6 Thomas Attwood Walmisley (1814–56) and John Goss (1800–80), the first Victorian generation

1 See N. Temperley, 'A list of T. A. Walmisley's church music', *English Church Music* (February 1957), xxvii(1):8–11. Cf. Temperley, 'Walmisley', *NG*, xx:183.
2 N.B. In T. F. Walmisley's edition of 1857, the source used for this study, the anthem is indicated as for the Queen's accession, and the text has been altered accordingly. This apparently led Bumpus to conclude erroneously that it was composed in 1838 in honour of Victoria's coronation. See J. S. Bumpus, *A history of English cathedral music* (London, 1908), p. 468. Cf. Temperley (1957) and Temperley, *NG*, xx:183.
3 J. C. A. Brown, 'The popularity and influence of Spohr in England', (Oxford University, unpublished D.Phil. dissertation, 1980), pp. 27ff, 52–3
4 W. E. Dickson, *Fifty years of church music* (Ely, 1894), p. 17. Cf. Temperley, *NG*, xx:182.
5 H. Watkins Shaw, 'Thomas Attwood Walmisley', *English Church Music* (February 1957), xxvii(1):5
6 W. Glover, *The memoirs of a Cambridge chorister*, 2 vols. (London, 1885), i:278–9
7 Bumpus (1908), p. 472
8 Watkins Shaw (1957), p. 3
9 H. Watkins Shaw, 'Church music in England from the Reformation to the present day', in F. Blume, *Protestant church music* (New York, 1974), p. 728
10 Bumpus (1908), p. 471
11 E. Dannreuther, *The Oxford history of music, vol. 6: the romantic period* (Oxford, 1905), pp. 304–9
12 This dating is implied by the chronological survey in F. G. Edwards, 'Sir John Goss', *MT* 698 (April 1901), xlii:226.
13 *MT* 125 (June 1854), vi:82; Bumpus (1908), p. 513
14 Cited in E. H. Pearce, *The Sons of the Clergy, 1655–1904* (London, 1904), p. 235

7 Samuel Sebastian Wesley (1810–76), a frustrated romantic

1 G. W. Spink, 'Samuel Sebastian Wesley: a biography', *MT* 1127 (January 1937), lxxviii:44
2 J. S. Bumpus, *A history of English cathedral music* (London, 1908), p. 370
3 Letter transcribed in *MT* 628 (June 1895), xxxvi:407; cited in P. Chappell, *Dr S. S. Wesley, portrait of a Victorian musician* (Great Wakering, 1977), p. 26
4 F. G. Edwards, 'Samuel Sebastian Wesley', *MT* 688 (June 1900), xli:374
5 BL Add. 35019, ff. 124–5; cited in Chappell (1977), p. 83
6 See F. G. Edwards, 'Metamorphosis of a well-known anthem', *MT* 690 (August 1900), xli:522–4, for a description of the differences between the published anthem and the version in the Hereford organ book, with numerous music examples from the latter.
7 *MT* 628 (June 1895), xxxvi:407
8 M. Elvey, *Life and reminiscences of George J. Elvey* (London, 1894), pp. 100–4
9 BL Add. 35019, f. 59; cited in Chappell (1977), p. 116
10 Chappell (1977), p. 39
11 Spink, *MT* 1128 (February 1937), lxxviii:150
12 W. Spark, *Musical reminiscences* (London and Leeds, 1892), p. 64
13 MS at the Royal School of Church Music; cited in Chappell (1977), p. 70
14 S. S. Wesley, *A few words on cathedral music* (London and Leeds, 1849), p. 61
15 Chappell (1977), p. 90
16 Cited in Edwards, *MT* 688 (June 1900), xli:371

17 S. S. Wesley, preface to *Cathedral Service in E* (London, 1845), p. v
18 Collection of John Dykes Bower; cited in Chappell (1977), p. 93
19 J. K. Pyne, 'Wesleyana', *MT* 676 (June 1899), xl:380
20 *ibid.*, p. 381
21 BL Add. 35020, f. 32; cited in Chappell (1977), p. 143
22 Spink, *MT* 1131 (May 1937), lxxviii:438
23 Pyne (1899), p. 377
24 *ibid.*, p. 378
25 *ibid.*, p. 380
26 Chappell (1977), pp. 151–3
27 *ibid.*, p. 152
28 *ibid.*, pp. 154–5, 166–8
29 H. Watkins Shaw, 'The achievement of S. S. Wesley', *MT* 1598 (April 1976), cxvii:304
30 *ibid.*
31 K. R. Long, *The music of the English Church* (London, 1971), pp. 345–6
32 Watkins Shaw (1976), p. 304

8 Sir Frederick Ouseley (1825–89): the timeless idiom and beyond

1 N. Temperley, 'W. S. Bennett', *NG*, ii:501
2 See the *Harmonicon* (1833), xi(pt 1):102; F. T. Havergal, *Memorials of F. A. G. Ouseley* (London and Hereford, 1889); J. Stainer, 'The character and influence of the late Sir Frederick Ouseley' (2 December 1889), *PMA* (1889–90), xvi:25–39; and F. W. Joyce, *Life of Sir F. A. G. Ouseley* (London, 1896).
3 From a letter of 1 December 1839 to the Countess de Montalembert, cited in Joyce (1896), p. 19
4 From two chapters on Ouseley as a musician, contributed by G. R. Sinclair to Joyce (1896), p. 243
5 *ibid.*, pp. 247–8
6 H. C. Colles in M. F. Alderson and Colles, *History of St Michael's College, Tenbury* (London, 1943), p. 7
7 Sinclair in Joyce (1896), p. 238
8 *Harmonicon* (1833), xi(pt 1):102. The march itself is printed in pt 2, p. 100.
9 Joyce (1896), pp. 26–7. N.B. F. W. Joyce, Ouseley's biographer, was the son of the Revd J. Wayland Joyce.
10 Stainer (1889), p. 37
11 Sinclair in Joyce (1896), p. 248
12 *Parish Choir* (1847), ii:46, 55. This journal published numerous reports on the state of church music in the nation's towns and cities, to the embarrassment of many a cathedral foundation.
13 Stainer (1889), p. 33
14 J. S. Bumpus, *A history of English cathedral music* (London, 1908), p. 539
15 See, e.g., a note by J. S. Bumpus in Joyce (1896), Appendix D, p. 258n.
16 Joyce (1896), pp. 77–8
17 Bumpus (1908), pp. 545–6
18 *ibid.*, p. 547
19 Sinclair in Joyce (1896), p. 250
20 Bumpus (1908), p. 549
21 Colles in Alderson and Colles (1943), p. 30
22 *ibid.*, p. 32

9 John Stainer (1840–1901) and Joseph Barnby (1838–96): the High Victorian idiom

1 J. Stainer, *The present state of music in England* (Oxford, 1889), pp. 11–12; hereafter referred to as Stainer (1889a)

2 *ibid.*, p. 12

3 *ibid.*, pp. 12–13

4 J. Stainer, 'The character and influence of the late Sir Frederick Ouseley' (2 December 1889), *PMA* (1889–90), xvi:34; hereafter referred to as Stainer (1889b)

5 See, e.g., Stainer (1889b), p. 36; and G. R. Sinclair in F. W. Joyce, *Life of Sir F. A. G. Ouseley* (London, 1896), pp. 252–4.

6 Stainer (1889b), p. 36

7 E. Chapman, quoted in F. G. Edwards, 'John Stainer', *MT* 699 (May 1901), xlii:308

8 Here and elsewhere these terms refer to the Prayer Book Psalter and Authorised Version respectively.

9 See, e.g., E. H. Fellowes, *English cathedral music* (London, 1941), p. 225; and K. R. Long, *The music of the English Church* (London, 1971), pp. 364–5.

10 E. H. Fellowes, 'Sir John Stainer', *English Church Music* (January 1951), xxi(1):7

11 Fellowes (1941), p. 224, citing W. H. Hadow, *Church music* (London, 1926), p. 24. N.B. Hadow's remark is a general statement. It is reasonable to suppose that he means to include Stainer, but he does not do so explicitly.

12 P. Charlton, *John Stainer and the musical life of Victorian Britain* (Newton Abbot, London, and North Pomfret, Vermont, 1984), p. 120; cf. P. Charlton, *The life and influence of Sir John Stainer* (Norwich, University of East Anglia, unpublished Ph.D. dissertation, 1976), p. 271.

13 Fellowes (1951), p. 4

14 Stainer (1889a), p. 11

15 *ibid.*, p. 15

16 See, e.g., Long (1971), pp. 360, 364.

17 *Daily Telegraph* (10 May 1930), cited in Charlton (1984), p. 202, n23; also Charlton (1976), p. 398n

18 Charlton (1984), p. 155; Charlton (1976), p. 398

19 Fellowes (1941), p. 225

20 J. Bennett, 'Sir Joseph Barnby', *MT* 637 (March 1896), xxxvii:154

21 *Lute* 97 (N.S.) (January 1891), p. 137

22 E. Walker, *A history of music in England* (London, 1907; also 2nd edn, 1924), p. 309. N.B. Omitted from 3rd edn, rev. J. A. Westrup (Oxford, 1952). Also in Fellowes (1941), p. 227; and Long (1971), p. 362

23 *MT* 460 (June 1881), xxii:315

24 Long (1971), p. 363

25 *MT* 302 (April 1868), xiii:346

26 *MT* 334 (December 1870), xiv:694

Select bibliography

The following list includes some books and articles which are not directly cited in the text, but which contributed to a fuller conception of the theory or practice of church music during the period. General reference works, dictionary or encyclopaedia articles, and smaller items from periodicals cited in the text are omitted. Also omitted are works ancillary to the principal period or subject of the study as a whole, but cited in the text and chapter notes where relevant to specific points. In cases where a work was published anonymously but attribution is not in serious doubt, the author's name is enclosed in brackets.

Alderson, M. F., and Colles, H. C. *History of St Michael's College, Tenbury* (London, 1943)

Banister, Henry C. *George Alexander Macfarren, his life, works, and influence* (London, 1891)

Barnby, Joseph. 'Church music', *CC* (Bath 1873), pp. 441-60. Reprinted in *MT* 369 and 370 (November and December 1873), xvi:267-72, 310-19

Introduction to *Hymn tunes* (London, 1897). Reprinted from *Original tunes to popular hymns for use in church and home*, 2 vols. (London, 1869 and 1883)

Barnett, S. A. 'Music as an aid to worship and work', *CC* (Carlisle 1884), pp. 321-5

Barrett, Philip. 'English cathedral choirs in the nineteenth century', *Journal of Ecclesiastical History* (January 1974), xxv(1)

Barrett, William Alexander. *English church composers* (London, 1882)

'Music in cathedrals' (3 April 1877), *PMA* (1876-7), iii:84-98

Bennett, J. R. Sterndale. *The life of William Sterndale Bennett* (Cambridge, 1907)

Bennett, Joseph. 'Sir Joseph Barnby', *MT* 637 (March 1896), xxxvii:153-5

'Victorian music', in eleven instalments:

      I. *MT* 647 (January 1897), xxxviii:10-12

      II. *MT* 648 (February 1897), xxxviii:84-7, ('The music of the church')

      III. *MT* 649 (March 1897), xxxviii:153-6

      IV. *MT* 650 (April 1897), xxxviii:225-8, ('Church music')

      V. *MT* 651 (May 1897), xxxviii:299-302, ('Church music')

      VI. *MT* 652 (June 1897), xxxviii:371-4, ('Opera')

      MT 653 (July 1897), xxxviii:443-5, ('Opera II')

      VII. *MT* 655 (September 1897), xxxviii:596-8, ('Orchestral music')

      MT 656 (October 1897), xxxviii:644-6, ('Orchestral music II')

      MT 657 (November 1897), xxxviii:734-5, ('Orchestral music III')

      VIII. *MT* 658 (December 1897), xxxviii:803-6, ('Chamber music')

[Bennett, Joseph.] *A short history of cheap music* (London and New York, 1887)

Bodley, G. F. 'The modes in which religious life and thought may be influenced by art', *CC* (Newcastle 1881, publ. 1882), pp. 325-30

Brown, John Clive Anthony. *The popularity and influence of Spohr in England* (Oxford, unpublished D.Phil. dissertation, 1980)

Bumpus, John S. *The compositions of the Revd Sir Frederick A. Gore Ouseley* (London, 1892)

A history of English cathedral music (London, 1908)

The organists and composers of S. Paul's Cathedral (London, 1891)

Chadwick, Owen, ed. and introd. *The mind of the Oxford Movement* (London, 1960; reprinted with slight revision, 1963)

The Victorian church, 2 vols. (London, 1966 and 1970)

Chappell, Paul. *Dr. S. S. Wesley, portrait of a Victorian musician* (Great Wakering, Essex, 1977)

Charlton, Peter. *John Stainer and the musical life of Victorian Britain* (Newton Abbot, London, and North Pomfret, Vermont, 1984)

The life and influence of Sir John Stainer (Norwich, University of East Anglia, unpublished Ph.D. dissertation, 1976)

Colles, Henry C. *Symphony and drama, 1850-1900*, vol. 7 of the *Oxford history of music* (London, 1934)

See also: Alderson, M. F., and Colles, H. C.

Courthope, W. J. 'Religion and art – their influence on each other', *CC* (Portsmouth 1885), pp. 192-6

Cox, H. Bertram, and Cox, C. L. E. *Leaves from the journals of Sir George Smart* (London, 1907)

[Cox, John Edmund.] *Musical recollections of the last half-century*, 2 vols. (London, 1872)

Crotch, William. *Substance of several courses of lectures on music, read in the University of Oxford, and in the Metropolis* (London, 1831)

Crowest, Frederick J. *Phases of musical England* (London, 1881)

Curwen, John Spencer. *Studies in worship music* (first series), *Chiefly as regards congregational singing* (London, 1880; 2nd. edn, enlarged and revised, 1888)

Studies in worship music (second series) (London, 1885)

Dannreuther, Edward. *The romantic period*, vol. 6 of the *Oxford history of music* (Oxford, 1905)

Dickson, W. E. *Fifty years of church music* (Ely, 1894)

Druitt, Robert. *A popular tract on church music with remarks on its moral and political importance and a practical scheme for its reformation* (London, 1845)

[Druitt, Robert.] *Conversations on the choral service; being an examination of popular prejudices against church music* (London, 1853)

Dykes, John Bacchus. 'Hymnology and church music', *CC* (Nottingham 1871), pp. 373-80

'Lecture on church music', *CC* (Norwich 1865, publ. 1866), pp. 290-310

See also: Ouseley, F. A. G., and Dykes, J. B.

Edwards, Frederick George. 'John Stainer', *MT* 699 (May 1901), xlii:297-309

'Metamorphosis of a well-known anthem' [i.e. 'Blessed be the God and Father' by S. S. Wesley], *MT* 690 (August 1900), xli:522-4

'Samuel Sebastian Wesley', in three instalments:
MT 687 (May 1900), xli:297-302
MT 688 (June 1900), xli:369-74
MT 689 (July 1900), xli:452-6

'Sir John Goss', *MT* 698 and 700 (April and June 1901), xlii:225-31, 375-83

'Thomas Attwood', *MT* 694 (December 1900), xli:788-94

'A visit to Tenbury', *MT* 693 (November 1900), xli:713-19

Ellerton, John, Stone, S. J.; and Hopkins, E. J. 'Hymns and hymn singing', *CC* (Stoke-on-Trent 1875), pp. 584-99

Elvey, Mary. *Life and reminiscences of George J. Elvey, Knt* (London, 1894)

Fellowes, Edmund Horace. *English cathedral music* (London, 1941; 5th edn, rev. J. A. Westrup, 1969)

'Sir John Stainer', *English church music* (January 1951), xxi(l):4-7

Foster, Myles Birket. *Anthems and anthem composers* (London and New York, 1901)

Fowler, J. T. *Life and letters of John Bacchus Dykes* (London, 1897)

Garrett, George Mursell. 'S. S. Wesley's organ compositions', *MT* 617 (July 1894), xxxv:446–9

Gauntlett, Henry John. 'The ecclesiastical music of this country', *MW* 17 (8 July 1836), ii:49–52

    'English ecclesiastical composers of the present age', *MW* 21 (5 August 1836), ii:113–20

    'The Gresham Prize', *MW* 19 and 20 (22 and 29 July 1836), ii:81–6, 97–101

Gedge, David. 'John Goss 1800–1880', *MT* 1647 and 1649 (May and July 1980), cxxi:338–9, 461–3

Gladstone, William Henry. 'Music as an aid to worship and work', *CC* (Carlisle 1884), pp. 308–17

Glover, William. *Memoirs of a Cambridge chorister*, 2 vols. (London, 1885)

Gurney, Edmund. *The power of sound* (London, 1880)

Hadow, William Henry. *Church music* (London, 1926)

Havergal, Francis T. *Memorials of Frederick Arthur Gore Ouseley, Baronet* (London and Hereford, 1889)

Haweis, Hugh Reginald. *Music and morals* (London, 1871)

    My musical life (London, 1884)

Hayne, Leighton George. 'Church music', *CC* (Bristol 1864, publ. 1865), pp. 303–7

Helmore, Frederick. *Memoir of the Revd Thomas Helmore, M.A.* (London, 1891)

Helmore, Thomas. 'Church music', *CC* (Swansea 1879, publ. 1880), pp. 585–94

    'On church music, with special reference to the joining of all the people in sacred song', *CC* (Wolverhampton 1867), pp. 334–51

Hodges, Edward. *An apology for church music and music festivals in answer to the animadversions of the Standard and the Record* (London and Bristol, 1834)

Hodges, Faustina Hasse. *Edward Hodges* (New York and London, 1896)

[Holmes, Edward.] *A ramble among the musicians of Germany* (London, 1828)

Hullah, Frances. *Life of John Hullah, Ll.D., by his wife* (London, 1886)

Hullah, John Pike. 'Church music', *CC* (Bristol 1864, publ. 1865), pp. 296–303

    The duty and advantage of learning to sing (London, 1846)

Hutchings, Arthur. *Church music in the nineteenth century*, Studies in church music, ed. Erik Routley (London, 1967)

    'In praise of John Bacchus Dykes', pamphlet offprint of an article in the *Durham University Journal* (March 1950)

Hutchings, Arthur, and Roe, William Gordon. *J. B. Dykes (1823–1876): priest and musician* (Durham, 1976)

    In memoriam, J. B. Dykes, M.A., Mus. Doc., reprinted from the *Literary Churchman*, 2nd edn (London, 1876)

Jebb, John. *The choral service of the United Church of England and Ireland: being an enquiry into the liturgical system of the cathedral and collegiate foundations of the Anglican Communion* (London, 1843)

    Three lectures on the cathedral service of the Church of England, 2nd edn with additions (Leeds and London, 1845), first published in the *Christian's Miscellany*, vol. 1 (1841)

[Jebb, John.] *Dialogue on the choral service* (Leeds, London, and Oxford, 1842)

Joyce, F. W. *Life of the Revd F. A. G. Ouseley* (London, 1896)

Kelly, Michael. *Reminiscences of Michael Kelly* (London, 1826)

Latrobe, John Antes. *The music of the church considered in its various branches, congregational and choral: an historical and practical treatise for the general reader* (London, 1831)

Long, Kenneth R. *The music of the English Church* (London, 1971)

Longuet Higgins, Charles. 'Church music', *CC* (Bristol 1864, publ. 1865), pp. 308–12

Lunn, Henry C. 'The music of the church', *MT* 249 and 250 (November and December 1863), xi:153–6, 173–6

Macfarren, George Alexander. 'The music of the English Church', in twelve instalments:
1. *MT* 287 (January 1867), xii:445–7
2. *MT* 288 (February 1867), xii:469–71
3. *MT* 289 (March 1867), xiii:5–7
4. *MT* 290 (April 1867), xiii:25–7
5. *MT* 291 (May 1867), xiii:49–51
6. *MT* 292 (June 1867), xiii:69–71
7. *MT* 293 (July 1867), xiii:93–5
8. *MT* 294 (August 1867), xiii:117–20
9. *MT* 297 (November 1867), xiii:189–92
10. *MT* 298 (December 1867), xiii:215–17
11. *MT* 299 (January 1868), xiii:247–9
12. *MT* 300 (February 1868), xiii:279–83

Mackerness, E. D. *A social history of English music* (London and Toronto, 1964)

Mackeson, Charles. 'The present cultivation of sacred music in England' (3 June 1878), *PMA* (1877–8), iv:126–39

Mainzer, Joseph. *Music and education* (London and Edinburgh, 1848)
Singing for the million: a practical course of musical instruction (London, 1841)

Marx, Adolf Bernhard. *General music instruction, an aid to teachers and learners in every branch of musical knowledge*, trans. George Macirone, Novello's library for the diffusion of musical knowledge (London and New York, 1854)

Metcalfe, J. Powell. 'Oratorio – its place in the Church of England', *MT* 340 (June 1871), xv:105–6

Monk, Edwin George. 'Church music', *CC* (Manchester 1863, publ. 1864), pp. 872–6

Monk, William Henry. 'The cultivation of church music' (5 December 1881), *PMA* (1881–2), viii:29–58
'The modes in which religious life and thought may be influenced by art', *CC* (Newcastle 1881, publ. 1882), pp. 330–8

Northcott, Richard. *The life of Sir Henry R. Bishop* (London, 1920)

Oakeley, Edward Murray. *The life of Sir Herbert Stanley Oakeley* (London, 1904)

'On cathedral services in general, and one by Mr Henry Smart in particular', *MT* 301 and 302 (March and April 1868), xiii:311–12, 343–4

Ouseley, Frederick Arthur Gore. 'Church music', *CC* (Manchester 1863, publ. 1864), pp. 161–72
'Church music', *CC* (Leeds 1872), pp. 326–34
'Considerations on the history of ecclesiastical music of western Europe' (3 January 1876), *PMA* (1875–6), ii:30–47
'The education of choristers in cathedrals', in *Essays on cathedrals by various writers*, ed. J. S. Howson (London, 1872)
'Musical training of the clergy', *CC* (Wolverhampton 1867), pp. 324–33. Reprinted in *MT* 297 (November 1867), xiii:194, 199–200

Ouseley, Frederick Arthur Gore, and Dykes, John Bacchus. *The choral worship of the church, two sermons preached in St Peter's Church, Derby* (Derby, London, Oxford and Durham, 1861)

Palmer, Roundell. 'English church hymnody', *CC* (York 1866, publ. 1867), pp. 322–43

Parratt, Walter. 'Music as an aid to worship and work', *CC* (Carlisle 1884), pp. 317–21

Parry, J. Gambier. 'The modes in which religious life and thought may be influenced by art', *CC* (Newcastle 1881, publ. 1882), pp. 338–43

Pearce, Edward Harold. *The Sons of the Clergy 1655–1904* (London, 1904)

Pears, Steuart Adolphus. *Remarks on the Protestant theory of church music* (London, 1852)

Phillips, C. Henry. *The singing church, an outline history of the music sung by choir and people* (London, 1945; with new material by Arthur Hutchings and rev. Ivor Keys: London and Oxford, 1979)

Pyne, James Kendrick, 'Wesleyana', *MT* 676 (June 1899), xl:376–81

Rainbow, Bernarr. *The choral revival in the Anglican Church 1839–1872*, Studies in church music, ed. Erik Routley (London, 1970)

The land without music, musical education in England 1800–1860 and its continental antecedents (London, 1967)

Raynor, Henry. *Music and society since 1815* (London, 1976)

Routley, Erik. *Church music and the Christian faith* (Carol Stream, Illinois, 1978; London, 1980)

The musical Wesleys. Studies in church music, ed. Erik Routley (London, 1968)

Scholes, Percy Alfred. *The mirror of music, 1844–1944, a century of musical life in Britain as reflected in the pages of the Musical Times*, 2 vols. (London, 1947)

The Puritans and music in England and New England, a contribution to the cultural history of two nations (London, 1934)

Shaw, H. Watkins. 'The achievement of S. S. Wesley', *MT* 1598 (April 1976), cxvii:303–4

'Church music in England from the Reformation to the present day', in Friedrich Blume, *Protestant church music, a history* (New York, 1974; London, 1975)

'Thomas Attwood Walmisley', *English church music* (February 1957), xxvii(1):2–8

Spark, William. *Henry Smart: his life and works.* (London, 1881)

Lecture on church music, more particularly the choral service of the Church of England as applied to parochial worship. (Leeds and London, 1851)

Musical memories 3rd edn (London, 1909)

Musical reminiscences: past and present (London, 1892)

Spink, Gerald W. 'Samuel Sebastian Wesley: a biography', in six instalments:
> *MT* 1127 (January 1937), lxxviii:44–6
> *MT* 1128 (February 1937), lxxviii:149–50
> *MT* 1129 (March 1937), lxxviii:239–40
> *MT* 1130 (April 1937), lxxviii:345–7
> *MT* 1131 (May 1937), lxxviii:432, 438–9
> *MT* 1132 (June 1937), lxxviii:536–8

Stainer, John. 'The character and influence of the late Sir Frederick Ouseley' (2 December 1889), *PMA* (1889–90), xvi:25–39

'Church music', *CC* (Leeds 1872), pp. 334–9

'Music, considered in its effect upon and connexion with, the worship of the church', *CC* (Exeter 1894), pp. 531–5

Music in its relation to the intellect and the emotions (London, 1892)

'On the progressive character of church music', *CC* (Brighton 1874), pp. 530–8

The present state of music in England (Oxford, 1889)

'The principles of musical criticism' (3 January 1881), *PMA* (1880–1), vii:35–52

[Stainer, John.] 'Sir John Goss', obituary, *MT* 448 (June 1880), xxi:269–71

Stanford, Charles Villiers. *Pages from an unwritten diary* (London, 1914)

Statham, Heathcote. 'St Michael's College, Tenbury – random recollections', *English church music* (May 1956), xxvii(2):34–7

Stewart, C. H. Hylton. 'Church music', *CC* (Rhyl 1891), pp. 279–87

'Music as an aid to worship and work', *CC* (Carlisle 1884), pp. 325–32

Stewart, Robert Prescott. 'Lecture on church music with illustrations', *CC* (Dublin 1868), pp. 405–32

Strutt, Richard. 'Music, considered in its effect upon and connexion with, the worship of the church', *CC* (Exeter 1894), pp. 552–4

Temperley, Nicholas. 'A list of T. A. Walmisley's church music', *English Church Music* (February 1957), xxvii(l):8–11

'Mozart's influence on English music', *Music and Letters* (October 1961), xlii(4):307–18

The music of the English parish church, 2 vols. (Cambridge, London, New York, and Melbourne, 1979)

Temperley, Nicholas, ed. *The romantic age, 1800–1914*, vol. 5 of the *Athlone history of music in Britain*, ed. Ian Spink (London, 1981)

Turpin, E. H. 'Uses of music in the services of cathedrals, town churches, and churches in rural districts', *CC* (Wakefield 1886), pp. 231–6

Vignoles, Olinthus J. *Memoir of Sir Robert P. Stewart, Kt., Mus. Doc., professor of music in the University of Dublin (1862–94)*, 2nd edn (London and Dublin, 1899)

Wackerbarth, Francis Diederich. *Music and the Anglo-Saxons: being some account of the Anglo-Saxon orchestra, with remarks on the church music of the nineteenth century* (London, 1837)

Walker, Ernest. 'Free thought and the musician', *Music and Letters* (July 1921), iii(3):254–60. Also in *Free thought and the musician and other essays* (London, 1946)

A history of music in England (London, 1907; 2nd edn, 1924; 3rd edn, revised and enlarged by J. A. Westrup, 1952)

Wesley, Samuel Sebastian. *A few words on cathedral music and the musical system of the church, with a plan of reform* (London and Leeds, 1849)

Preface to *A morning and evening cathedral service* [in E] (London, 1845)

A reply to the inquiries of the Cathedral Commissioners relative to improvements in the music of divine worship in cathedrals (London, 1854)

Wienandt, Elwyn A., and Young, Robert H. *The anthem in England and America* (New York, 1970)

Young, Edward. *The harp of God: twelve letters on liturgical music, its import, history, present state, and reformation* (London, 1861)

Index of compositions

Page references with an asterisk indicate music examples

General index

academicism in English musical culture, 51-2
Aldrich, Henry, 42, 69
All Saints, Margaret Street, *see* Margaret
   Chapel
Anglican Psalter Chants, ed. F. A. G.
   Ouseley and E. G. Monk, 79
Apologia pro vita sua, J. H. Newman, 1
Apology for church music, An, 23-4
Armes, Philip, 10, 80
Arnold, George Benjamin, 77-8
Arnold, Matthew, 57
Arnold, Samuel, 22, 101
Attwood, Thomas, 48, 67-8, 80, 84-102, 103,
   104, 105, 106, 108, 112, 115, 116, 120, 125,
   157, 160, 172, 175, 180; assessment by later
   Victorian writers, 100-2; contrapuntal
   technique, 91-7: influence of Mozart, 87-9;
   life, 84; obituary, 102; symphonic anthem
   technique, 98-9
Avison, Charles, 36, 60
Ayrton, William, 85, 120, 149-50

Bach, Johann Sebastian, 67, 113, 140, 154,
   169, 184, 185, 187, 191
Barnby, Joseph, 49, 73, 80, 126, 170,
   191-200; at St Andrew's, Wells Street, 10,
   14, 191: at St Anne's, Soho, 14, 191; form
   in anthems, 192, 195, 196-7; influence of
   Gounod, 75, 198-9; influence of Mendelssohn, 193; life, 191-2; lighter style,
   199-200; on contemporary style, 78; part-
   song style, 195-6; tonal and harmonic
   techniques, 193, 196-7
Barrett, William Alexander: on Thomas Attwood, 100-1; on glees, 94; on propriety, 73;
   on Henry Smart, 80
Battishill, Jonathan, 67, 68, 101
Beethoven, Ludwig van, 35, 38, 53, 67, 87,
   106, 120
Bennett, Joseph: on Thomas Attwood, 102;
   on Joseph Barnby, 192; on Barnby and
   Stainer, 75-7: on influence of Mozart, 88;
   on propriety, 74; on Henry Smart, 79-80
Bennett, William Sterndale, 19, 51, 132, 147,
   148, 149, 199
Berlioz, Hector, 53, 88, 149, 171
Bickersteth, Edward Henry, 26

Biedermeier as parallel to Victorian, 53
Bishop, Henry Rowley, 132, 154
Blow, John, 22, 63
Blume, Friedrich, on classicism and
   romanticism, 52
Bodley, G. F., 23
Book of Common Prayer: background and
   history, 11-12; choral offices, 12-14;
   equally applicable to cathedrals and parish
   churches, 26
Bowra, C. Maurice, on romanticism, 49, 51
Boyce, William, 22, 67, 68, 69, 101
Brahms, Johannes, 57, 88
Bumpus, John Skelton: on Thomas
   Attwood, 87, 88, 101-2; on F. A. G.
   Ouseley, 154, 161, 164; on Henry Smart,
   80; on T. A. Walmisley, 110, 115
Byrd, William, 68, 115

Cambridge University, 9, 103, 132
Cathedral music, Thomas Attwood, 97
Cathedral music, F. A. Gore Ouseley, 152,
   156
Cathedral music, T. A. Walmisley, 104
cathedrals, conditions and reform, 8-9,
   10-11, 70
Chadwick, Owen, on the Tractarians, 53
Chapel Royal, 84, 88, 101, 103, 129, 153
Chappell, Paul, on S. S. Wesley, 131-2, 143
Charlton, Peter, on John Stainer, 182, 189
choral service: attacked, 27-8; cathedral
   ideal, 8-11, 47, 191; defended, 24-6, 29-32,
   35-6; devotional theory, 14; ecclesiological
   ideal, 7-8, 9-10, 42, 47, 191; increase in
   communion settings, 14; structure, 12-14
Choral service, The, John Jebb, 30
Christ Church, Oxford, 151, 152
church choral festivals, 10, 167, 197
Church Congress Reports: 1863
   (Manchester), 78; 1864 (Bristol), 42; 1867
   (Wolverhampton), 31; 1868 (Dublin), 86;
   1871 (Nottingham), 29, 79; 1872 (Leeds),
   44, 71-2, 79; 1873 (Bath), 72, 77; 1881
   (Newcastle), 26; 1884 (Carlisle), 29, 46, 56;
   1885 (Portsmouth), 27, 57; 1891(Rhyl), 31;
   1894 (Exeter), 31
Church of England: liturgy, 11-14; parties in